Malcolm Brodie ɑ

Published by: *dimedio*

ISBN 9798692200778

Also by *dimedio*

An Ulsterman In the West Indies, Ireland's Caribbean Cricket Crusade
An Ulsterman in Japan, Ireland's Search for the World Cup Semi-Finals

'Become what you respect,
mirror what you admire'

(Brighton Keller)

PROLOGUE

A gentle tap on the shoulder, then: "...and this is our sports editor, John Laverty.

"John, say hello to our special guest, Mr Ben Bradlee..."

What a surprise. I'd no idea the Washington Post legend was in town, let alone standing two feet away and accompanied by senior executives from Independent News & Media.

"Mr Bradlee, it's an honour to meet you, sir..."

In journalism terms, this was royalty; Benjamin Crowninshield Bradlee, the editor who published the Pentagon Papers that hastened the end of the Vietnam War, whose paper's incisive coverage of the Watergate scandal ultimately brought down President Nixon and under whose guidance the Post scooped 17 Pulitzer Prizes.

An honour indeed. I was awestruck – something that never happened in the presence of world-famous sports stars – and momentarily tongue-tied.

I remember thinking, abstractly, that the then 83-year-old didn't look much like Oscar-winning Jason Robards, who played him in All the President's Men.

All I could manage: "I'm surprised you've even heard of the Belfast Telegraph, Mr Bradlee".

"Oh, of course I have," the iconic Bostonian replied, adding: "Tell me, does Malcolm Brodie still write for the paper?"

CHAPTER 1

Malcolm, who was friendly with my dad, got me a summer job as copy boy with the Tele sports desk. Wow! He knew that was all I ever wanted. He later told me to work for him directly as a sports reporter. "Forget the training," he said...
(Alan Green, BBC)

"Bout ye?"

"Oh I'm grand, Malcolm, and can I just say how delighted..."

"Ye'll be here in a couple o' weeks, right?"

"Well, uh, yes, a week on Monday in fact and..."

"So ye'll do the junior football and cricket?"

"Yes indeed Malcolm, and I'm glad you brought that up because I've a couple of idea..."

"Right, that's it. Sammy will show ye round. Arrivederci."

'Right, that's it'? What do you mean 'that's it'? And what exactly was *that* anyway?

That was my interview for a job on the sports desk. And my inaugural face-to-face meeting with the legendary Dr Malcolm McPhail Brodie, MBE.

I should have known from the brevity of earlier phone conversations that 'MB' was no fan of small talk.

"Get tae the point... pronto" was something he'd say.

And no, he wasn't of Italian extraction, hadn't changed his name from 'Brodi' but would regularly prefix a conversation with 'buongiorno' (Italian for 'bout ye') and end it with 'arrivederci'.

'Pronto', 'spaghetti', 'jacuzzi', 'pizza' and 'magnifico' just about completed his bilinguality. What's left would be in English with 'o' bolted on, as in "soup-o with bread-o" and "steak-o-well-done-o".

But we both understood what arrivederci meant: the 'interview' – one I'd prepared and rehearsed long hours for – was over.

Within seconds, Malcolm had returned to a half-eaten ham sandwich sitting on his desk.

Right, that's it, indeed.

I wasn't sure how to react. Elation? Well, I must have got the nod, because he did say "you'll do the junior football and cricket". But was that a statement or a question?

It didn't help either that, throughout the brief encounter, conducted in an office not much bigger than a cubby hole, Malcolm had the little finger of his left hand lodged firmly in his left ear. The breadcrumbs on his chin also caught the eye. And those dark, bushy eyebrows.

His light blue shirt was unbuttoned – from the middle down – thus exposing a considerable proportion of the fabled MB belly that was clearly no stranger to steak-o-well-done-o.

Mark Robson of UTV once introduced Malcolm at a formal dinner thus: "Brodie almost didn't make it tonight. He has a bad stomach... and now you're all going to see it for yourselves."

Below that magnifico mass of flesh, his trousers – taupe – were threatening to descend because, despite that bulky upper body, the man's legs were disproportionately skinny.

The belt was positioned well below the bowling-ball belly, ergo redundant. And, when he stood up, his trouser bottoms completely covered the patent leather shoes beneath them.

(An after-dinner speaker once quipped that Malcolm was the only man who got his trousers soled and heeled).

Having finally met him, I was convinced there was truth in the tale that his trousers fell to half-mast in a Heathrow arrivals lounge.

Legend has it that, instead of setting down his suitcases and taking remedial action, MB simply muttered "Ah, fer fuck sake" in that unmistakable Glaswegian accent and waddled off like a penguin, strides around the ankles, to the nearest rest room.

Legendary Daily Mail sports columnist Ian Wooldridge once described Malky as "a man who walked on the balls of his feet, shoulders hunched, like a boxer advancing from his corner, and talking incredibly fast in a language I'd never heard before".

Sammy Hamill (assistant sports editor, motorsport and table-tennis correspondent) sensed bewilderment as I emerged from MB's cubby hole into an open plan space the size of a large assembly hall.

"We call this The Big Room", said Sammy, cigarette in hand, gesturing towards coffee-stained carpet, a nicotine-kippered ceiling and banks of colleagues with cigarettes in hand. Quieter than I'd imagined (my thoughts having been influenced by the Washington Post office depicted in All The President's Men), but computer keyboards had only recently replaced scores of clattering typewriters.

"This is where you'll be sitting, wee man."

He introduced me to Colin McMullan (racing and athletics), whom I didn't recognise. Fortyish, bearded, baggy-eyed, permanently pissed-off-looking.

Despite a firm handshake, my immediate impression was that the grumpy bastard didn't like me.

The next few minutes, however, were ethereal.

Jimmy Walker, Jack Magowan, Jim Stokes, Jim Gracey, Ronnie Harper, John Campbell, Bob Fenton, Graham Hamilton and of course Sammy, who'd been showing me around... icons.

The only time I felt similar awe was eight years earlier when, as a promising – but ultimately not delivering – teenage footballer, I was introduced to the first team squad at Manchester City's training ground. I never really believed I was good enough to be another Kidd, Barnes or Hartford – and I was right – but here I was, at 24, about to become the youngest member of the dream team of local sports writers; the guys who mixed with the stars and waxed lyrical about them.

These were the days before internet, 24-hour rolling news, lockdowns and slack-jawed zombies staring vacantly at screens; when 'Zoom' was just a hit single by Fat Larry's Band; remember the good old days when you 'read it first' in a printed newspaper?

And the main contributors to that medium were as recognisable as anyone on local telly.

We were still in the midst of the Troubles, and the Belfast Telegraph's daily circulation was huge – something north of 160,000.

Consequently, front-line news reporters had high profiles, but the established sports guys were even better known.

People spoke of them in reverential tones; it was like having A-listers in your midst when one of them turned up at an event.

And the king, the big cheese – the *doyen* – was Brodie.

At this point in his life, September 1987, he was approaching his 61st birthday and still one of the best-known, most respected – and richest – journalists in the Britain Isles.

Despite spending the thrust of his career with a provincial paper, he had a higher profile and better contacts than the so-called cream of national sports writers.

He'd been in situ since the early 50s, had written books, covered hundreds of Northern Ireland internationals, numerous World Cup tournaments, European and FA Cup finals, was on first-name terms with

Blatter and other FIFA big-wigs, giants of journalism like Bradlee (who was chairman of the international advisory board of INM, owners of the Tele, when I met him), was always on telly and radio, was best friends with legendary West Indies cricketer Sir Everton Weekes (yes, he of The 3Ws) – and even received fan mail.

His unparalleled achievements had been recognised with an MBE in 1979 (and would earn him an Honorary Doctorate from the University of Ulster 20 years later).

My late father was among those diehards who stood on street corners, waiting for the 'Ireland's Saturday Night' van to arrive, eager to read what Brodie had written.

Ballymena labourer Joe Laverty's middle son therefore felt privileged to be working with the great Scot, proud to be one of the chosen few, delighted I could call him 'Malky' or 'MB' like other members of the exclusive inner circle.

I wasn't interested in succeeding him, though – well, not then – and, anyway, who could? He was a one-off, a unique product of his time, a man who epitomised a long-gone golden age.

After the introductions (I already knew Bob from his occasional visits to the Ballymena office, and Jim, whom I'd met at NUJ meetings but who was "away in Finland or somewhere like that"), I sought a quick word with new pal Colin who, like Sammy and Ronnie, was a former editorial assistant (or 'copy boy') and had since worked his way up a 'ladder' that had long been pulled away.

"What advice would you give to a young buck like me, Colin?"

He didn't look up from his new PCS (Press Computer Systems) screen. (The days of 'casting off' and mentally calibrating headline sizes had gone).

"Simple," he said, "learn to write like Jack, and operate like Jimmy".

What about Malcolm, I wondered out loud.

"And what can the big boss man teach me?"

Colin: "Well, that name-dropping will become second nature... nah, just learn to walk first, sonny..."

"Thanks, Colin, I'll try."

Sonny, eh? Patronising shit! You fools don't know it yet, but Malky has just signed Maradona. You'll know soon enough.

Emboldened by that thought, I wafted out of the century-old, five-storey, red sandstone building.

There was a pile of newspapers by the exit; on the back, Jim Gracey was indeed slumming it in Finland with the Glens and Brodie had written that, with an Ulster Cup final against Larne looming, Coleraine were sweating on the fitness of promising young midfielder Michael O'Neill, who lived next door to my girlfriend in Brigadie Gardens, Ballymena.

"Well, how'd it go?" asked Joe. (I'd stopped calling him 'Dad' by then).
"Great. Everybody was really nice, especially a guy called Colin. I think I'm going to enjoy working with him."
"What about Brodie?"
"Aye, he was brilliant. He said he wants me to write about junior football and cricket."
"That's my boy. What else did he say?"

CHAPTER 2

"Our stars included centre-half David Jeffrey, while Terry Gibson was impressive for England. We had a great squad that year. During the trial games John Laverty, a young striker from Ballymena, excelled, but failed to impress in the final stages..."
(Former Northern Ireland schoolboy international manager Ian Russell)

"... and this is ma son, Victor..."
Malky never had to introduce himself. He did, however, start phone calls with "is that you, John?" (superfluous), followed by "MB here" (ridiculous).
And, when he called Mrs Brodie from abroad: "Is that you, pet?"
I never heard the soft-spoken, mild-mannered Margaret's reply but fervently hoped that, just once, she'd bellow back from the hallway in Rochester Drive: "who the f*** did you *think* it was, you short-arsed Scottish eejit? Have you forgotten who you carried over the threshold of this house in September 1949?"
The "ma son Victor" introduction was often used in the magnificent Ulster Reform Club.
I mention that blithely, as if the prestigious, members-only Royal Avenue establishment was a regular haunt, like The Blackthorn across from the Tele with its 'steakette and chips' plat du jour-after-bloody-jour.
It wasn't, but Malky relished the ambiance and fine dining experience synonymous with a lauded premises which first opened its imposing doors in 1885.

You knew when a Reform visit or something equally prestigious was in the diary; MB would arrive in the office wearing The Shiny Suit – a silvery grey ensemble the late Marc Bolan of T Rex would have coveted.
And, every so often, he'd introduce "Victor" after saying "a-lo-dah" (I think that meant "hello there") to pinstripe-suits at the bar. They'd look confused because (a) I'm not Malky's son and (b) my name isn't Victor.
It was common knowledge that Malky and Margaret were biological parents to Iain (accountant, born October 31, 1953; "Dad always remembered my birthday; it was Halloween"), Kenneth (civil servant, September 17, 1956; "I was due to arrive on my parents' seventh wedding anniversary but was a few days late") and Steven (computer

operator, July 21, 1962; "Big Mal would sometimes forget my birthday. It was easier for him to recall when my daughter Claire arrived – September 11. She'd just turned four when that date became unforgettable. Dad loved New York").

"Tell them why Ah call ye Victor, John," Malky would say, like Captain Mainwaring.

Then, to the audience: "It's yer quintessential coming-of-age tale; Ah call it *Victor's Redemption*".

I call it St Louis Sports Day, May, 1977. Here goes...

I'd only deigned to go in that day because, technically, school wasn't on. After a decade of being good, the delights of truancy were embraced, then flouted so much that this one-time model student was threatened with expulsion.

The 'mootching' escalated in the days leading up to that sports day; absentees had a ready-made excuse – the United Unionist Action Council (UUAC) strike.

An attempted emulation of the 1974 Ulster Workers' Council disruption, which scuppered the Sunningdale power-sharing agreement, this one wasn't as effective, but still led to mass intimidation by sinister figures wearing sunglasses and three-quarter-length trousers; history will record that Northern Ireland was paralysed twice in the 70s by people who looked like a cross between Lou Reed and the Bay City Rollers.

There was tension in the air... or at least that's what it said in the Belfast Telegraph.

Concerned parents opted to keep their children at home. Not mine.

"There's nothing to be scared of," said Mum, as tractors and hijacked lorries began blocking off Ballymena's streets.

She was right; when Ian Paisley came past our boarding house in Hill Street, having roused a rabble, the first thing he did was embrace Mrs Mary Laverty, who'd been gently heckling The Big Man from her doorstep.

Paisley and mum were well acquainted; the firebrand DUP leader's boyhood home in Mount Street backed onto ours.

Bizarrely, a few days later I'd see her hugging a man Paisley later derided as "the Black Pope of republicanism" – Cardinal Cahal Daly, whom she grew up with in Loughguile, Co Antrim and who, like her, occasionally returned to his native parish for Mass.

Myself and two pals, Martin Davis and Liam Ward (aka 'Budgie') also brokered cross-community relationships during the strike.

11

Farrah Fawcett was now competing with Kevin Keegan on bedroom walls and, after we arrived at the People's Park for some serious mootching, three girls from the local Protestant school hove into view.

It was Martin who spied them first. "Oi, sham, glope the tone donors on the far dreg", he said, adding: "You think they'd be up for a bit of facing?"

An epic stand-off ensued, featuring a number of abortive "you go over, no YOU go over" moments.

Finally, Budgie produced a transistor radio, strode purposefully across No Man's Land and: "Hey, wanna listen to our tranny?"

Hotel California and Sound and Vision were played a lot, probably because they had unusually long intros Radio 1's Smashys and Niceys could talk bollocks over.

My donor, Sandra ("say skelps about her being a Prod, sham"), who looked mighty 'tone' indeed, told me her brother recently took her to Newry to see 'the border' for the first time.

She'd heard Paisley say Protestants "would never forsake the blue skies of Ulster for the grey mists of an Irish Republic", and wanted to witness this meteorological phenomenon for herself.

But all she got was a bureau de change, a petrol station and an Army checkpoint. The roads on the Republic side were "keek" though, riddled with potholes and obviously built by gypsies.

I was reclining on a grassy bank – 'social distancing', they might call it these days – near the running track when grey-suited St Louis Grammar School vice-principal Jim Keenan approached.

"Are you competing today?" he asked in a measured, non-threatening way.

"No sir, not today", I replied, settling back into a supine position.

Mr Keenan didn't budge.

"I think you should; didn't you win the 100m last year?"

"Yes, sir, but I can't be arsed this time."

"Well that's a pity, John, because your parents aren't too proud of you these days, and this would be an opportunity to change that."

Bastard! Who does this tosser think he is, and what would HE know about my folks?

Outraged, I dashed home, got changed and won the 100, 800m, long jump, triple jump and 'Victor Ludorum' – school champion athlete – titles.

"He just wound me up, yakking about how 'your parents' would feel," I told Mum later that day.

"Like, what would he know?"

"He stayed with us, John."

"He *what*?"

"He was a lodger in our house when you were a baby; didn't I tell you that?"

"Er, no, I think I'd have remembered..."

"He was really nice. He'd babysit in the evenings. Funny, he was talking about that when I bumped into him in Stewarts the other day..."

Then Dad chipped in: "Now that you're – what is it, Victor Ludorum? – maybe Malcolm Brodie will do a big interview with you."

"Who's Malcolm Brodie?"

A couple of hours later, after finishing that day's paper round, and sat on a stone wall in Carniny flicking through a leftover copy of the Tele. On the back page, Malcolm Brodie – so THAT's who he is – had written that two Northern Ireland youngsters, Martin O'Neill and Gerry Armstrong, would be blooded in the Home Internationals. He also previewed that night's Liverpool v Borussia Moenchengladbach European Cup final – in Rome.

'Victor' devoured every word, then: *"That's* the job for me..."

"Ha-ha-ha-HA!" (Always four notes, last one raised).

"See, Ah told ye it was a great yarn," said Malky, taking a triumphant swig of Johnnie Walker Black and water, his pinkie finger pointing towards the rapt audience.

"Ma boy knew, even when still a bairn, that he wanted tae be a writer like MB."

CHAPTER 3

28th June 1983

Dear Mr Brodie,
I am writing to enquire as to whether there are any positions available,
either full or part-time, in the sports desk of the Belfast Telegraph.
I am a great admirer of your work, having seen you many times over
recent years at Ballymena Showgrounds when Linfield or Glentoran came
to play my home town club Ballymena United.
I was also very impressed with your coverage of last year's World Cup
tournament, especially your match report following Northern Ireland's
victory over Spain.
My name may not be familiar to you, but it was my recent story in the
Ballymena Guardian (Tony McCall leaving Irish League football for a new
life in America) which you followed up and used as a back page main
story in the Belfast Telegraph.
I have just finished the NCTJ (National Council for the Training of
Journalists) course in Belfast and, I'm pleased to say, passed all the exams
and now have the certificate which, I understand, is an essential
requirement for employment at Belfast Telegraph Newspapers Ltd.
I have a strong working knowledge of most sports, particularly football,
and would be available to report on matches at the weekend or in
midweek.
I am looking forward to hearing from you in the near future.

Yours faithfully,
John Laverty

After that cathartic moment in May 77, I vowed never to disappoint my
parents again, returned to being a model student, studied diligently for
my O and A levels and, on the final day, got a huge bear hug from Mr
Keenan, tears streaming down his cheeks. "I KNEW you could do it," he
sobbed.
None of that actually happened.
Mr Keenan left for pastures new and I was finally bounced out of St Louis
in 1979. I had to do my A Levels at the local tech, and enjoyed the
cosmopolitan (by Ballymena standards) atmosphere of the place.
It was different on the streets. In those troubled times, you were one side
or t'other... Broadway or Harryville 'Boot Boy'.

14

Coming from the 'Top of the Town', you had to side with the Broadway lot and, although I'd no discernible nationalist leanings, I still enjoyed taunting the enemy when they ventured into 'our' territory.

With most of them being diehard Ballymena fans and me a signed player at the club, this was a tad schizophrenic.

We often chased them down Church Street from Broadway; they reciprocated if we encroached south of Mill Street, the unofficial demarcation line. This was more Clan Dew-fuelled cowboys and Indians than Taigs and Prods.

The fun stopped when I got caught near Harryville Bridge one night.

Keep walking John, you've got your snorkel jacket zipped up... they might not have spotted you... oh shit, at least two of them are crossing the road... fuck... I don't like the look of... smack, blinding flash, oh Christ no, teeth slicing through lip.

So keen was this mob to knock the beJesus out of me, some ended up kicking each other. I crawled out from beneath a forest of legs and 'took to the beaters' towards the bridge.

Wrong direction. But escape was all that mattered; for once, the Victor Ludorum velocity came in handy.

I'd been drinking, though, and the assailants were gaining ground. "Toss the bastard over the bridge", was one audible suggestion.

This was Very Bad News Indeed because even if I survived the 25-foot drop into the Braid, I possessed the swimming prowess of a paperweight. The end was surely nigh.

Then a car drew up, driven by John Davis – younger brother of Martin from those halcyon days in the park.

Having seen my blood-drenched body, he uttered the most gratuitous question in history: "You need a lift, sham?"

I dived into the back seat, my hero floored it and then I fainted. So much for cowboys and Indians.

I should have realised how bitter things had got in Ballymena when another Broadway teenager died after choking on his own vomit at a house party; the following day, Harryville gang members sent his grieving mother a box of Good News chocolates.

Irony times-two regarding my close encounter with brutal sectarian violence:

1. At the time of the attempted swimming lesson, my already flimsy Catholicism had lapsed. I'd grown to resent fingers pointing to that framed needlework on the wall which quoted 1950s 'Rosary Priest'/CIA agent Fr Patrick Peyton...

The family that prays together, stays together.

As if enforced piety was one of the Commandments.
I even penned an angst-ridden poem (it won a Seamus Heaney sponsored award) which began thus:
Give us this day our daily bread
For Christ sake, get this Rosary said...

2. Myself and my would-be murderers were, in those days (early 80s) united by Ballymena United.
As a young teen, I loved watching Alec Donald, Arthur Stewart, Bobby Averill, Quentin McFall, Jimmy Martin *et al.*
I even joined in with the Harryville boys in the 'clock stand' when they sang "Sammy, Sammy, show us your chest". Sammy Frickleton, long-haired Scottish loyalist and terrace hero, would then pull up his light blue shirt to reveal a huge torso tattoo of King Billy.
And I cried when Jimmy Martin ("he's here, he's there, he's everywhere, he's always scoring goals. And as for Dessie Dickson, you can stick him up your hole...") left for the Blues; why would anyone WANT to leave Ballymena?
I signed schoolboy forms for the club in 1978 – the same day as Tommy Sloan departed for his short-lived stint at Manchester United.
At the time, the Braidmen were managed by Billy Johnston, a man I clearly didn't make much of an impression on despite being top scorer in the hugely successful youth team – also known as 'Star United' – that included the likes of Tony McCall, Davy Smyth and Steve Penney.
(Years later, at a function, Malky would 'introduce' me to Johnston, prompting the reply: "So you actually exist, then? I thought 'John Laverty' was another Brodie pseudonym...")
There was always a buzz when the Blues, Glens or Coleraine came to town, and Ballymena got into the habit of regularly beating them after Alan Campbell replaced Johnston.
Those were the days of the 'Argentina' strip, of George Beattie, Nigel Worthington (we called him 'Worth-nothing', prior to his record-breaking transfer to Notts County), Graham Fox, Ronnie ("forget about the ball, Ronnie, and get on with the game") McCullough, John Sloan, Tony McCall, Paul 'Maloney' Malone and Gerry Mullan, of finishing runners-up in the league and actually winning things, including the 1981 Irish Cup, not long after Campbell almost died in a car crash.

16

That was the day my late, great friend and Eric Clapton/Jesus lookalike Davy Smyth was drafted in by acting boss Ivan Murray to face Glenavon (replacing my other great – but injured – mate Tony) and, courtesy of Sammy McQuiston's late goal he became, at 17, the youngest Irish Cup winner.

Brodie would be at the Showgrounds when Linfield visited. Short and squat, he sat behind the press box glass like Jabba the Hutt.
We'd turn round, point at him and chant "Brodie, BRODIE, what's the score?" when United were fortunate enough to take the lead.
'Brodie the Blueman' was one of several myths debunked when we worked together.
He didn't support Linfield, or *any* team. He was merely the top writer, covering the top club, going to the top matches. End of.
After I replaced him, fanzines like The Wee Red constantly reminded their Cliftonville-supporting readers of this one-time All Saints altar boy and Glenravel GAA player's apparent Blue bias.
If I'd had any leanings towards Linfield, they'd have been eradicated on December 29, 1979 – the day I saw Blues manager Roy Coyle showered in spittle by so-called supporters as he trudged down the touchline after a 5-0 loss to 'Argentina'.
Even one of the disabled Linfield fans, whom we knew as 'Geordie No Legs', angrily propelled his wheelchair in Coyler's direction that day.
Why did Blueman Brodie not put THAT in the 'Ulster'?
At that time, I'd been vacillating about taking the NCTJ course at the College of Business Studies.
The Ballymena Tech years yielded A Levels good enough for third-level education, but I ended up forsaking a university place – and that NCTJ application form remained blank.
The reason? I'd been offered a job – as manager of the town's new Grouse Inn.
Of course I accepted. It was better than stacking shelves in Crazy Prices, and what was the sports journalism aspiration anyway except, as Carly Simon sang, 'clouds in my coffee'?
Back then, I'd more time for the front end of newspapers, and 1981 provided plenty of reading: the hunger strikes, Paisley's 'Third Force', gleaming DeLoreans in Dunmurry, Charles and Di getting married, the inner-city riots that epitomised Thatcher's most difficult year in office, the Space Shuttle, Rubik's Cube.

Here's another story: the Grouse owners decreed that I was too young, too big a risk, to manage their new project.

Panic ensued. I'd wagered my immediate future on the Grouse gig, it was too late to rescue the NCTJ course (some bloke called Eamonn Holmes got in that year) and a big, bugger-all lay ahead.

Suddenly, I had to become a journalist. Not a famous, Brodie-type one, just *any* type. A sense of purpose finally kicked in.

Briefly: I signed on the dole, returned to the Tech for night-time typing and shorthand, was rushed to hospital after rupturing my appendix, endured my first 'it's not you, it's me' heartbreak, re-applied for the NCTJ course...

Saturday morning, June 26, 1982. I dare not budge. Some bastard had put a mercury tilt switch in my head. The slightest movement would bring an explosion of pain. Just lie on, John, perfectly still. Preferably forever.

We'd been watching a big World Cup match at The Countryman. In those days you could get three pints of Harp for less than a fiver. But I was paying for it now.

It was well after lunchtime before I sought rehydration downstairs. There was a letter, addressed to me, beside the telephone (olive, rotary dial) in the hall. And the Tele had just dropped through the letter box.

Dear John,

We are delighted to offer you a place in the forthcoming National Council for the Training of Journalists course for 1982-83.
Please complete the enclosed acceptance form and return as soon as possible.
I will write to you in due course regarding starting dates and times.

Yours sincerely,
Joan Fitzpatrick
Course Co-ordinator

Wow. Only 12 places available, and I'd bagged one. Whoever you are, Joan, I love you already.

And watch out, Brodie! I'm coming for you now. Wonder what Jabba has written in the Tele today?

HAIL THE NEW IMMORTALS

By Malcolm Brodie in Valencia

It is almost dawn.
Seven hours have passed since Northern Ireland last night defeated Spain to top Group 5 of the World Cup and qualify for the second phase.
Yet, in the stillness of the room, with the Mediterranean only a few yards away, the heart still pounds, the pulse races, the game is relived in the mind like a constant video replay...
Northern Ireland not only achieved soccer history, but produced one of the greatest ever performances of a British team in any World Cup...

Mmm.

I moved to a rented house in Edinburgh Street off the Lisburn Road with Davy and Kieran 'Ears' McLaughlin, topped the NCTJ class in everything (except shorthand; Teeline, by the way) and had a one-week placement with the Ballymena Guardian in March 1983.

Around that time, Tony decided he'd had enough of the bombs, bullets, barriers and bigotry of Northern Ireland.

"It's like being stuck in one of those Billy plays," he said, after letting it slip that he'd accepted a job coaching 'soccer' to college kids in the States.

"Have you told anyone else about this?" I asked.

"No, just my folks and you."

"Good. I've got a placement at the Guardian next week, and that would be a ball-breaker of a story to bring in."

"Go for it, sham."

The boys at the Guardian couldn't believe this big exclusive from the work experience guy. After all, the outrageously gifted but injury-prone McCall was one of the biggest names in the local game. Yet here he was, sensationally quitting in his early twenties.

The Guardian hit the streets midweek – and my story was the back-page splash in that evening's Tele.

McCALL OFF TO THE UNITED STATES

By Malcolm Brodie

Ballymena United midfielder Tony McCall, one of the best players in local soccer, is to quit the Irish League for a new life in America.
McCall, who is still in his early 20s, has accepted a job coaching in the US and is expected to cross the Atlantic in the next few weeks.
The news has shocked Ballymena, who said they had no idea the former Northern Ireland youth international was planning to emigrate.

During my stint in the Guardian, there was a brief exchange between Ballymena-born TV presenter/former Irish League star Jackie Fullerton (whom I recognised but hadn't met), who was producing football stories for the paper, and the confrontational, Kenny Rogers-lookalike editor Maurice O'Neill.

Jackie: "Could you leave my byline off the back page from now on, Maurice? I'm getting a bit of stick from the Ballymena fans..."

Maurice: "It's like this, Jackie... your stuff is shite. The only reason I use it is because your name's on it."

Jackie: "I'll assume that's a 'no' then..."

Sliding Doors Moment 1: I'd passed exams in newspaper law, politics and story writing. The shorthand result could come through the post. No percentages, nothing to say how close you'd got; just a simple, one-word, 'PASS' or 'FAIL' on a postcard. It was touch and go.

The day before the cards went out, I was in Belfast with Davy.

He had some student business at Queen's, I was at a loose end. A pint in Robinson's beckoned.

Robinson's is close to the College of Business Studies – maybe I could collect my shorthand result in person?

Joan Fitzpatrick – fiesty, no-nonsense, ex-News Letter, old-school hardened hack – was sifting through the postcards when I got there.

"Okay, Joan, put me out of my misery."

"Let's see... John Irvine, Karen English, Nigel Gould... yes, here we are... sorry, John, it's a fail..."

"Oh."

I still don't know what made me ask the next question.

"How'd the others do?"

She went through the cards. "Pass, pass, fail, fail, pass..."

Then: "Oh, Jim Laverty got a pass."

"*Jim* Laverty? But Joan, I don't think he even stayed to the end of the exam. Could they have mixed the cards up?"

28th June, 1983

Dear Mr Laverty.

Thank you for returning the card with the incorrect result of the shorthand examination you took on the 3rd June, 1983. You are no doubt aware that we had papers to mark for two trainees with the same initials and surname.
We sincerely apologise for sending you an incorrect result, you have in fact passed the 100 w.p.m shorthand examination and enclose herewith your result.

Yours sincerely,

Frances Robson (Mrs)
Shorthand Examinations

No shorthand pass would have meant no NCTJ certificate, and no certificate meant no employment at the Tele or any of the Antrim Series Weekly Newspapers (Ballymena Observer, East Antrim Times) they owned. Now, however, I could dare to dream.

July 5, 1983

Dear Mr Laverty,

Thank you for your letter dated June 28. I regret to inform you that we are currently well covered for writers in football and all other sports.
I do, however, wish you all the best for a future career in journalism.

Regards,

Malcolm Brodie,
Sports Editor

CHAPTER 4

You miss 100% of the shots you don't take.
(Wayne Gretsky)

"So, what's your girlfriend's name?"

"It's Cathy. Her name's Cathy."

"Cathy who?"

"Cathy Smith."

"Smith. Mmm. Don't think I know any Smiths from Jordanstown."

"She's actually from further down the road. Greenisland. Works in a solicitor's office. In Carrickfergus."

"Which one? I know a few down that way."

"Sorry, Jim, I've just had a mental block and can't remember the guy's name. Big bloke, dark hair. Plays rugby. It'll come to me..."

God, how I wish Jim Gray would stop asking stupid questions. The more he asked, the more lies I had to come up with.

There was no girlfriend called Cathy Smith from Greenisland.

But Greenisland wasn't far from Jordanstown, and Jordanstown was home to Jim Gray, Belfast Telegraph deputy editor, who'd come up to see how us boys on the frontier were doing following a bitter, Wapping-style dispute over 'direct input' PCs.

And I was giving him a lift home. From Stroke City. In a blizzard, in February 1987.

Jim was rather surprised when I offered.

So was Frank Curran Jnr, sitting across from me.

"How are you getting home, Jim?" John Dinsmore had asked.

Jim: "The train, I have a return ticket."

Me: "I'll give you a lift."

Jim: "What, to *Jordanstown*?"

Me: "Yes, my girlfriend lives there. I'm seeing her tonight. I could drop you off. It's no bother, honestly."

Frank looked bemused. Like someone who knew I was talking bollocks. In six months of downing pints with him, the 'girlfriend from Jordanstown' hadn't merited a single mention.

Yet here was I, so keen to see her – and on a school night too – that I'd risk a 150-mile round-trip, treacherous Glenshane Pass *et al,* for a few fleeting hours with her.

Yep, Frank knew I was lying, but also that I was desperate to get out of the north west, and wasn't going to pass up the opportunity to ensnare someone who could possibly help.

Having accepted my kind offer, Jim Gray would be my prisoner for three hours. Sufficient time, surely, to get the message across.

My first rant was about the unsuccessful attempt at finding out who in Belfast had changed 'Derry' to 'Londonderry' in copy I'd filed a few days earlier.

Our house style was Londonderry in the first par and Derry after that – but somebody had altered a nationalist politician's quotes, making idiots of us both.

"Are you a fucking retard?" was SDLP man's opening gambit the next day. In those pre-historic times, hacks' copy was retyped by members of the once-powerful NGA (National Graphical Association), whose jobs were under threat due to the inevitable introduction of direct input. Was a saboteur at work?

Despite valiant efforts, Jim Gray couldn't identify the culprit.

"It's an awkward time up there at the minute," he said.

Jim didn't ask me if 'Cathy' liked Derry. I'd have happily answered on her behalf.

"Hates the place. Brought her once, couldn't believe how divided it is," I didn't get to say.

"Catholics on one side of the Foyle, Protestants on the other. Thinks it's a big city, but has a small village mentality. Cityside or Waterside, nobody speaks to the blow-ins. It's 1987 and they can't even agree on what the damned place is called, although no one cared about that before Duke Street and Burntollet Bridge and that Gerry Mandering bloke, ha-ha. Hatred of Belfast unites them, though. About 90% of our stories are someone or other moaning that {puts on Derry accent} 'Belfast gets ev'rythin', Derry gets nothin'. Been that way since Stormont gave the new uni to Coleraine and allowed the shirt factories to perish. And they call that blink-and-you-miss-it landing strip at Eglinton an 'airport', like it's fucking Aldergrove or something. And everyone's Gallagher or Doherty, and they get hammered in McKenna's, warble The Town I Loved So Well – although they can't wait to get out of it – and John Hume, Dana or that floppy-haired git from The Undertones should be the next Irish president. No, Cathy would NEVER want to settle here..."

The north west office was a drab, standalone, two-storey, flat-topped building in a small commercial centre just off Glendermott Road on the Waterside.

Boss man John Dismore was meticulous, resourceful, highly-respected; I became a better hack because of him.

Tall, slim, distinguished, middle-aged, softly spoken, rugby-mad and bald, he was editor of the north west edition, which had its own, separate, 'slip page'. The front page was also 'editionalised' with its own masthead.

If you got a really good story, however, it went 'all editions'. This meant that there'd still be space to fill on the slip page. Thank goodness for the new Foyle Bridge, the Apprentice Boys, non-stop rows about 'Derry/Londonderry' and, this being 1986, on-going Unionist fury about Maggie's treacherous Anglo-Irish Agreement.

It didn't feel like a step-up from Ballymena, though; another divided town, familiar issues. The office was similar too; advertising downstairs, editorial on the first floor. Six desks in total; even smaller than the Ballymena place, in fact. If this was a higher level, I hadn't noticed.

The main difference was, you had to deliver daily, and to tighter deadlines. And come up with stories that – intentionally – weren't good enough for all editions, but could carry the slip page.

John, and his likeable deputy Charlie Haslett, a chain-smoking caffeine addict with thick-lensed glasses, were adept at this.

In Derry, if you rang about a story, you got a story – even if it wasn't the one you were chasing.

Example: John heard a whisper that a new hotel was to be built on the Foyle's west bank.

I called the builder supposedly behind this.

"Are you planning to build a new hotel on the west bank?"

"No, definitely not. Where'd you hear that?"

I ambled over to the boss's desk.

"There's no story, John. He isn't building a hotel."

"What IS he building?"

"I don't know. I didn't ask..."

"Call him back."

Two minutes later: "Definitely no story, John. Says he's only building a dozen cottages this year..."

"Only a dozen? Why so few? Call him back..."

Two hours later, a 600-word lead on 'Londonderry's housing shortage' had been rattled out on my Adler, placed in a big brown envelope and sent to Belfast in the 'Derry van' that had arrived earlier, bearing copies of that day's north west edition, printed in the 'other' big city.

Belfast gets ev'rythin, Derry gets nothin.

Let's rewind a little for Sliding Doors Moment 2: late August, 1986. I'd been with the Ballymena Times (formerly Observer, part of Antrim Series, owned by the Belfast Telegraph) for two years and 51 weeks.
This is important. It wouldn't have been, except deputy editor Russell McLernon came out with something seemingly innocuous, over a pint, at the 1985 office Christmas party.
"You're too good for the weeklies," he said.
"Lyle won't tell you that, because he doesn't want you to leave.
"But my advice is: don't stay here longer than three years."
That spooked me. Things were good in the Observer/Times. I lived close by, was developing a high profile (in Ballymena terms) and even had my own column, Observations, which featured quirky snippets from around town.
Not only that, but I was learning the trade from experienced colleagues such as Stephen Kernohan, Dessie Blackadder, Billy Spence, Russell and editor Lyle McMullan in the smoke-filled first-floor Ballymoney Street office.
The unmistakeable smell of ink on paper, that unforgettable cacophony of clattering typewriters; the satisfying feeling of physically creating something.
Morning routine: down a coffee, shoot the breeze with Lyle and the boys, load a sheet of horizontal A5 paper into my Adler Universal 200, turn the cylinder (or platen) until the virgin sheet emerged, ready for that orchestra pit of tiny metal arms to strike as your fingers danced on the spring-loaded keys. Clackety-clack, then ding! Hit the carriage return lever to move the cylinder back to the right.
You left extra space on the first sheet (of carbon paper; a copy had to be kept) for subbing instructions, then typed the story's catchline and page number on the top right: *Robbery....1*, etc.
The only place you'll see those magical appliances now is in an antique shop, alongside old Singer sewing machines.
I recently came across an ancient Olivetti while visiting a market with my young daughter.
"That's what Daddy used, before computers..."
"But where's the screen, Daddy?"

(Come to think of it, where's the cut and paste, spell checker, autosave, control and Z and autocorrect? What on earth is Tippex?)
"No darling, it just types words onto a page – but at least you don't need a printer..."

It was worth coming into the office for Billy Spence's dry wit alone, never better exemplified the day he was publicly lit upon by a Ballymena keeper (I believe it was Damian Grant) furious at being given only four out of ten for his performance the previous week.
"You clearly didn't see those two great saves I made towards the end of the match," said the keeper.
"Au contraire," said Billy, "That's what brought you up to four..."
I felt a sense of loyalty towards Lyle who, back in September 1983, had given me the job after verbally promising it to someone else.
"I had to go with my conscience... so don't make me regret this."
Then, two years and 51 weeks into my Ballymena Times career: "There's a job going in the Tele's Derry office," said Dessie.
"I've applied for it, and so's Stephen. The bloke who runs the north west edition is interviewing tomorrow".
"Wow! Good luck, Dessie. The *Tele*, eh?"
The interviews didn't last long. Both candidates, having slept on it, respectfully informed John Dinsmore that moving so far away wasn't for them.
By the time the visitor came to collect his coat, there was only him and me left in the office; I was only there to kill time before the stock car races.
"Bit of a wasted journey," he said ruefully.
"Did you have someone in mind for the job, Mr Dinsmore?"
"Not really. I'd heard those two were the pick of the weeklies..."
Oh you did, *did you?*
"Well, what about interviewing *me*, seeing as you're already here?"
"*You*?"
"Sorry, my name's John Laverty. I'd have applied, only Dessie and Stephen were ahead of me and I was sure one of them would've got it. But I'd love to work in Derry. I've been there many times; it's a wonderful place. My girlfriend's from Limavady, you know..."
40 minutes later: "I'll speak to Roy Lilley, and they'll be in touch. You may get a second interview, I don't know. This is highly unusual. What did you say your name was?"

28th August 1986

Dear Mr Laverty,

Further to your interview with our Londonderry Editor, Mr J Dinsmore, I am pleased to offer you a position on our Londonderry staff, effective from Monday, 8th September 1986.
Your salary will be increased to £8,967.
I would be grateful if you would please confirm to me your acceptance of this offer, in which case would you then contact Mr Dinsmore on his return from holiday on 1st September to make detailed arrangements for your move.
Meantime, may I take this opportunity to wish you every success in your future career.

Yours sincerely,

RH Lilley,
Editor

On Friday, October 24, 1986, the Antrim Series staff were summoned to the Chimney Corner Hotel, where it was announced that the papers, which had suffered trading losses of £67,000 in the previous calendar year, had been sold to the Morton Newspapers group for £220,000.

Thursday, 8th January, 1987

Dear Mr Laverty,

I wrote to you on Monday, 5th January outlining the situation with with regard to the editorial direct input system. In my letter I asked you to confirm by noon today (Thursday) that you would present yourself for training when required to do so.
I regret that I have not received such confirmation from you.
This letter, therefore, is a final warning that if you do not undertake training on Monday, 12th January your employment with this Company will be terminated.

Yours sincerely,

RH Lilley,
Editor

After that scary sabre-rattling, the NUJ and company bosses reached an awkward but acceptable compromise.

In early April I was sent to cover what would become a four-day siege at Magilligan, when loyalist inmates took a prison officer hostage over a segregation dispute.

"Deal directly with Belfast," said Mr Dinsmore, adding: "They're going to splash all editions with this."

My first all-editions splash, eh?

Not only that, but Jim Gracey had been on first thing about a story I'd filed the previous afternoon regarding the possible sale of Derry's Yugoslavian striker Alex Krstic to a foreign club.

"We'll probably make that our main story," said Jim.

I stopped at a phone box to call Dad.

"You'll never guess, Joe... I'm doing the front page AND back page splashes today. How cool is that?"

Front page that day...

Protesting loyalists capture prison officer

By David Lavery

Christ, they got my fucking name wrong! Today of all days. I'd have forgiven 'Lavery' – but *David*?

How it happened: "Oi, what do you call the new bloke in the Derry office?"

"Lavery, I think; it'll say on the copy."

"No, he phoned it in and Joyce wasn't sure. First name, anyone? Come on, come on, we're on deadline here... what was that; *David*? Yeah, I *think* that's right..."

Back page...

SPANISH EYES ON KRSTIC

By Malcolm Brodie

To be fair, he gave me a mention halfway through:

My colleague in the north west, John Laverty, tells me...

The Tele did very little on Derry City; strange, because they were drawing huge crowds home and away and, with Dubliner Noel King in charge, were well on their way to the south's Premier League.
Even the New York Times was intrigued by a border-town club that bowed out of the Irish League, homeless and penniless, in 1972 – the worst period of the Troubles – yet rose again, phoenix-like, 13 years later.

"John Laverty, please."
"Speaking."
"Is that ye, John? Malcolm Brodie here."
"Malcolm! This IS a surprise. I don't think we've ever spoken..."
"So tell me, John, how are the oul' Candystripes doin'?"
"They're really going places, Malcolm. Fantastic crowds. Krstic and Da Gama are worth the admission money alone."
"Ah heard that. In fact, Ah had a story aboot Krstic in the paper a couple o' weeks ago."
"Yeah, Malcolm, I saw that..."
"Aye. Anyway, Ah hear ye're the boy who'd know the best place tae get a cremated steak an' chips up there."
"Well, I do like the Inn at the Cross..."
"Good, can ye book a table for two this Sunday, like a fella. Ah'm comin' up for the match."
Like a fella?
"Sunday? Well, I'm not usually around, but..."
"It would be for MB an' his oul' mate Frank Curran. A character. Ye ever see him?"
"Well, yes, now and again. I work with his son, Frank Jnr."
"Course ye do. Oh, John, could ye ask them tae play Sinatra though the speakers on Sunday?"
"Sinatra? Well, Malcolm, I'm sure I could make a call..."
"Ha-ha-ha-HA! Nah, Ah'm only pullin' yer leg. Right, that's it. See ye anon."
Click.

"John, Jim Gray here."
"Jim! How are you?"

29

"I'm grand. How are you – and, more importantly, how's Cathy?"

"Cathy? Oh, yes... Cathy. She's great. What's up?"

"I said I'd keep you informed, remember? Bob Fenton's moving to features."

"Bob's leaving sport?"

"Yes, and your name has been mentioned as a possible replacement."

"Really? So, what happens now?"

"Send a letter to the editor, expressing your interest. You ARE interested, aren't you? I know it's not news reporting..."

"I'm not bothered about that. I'm sure I could adapt."

"Good. One thing, though... Malcolm Brodie has the final say. You'll probably have to go through an in-depth interview with him. My advice, John? Be prepared..."

CHAPTER 5

If a halfpenny paper is issued as near as three in the afternoon as
possible, it should command a good sale. A well selected little paper
might make a position to itself. There could be no risk and it might turn
out satisfactorily. Let me know what you think about it. I would call it the
Belfast Evening Telegraph.
(Letter from George Baird to William Baird, August 9, 1870)

Malky admitted earlier that "the aura" was upon him. Ergo, many drams
to be had.
"Right, it's time tae join MB in another toast."
With that, he lifted his glass in the direction of the magnificent Dom Luís I
Bridge.
"Tae Neil Franklin – the man who made it all possible."
This was awkward. Who the hell is Neil Franklin? And what exactly did he
'make possible'?
It can't have been the bridge; I knew, from the huge travel book Ronnie
Harper had selflessly donated, that the awesome century-old structure
spanning the Douro River in Porto was the brainchild of Gustave Eiffel
(yes, he of the tower) and disciple Theophile Seyrig.
"Well said, Malky. To Neil Franklin, a true great."
My ex-boss wasn't buying it.
"Ha-ha-ha-HA! Schemer hasnae a clue who Neil Franklin is."
(Malky's preferred pet-name in later years was 'Schemer', because "ye're
a wee ballix who's always up tae no good...")
"No, Malky, I don't know who that is."
As we sat outside a quaint little tavern on a cobbled street in the old
town, he told the story in the same way he wrote match reports; with
teasing, delayed delivery.
The late Cornelius 'Neil' Franklin was a centre half for Stoke City and
England in the post-war years. Some say he was even better than Bobby
Moore.
In 1950, however, 27-year-old Franklin caused a sensation by walking
away from England's World Cup preparations and selling his soul to
Colombian club Independiente Santa Fe for an eye-watering £3,400
signing-on fee and a contract worth £170-a-week (the English maximum
wage in those days was £15).
The El Dorado dream soured quickly; Franklin couldn't adapt to the

6.30pm curfew in the war-torn South American country and his pregnant wife and six-year-old son got terribly homesick. The trio upped sticks after just two months.

It wasn't a happy homecoming; Franklin was branded a national disgrace, banned and ostracised by Stoke as well as every other top-flight club who'd hitherto coveted a man described by Sir Tom Finney as "the best defender I've ever played with or against."

He eventually joined Second Division Hull for £22,500 – a world-record fee for a defender – and later emigrated to New Zealand. He died in 1996.

Intriguing tale – but what did this have to do with Malky?

"When Franklin buggered off tae Colombia, we covered it in one paragraph. Can ye believe that? The biggest story in English football, and we gave it one measly par..."

And?

"MB took his life in his hands, told RM Sayers, absolutely straight, that it was a disgrace, and that the time had come for the paper tae have its own dedicated sports department."

The good news: the editor agreed.

The bad news: he wanted someone other than Malky to put it together.

"Aye, that was a fight. He wanted tae keep me in news, but MB eventually wore him down. It took months, mind..."

Malky – who regularly drifted between the first and third person – said it was the proudest moment of his life when, at 24, he got the go-ahead as (deep breath) the UK's first regional specialised sports editor in late 1950, although the department wouldn't be fully up and running until early 1952.

"MB knew from those days at Park Parade that he'd never be good at sport but, even before then, Ah knew Ah wanted to write aboot cricket, football and boxing," he said.

"Ah couldnae be happier when Sayers gave the nod, but he expected me to walk the walk, and quickly. 'We have to be the best, young Brodie', he'd say. 'If it's not in the Tele, it hasn't happened. Are we clear?' MB felt the pressure from day one, but he knew who he needed."

Among early recruits were Jack Magowan, Billy McClatchey (aka 'Ralph the Rover') and the first deputy sports editor Brian Munn, who'd served with distinction in Burma during World War II.

There was also a four-strong racing team – Eddie Lowry, Johnny Boyd, Joe Sherlock and Billy Jess.

(With no 'proper' bylines back then, sports reports in the Tele and Pink were brought to the masses by the likes of 'The Timekeeper', 'Wanderer', 'Beacon', 'Franc', 'Fairway', 'Featherfly', 'Backhand Flip', 'Crank', 'The Squire', 'Iron Arm', 'Porpoise' and 'Solid Man'. The only name guaranteed to run on the back page every day was that of private detective Paul Temple – hero of the popular comic strip).

"MB told Sayers, absolutely straight: Ah want THAT-and-that-and-THAT-and-that... full point, end par."

Malky jabbed at a beer mat with his forefinger in time with the 'thats'. (Always four, just like 'ha-ha-ha-HA').

"Ye know, they didnae bat an eyelid when Ah said Jack should cover the 1952 Olympics in Helsinki. Did ye know Jack {who reported from Finland under the byline 'Belfast Telegraph Sports Reporter'} nearly got there as a member of the actual team? He was a promising athlete in his day.

"Right, waiter, get ma son another vodka an' diet coke, like a fella. Pronto..."

Malky could be rude to waiters.

Once, in business class on a transatlantic flight, he tugged at the white shirt of a distinguished-looking man striding purposefully down the aisle.

"Right, Johnnie Walker Black wi' water – no ice – for me, and a vodka an' diet coke for ma colleague here. Oh, and some more peanuts..."

"Malky, that's the pilot."

"Whaaa?"

The pilot, resplendent with those tell-tale epaulettes, was commendably unruffled.

"Your colleague is correct, sir. For my sins, I'm responsible for getting this wonderful machine across the pond. I've just escaped the cockpit to stretch the old legs for a minute, but I'll happily fetch you a waiter..."

We were airborne a lot.

Taverns would be located, tales told, toasts made, in Belgrade, Boston, Odense, Glasgow, Bremen, Tirana, Dublin, Vilnius, Riga, Seville, Copenhagen, Providence, St Etienne, Los Angeles, Suwon, London, Vienna, Vaduz, Birmingham, Nuremberg, Miami, Palermo, Kiev, Amsterdam, Liverpool, San Bernardino, Bordeaux, Frankfurt, Rotterdam, Daejeon, Lisbon, Santander, Manchester, Las Vegas, Paris, Istanbul, Helsinki, Orlando, Tokyo, Stockholm, Toulouse, Tallinn, Gelsenkirchen, Chisinau, Dortmund, Ta' Qali, Reykyavik, Albacete, New York, Seoul, Cologne, Zurich, San Francisco...

"Ah was there" was a classic Brodie catchphrase.

"So was I" might have be mine.

Did I leave out Porto?

That was memorable, not least because our boys grabbed a deserved 1-1 draw (Michael Hughes second half equaliser) when we'd been expecting a right tanking in the Estadio das Antas.

The night before that Euro 96 qualifier – and long after we'd toasted Neil Franklin – other guys from the press corps, including Jeekie ("I've got a programme, Mark – *you've* only got a slot") Fullerton, joined us.

My mum was a big fan of Jeekie, especially when he was on UTV. She loved it when he tilted his salt and pepper head, winked to camera and said: "We'll be RIGHT back, after the break..."

Having defected to Ormeau Avenue, Jeekie loved winding up UTV rival Mark Robson – and Malky.

On one occasion, in Spain, Malky asked Jeekie if he knew where the entrance to the stadium press box was.

"It's right over there, Malcolm," said Jeekie.

"Do you see the sign... 'Jugadores'? That means 'media' in Spanish. Go through there."

Malky then explained to Spanish security that he was one of the 'jugadores'.

"You no jugadore," said the burly guard as the short Scottish pensioner in front of him repeatedly pointed to the accreditation badge resting on his legendary belly, insisting "Ah AM jugadore; Brodie, Ireland – and ye, sir, are makin' a career decision by standing in ma way..."

That was The Day Malky Tried To Convince A Spanish Security Guard He Was A Footballer.

But Porto, September 2, 1995 brought The Night Malky Toppled Over In Mid-Boast.

Dressed in his trademark away kit of polo shirt, blue tracksuit bottoms and patent leather shoes, the 'aura' was indeed upon him, the audience rapt.

Then Jeekie said: "Malky, don't you think it's time you let the young pretenders take centre stage?"

Malky was livid. He set down his whisky and water and leaned back, demanding sufficient room to puff himself up like a corpulent peacock.

"Whaaa? Young pretenders, ma arse. Ye can keep yer Schemers and yer Graceys and those 18-carat-gold diddies fray the tabloids. Let me tell ye this Jeekie, absolutely straight; at the end o' the day, no one will ever, EVER, achieve what MB's done. Absolutely, completely, end o' ball game. Quite frankly, Ah am the BES..."

And with that, the chair gave way. Momentarily, Malky disappeared.

He'd toppled onto his back. Attempting to extract himself from the wreckage, arms and legs flailing, he resembled a flipped-over beetle.

"Uh, can ye help me up, Jeekie?"

But the creased-up commentator had turned away. He was laughing so hard, I thought his (latterly troublesome, ultimately repaired) ticker would explode.

Eventually, I reached down to help 'the BES' regain his decorum.

"Cheers. Ah, took a wee bit o' a tumble there. Did ye see that? No, no, Ah'm absolutely fine. Right, what was Ah talkin' aboot?"

CHAPTER 6

You don't always need a plan. Sometimes you just need to breathe, trust, let go and see what happens.
(Mandy Hale)

We traversed the globe in planes but, back in Belfast, my relationship with Malky initially failed to take off.

Indeed, for much of my first year we barely spoke on a one-to-one basis. He wasn't unfriendly though; not by any means. And, when Friday came and I'd bounded two floors up to the Ink Spot (try telling today's bottled-water-and-skinny-decaf-latte brigade that the Tele had its own in-house pub), the wee boss man would be holding court, ensuring my glass was forever charged.

There were always nuggets of advice to be had.

"Only one rule in journalism," he'd say, "apart from being accurate, never leave an unanswered question in the mind of the reader."

Colly: "Is that not *two* rules?"

In those days – before "ma son Victor" – Malky's inaugural, short-lived nickname for me was 'EW Swanton', after the renowned Daily Telegraph cricket correspondent.

It was a sardonic sobriquet; he was well aware of my limitations in that particular sport.

The first match I covered was between local big guns North and Waringstown; deploying football logic, I went early "to avoid the crowds". There were about 10 people watching this early-season clash of the titans.

The following Monday, a copy of 'The Bluffer's Guide to Cricket' was sitting on my desk. "To EW, from MB", he'd written on the inside cover. There was always a 'bout ye?', but little meaningful dialogue.

I'd have appreciated him reaching out, as Americans would say, a little more. Those nights in the fifth floor Ink Spot Sports & Social Club (established in 1973) were enjoyable but I felt more like one of the audience rather than a genuine friend.

This perceptible distance between us would change remarkably, but not immediately.

Nine months into my sports desk adventure, Malky invited me to go with him and Jim to Dublin for the 1988 FAI Cup final between Derry and Dundalk at Dalymount Park, which the latter won courtesy of a hotly-disputed penalty.

There were memorable Brodieisms en route ("That man cannae be gay – Ah know his father"; "does that racehorse live here?"; "May McFettridge? Ah cannae stand that woman..."), typical Brodie largesse (steak dinners in the Monasterboice Inn), a first sighting of the fabled Shiny Suit and my inaugural 'MB driving experience'.

"Malky, we're down to 20 miles an hour..."

"Whaa? Right, right... leave that with me."

Whoosh. The foot went down, and the smooth, two-litre engine in Malky's shamefully underused, charcoal grey, automatic Honda Accord would propel us back to 80 mph in seconds.

But, as the chattering continued, the car eventually receded to funereal pace. Step and repeat, throughout the 200-mile round trip.

Jim: "I was with him the day he reversed up an M2 slip road after taking a wrong turn. We'd just come away from Coleraine v Spurs in the Cup Winners Cup; September 1982. I remember the date because he was attempting this kamikaze manoeuvre the day Princess Grace died in a car crash..."

I never encountered Malky at his brilliant best.

He was heading towards 'retirement' and getting dates, scores and names wrong; something I was assured the younger MB would never have done.

Other things caught the eye that first year.

His arrival time, for one. Everybody else, 7.30am – but Malky didn't surface until three hours later.

By then, the first deadline – there were five editions – was a mere hour away.

It was clear that Jimmy (unaffectionately known as 'Walker') and Sammy ran the desk.

Malky was the bloke who wrote the big stories. But who was providing the background info?

From what I could see, Jim was on the phone from minute one, hoovering.

Jim, who joined the sports desk in 1979 (the same day as Jim Stokes), was latest in a line of 'MB leg men' that included Billy McClatchey and Billy 'Bill' Ireland.

Malky told me about the awkward changeover between the two Billys in 1962, after 'Ralph the Rover' retired – but continued to come in every day. Eventually Malky had to do a precursor of the legendary Del Boy-

Rodney moment; "Billy, Ah'm sorry but it's ma formal duty tae tell ye this... ye don't work here anymore."

The 'leg man' job didn't seem particularly rewarding, with your best stories being taken away every day. Like removing new-born kittens from their mother.

Jim was five years older than me, and taller. Shorter temper.

His fair hair and blue eyes made him look Aryan; Ronnie Harper called him 'Hitler's wet dream'. But not to his face. 'Jurgen from Lurgan' was another label.

Morning ritual: Malky would sit in his cubby hole, slurp tea brought to him by sports desk secretary Angela Klein, then stride over to Jim: "Right, what have ye got?"

Jim would say he had A, B, C and D.

Malky: "Right, I'll do A, you do B, C and D", at which point Jim would relate story A, quotes and all.

Malky would then sit with Angela and dictate A to her.

There was a palpable sense of relief when impeccable, faultless Angie was copytaker.

The great man's shorthand was peerless, but his typing was diabolical. Half a century in journalism, and he still hadn't mastered the spacebar.

He did of course bring in his own stories – some big ones too.

On the other hand – Lee Doherty's groin strain. One season, we led the back page no fewer than 23 times with stories about the Linfield midfielder's fitness or lack of.

Ronnie Harper: "The punters know more about Doherty's groin than his own missus."

One day, a Harper headline – about Doherty, *mais oui* – fell well short of the space allocated. Ronnie was asked to extend it, pronto.

'Hot metal' had been replaced by the 'paste-up' process, whereby text and headlines would arrive on photographic paper, cut into strips and pasted by compositors onto the page plate... literally cut-and-paste.

There was a computer screen nearby where you could make corrections. With the deadline closing in, and stick-thin Ronnie feeling the heat from the waiting 'comps', he changed 'Doherty an injury doubt for Big Two game' to this:

Doherty is an injury doubt for the Big Two game, so he is

"It was all I could think of at the time," explained a preposterously earnest Harper, oblivious to the hardened, seen-it-all comps such as

Norman Stockman, George Newell, Gordon Robinson and John Hull disintegrating in front of him.

Ronnie, who died in October 2018, aged 77, had an endearing knack of being both unintentionally and intentionally hilarious.

One of his claims to fame was moonlighting as Alex Higgins' first manager in the late 60s. Ronnie promoted and handled bookings for the outrageously gifted but irritatingly unreliable youngster – until the day Higgy embarrassed his manager by failing to show up for an important event.

Ronnie promptly resigned after swearing down the phone to the snooker prodigy, ending the call with: "you may make it as a pro, Alexander, but you're an amateur human being."

The Hurricane went on to become a double world champion and the biggest draw in the game, but Ronnie wasn't wrong about him.

One day in 1987, I took a call about a former Irish League player who'd died. I'll not embarrass the deceased's family; let's just call him Jimmy Kelly. Of Distillery.

"It was before your time, but Malcolm will know all about him," said the caller.

Later: "Malky, Jimmy Kelly has just died."

"Who?"

"Jimmy Kelly. Apparently, he was a terrific inside right for the Whites in the 50s."

"Never heard o' him. Angie, see if we've a file on a Jimmy Kelly. Frankly, Ah doubt it."

Angela returned from the fourth-floor library with a thick cuttings file. Two hours later, on the inside back page: "Who could ever forget the immortal Jimmy Kelly? I loved watching this majestic will o' the wisp bamboozle opposing defenders at Grosvenor Park. His two sweetly taken goals against Linfield in 1956 are forever videoed in my memory..."

Like the caller said, Malcolm will know all about him.

Walker, who sat immediately to my right, was never slow to cast doubt on the veracity of some 'Brodie stories'.

"He's supposed to have interviewed Glenn Miller, but would have been 10 years old at the time," said Jimmy – who'd then launch into his impression of a squeaky-voiced, pre-pubescent Malky with runny nose, short trousers, colouring-in book and pencil, peering up at the legendary American band leader.

Walker looked – and often acted – like Doc Brown in Back to the Future;

his impression was both grotesque and wickedly hilarious. Comedian Roy Walker would have been proud of his London-born cousin.

But was Walker right?

US Captain Alton 'Glenn' Miller *did* visit Northern Ireland... in August 1944, when he and his Army Air Force Band entertained audiences with swing classics such as In the Mood and Chattanooga Choo Choo at Langford Lodge base in Co Antrim, and Belfast's Plaza Ballroom.

That was a few months before the prolific 40-year-old chart-topper died in a plane crash... and about a year after Malky joined the Tele, aged 17.

"Hitler's gift to Ulster" (his own description) arrived, along with brother Allan, in Belfast just as war was threatening in 1939.

Malky was 13, some 18 months older than Allan, when parents Jack, a shipyard worker at John Brown's on the Clyde, and housewife Sarah, decreed that their young boys would be safer flitting the family's small tenement home at 771 Dumbarton Road for safer environs.

"They were worried the Germans would bomb the Clyde shipyards," recalled Malky. "Someone in Glasgae forgot tae tell them about Harland & Wolff..."

Malky and Allan went to live with their father's siblings, 'Auntie Kate' and 'Uncle Malcolm', in 122 Ravenhill Avenue, a spacious, four-bedroom corner house.

The young evacuees' grandfather was still around too, as clerk of works at the nearby Co-op bakery, which would later employ Allan as a bread server. Uncle Malcolm was a carpenter, while Auntie Kate would marry a soldier with the Argyll and Sutherland Highlanders.

Young Malky, however, wanted to be a journalist. He mastered shorthand and typing under the tutelage of 'Miss Gillespie' at the Connell's Institute on Royal Avenue and, despite his youth, talked himself into a job as cub reporter with the Portadown Times.

"Ah got the train down every day," he recalled.

"After a while Ah got tae know the conductors. They'd feed me stories, even hold the train a few minutes when Ah was runnin' late. It didnae happen both ways, though, and manys a night Ah had to sleep in the Portadown office after missin' the train."

Then Robert McMaster 'RM' Sayers – who succeeded late brother John as editor in 1939 and was replaced by John's son (John Edward 'Jack' Sayers; Malky's favourite boss) in 1953 – came calling from the big evening paper the Baird brothers had started, back in 1870.

"The first time Ah saw the Tele office was Sunday, September 3, 1939," said Malky.

"An easy date tae remember – the day war was declared. Ah was walkin' up Royal Avenue after mornin' service at the United Church of Scotland in Clifton Street, an' thinkin' the Belfast Telegraph was a really imposin' buildin', but the big clock made it welcomin' at the same time.

When Malky started in '43, paper rationing had restricted the Tele to four pages a day.

It would be another six years (Monday, October 10, 1949) before the name 'Malcolm Brodie' first appeared – in a report of his brother-in-law Samuel Stevenson's marriage to Martha 'Ciss' Davidson at Ballyholme Methodist Church...

'Mr David Davidson was best man and the groomsman was Mr Malcolm Brodie'.

He didn't get his first 'proper' byline until Thursday, May 21, 1953 – the year news stories finally replaced adverts on page 1.

Ireland win two-nil, but forward changes are still to come

From Malcolm Brodie, "Belfast Telegraph" staff reporter, who is accompanying the Ireland footballers

Toronto, Thursday – Ireland selectors are still far from satisfied with the displays of the touring side.

Colleagues from that 50s era included WD 'Billy' Flackes and John Cole, both of whom would become political behemoths with the Beeb, and the innovative Freddie Gamble, better known to the public as John Pepper, columnist and author renowned for his research of Ulsterisms/Pepperisms.

"RM Sayers put me on the political staff; in those days the Tele also produced a daily for locally stationed American troops called The Stars and Stripes," Malky told me.

"It was their editorial guys who tipped us off aboot Bob Hope {July '43} Irving Berlin {January '44} and Glenn Miller comin' here. After getting a word wi' big stars like them, and still in ma teens, everythin' afterward was bound tae be an anticlimax."

Hope and Berlin's morale-boosting visits were well documented in the Tele – and, despite the absence of a byline, the use of atypical 'second par quotes'...

Bob Hope is yearning for a day on one of Ulster's golf courses.
"I haven't had a round in six weeks, and would love one slap of a ball on a
links course," said the famous American screen and radio star in the wings
of the Hippodrome stage.

... hinted at a writing style that would become familiar to readers in years
to come.

Miller's visit, however, didn't rate a mention in the paper (although the
Northern Whig reported it), nor did his disappearance over the English
Channel four months later (which both the Whig and News Letter
recorded).

Walker, who rated the Whig's news gathering operation as superior to
that of the paper he left it for, mockingly likened my wide-eyed credulity
to Dorothy's – prior to her discovery that the 'wonderful Wizard of Oz'
was actually a wee man pulling levers and pushing buttons from behind a
curtain.

CHAPTER 7

Your best teacher is your last mistake.
(Ralph Nader)

There's a pivotal scene in the 1984 movie Amadeus when Salieri, brilliantly played by F Murray Abraham, snaffles Mozart's sheet music and starts reading.

As the ethereal notes drift through his head, Salieri's face is a picture of astonishment, morphing into anger, envy, humility, sorrow, humiliation – and, ultimately, grudging admiration.

Abraham bagged an Oscar; he deserved it for that wordless scene alone.

My own 'Salieri moment' arrived not long after I joined the sports desk.

Female with southern Irish accent: "Could I speak to Jimmy Walker, please?"

"He's in the building, but not at his desk right now. Can I take a message?"

"Indeed you can. This is the Irish Press sports desk. We'd like Jimmy to write a lengthy feature on the relationship between the Dunlop brothers. 2,000 words... sorry! And we need it within the next couple of days."

"Got that. Wait, Jimmy's just walked back in. You can tell him yourself..."

Jimmy: "Who's this? Hello, yes? Right... right... 2,000 words. Put me through to a copytaker..."

He's not, is he? He's not really going to dictate a feature-length article, at 10 seconds notice, with no notes in front of him? Christ, he IS!

Shock and awe. This couldn't be happening. People can't do this, can they? NO ONE can do this!

But Walker can; there he is, lounging back on his swivel chair, doing it. Effortlessly. Bastard.

Now I know how Salieri felt.

It was only a few days since 'Diego Maradona' had floated out of the building, vowing to show those old codgers.

Now I felt more like a Carrick reserve than a World Cup winner.

What had I been *doing* the previous four years? Clearly not 'journalism'. THIS is journalism; 'the next level' I didn't experience in Derry.

And fuck you, Walker, for making me feel so inconsequential. You did it deliberately, didn't you; let's put the uppity wee shit in his place, is that it?

The 'finished article', my arse.

43

"Learn to operate like Jimmy..."

Wasn't that what Colly said? Colly 'Colin' McMullan, for whom I'd mistaken grumpiness for refreshing honesty.

But no one could operate like Walker. My mistake that chastening day was thinking he was typical of a Tele hack. There was consolation in realising he was Wolfgang Amadeus Mozart.

Walker, who'd just turned 50, was also obnoxious, arrogant, impatient, condescending, bipolar and insane.

I liked him very much.

Perhaps I've always been forgiving of those who can back up their arrogance. In our business, there's nothing worse than someone for whom ability and ego are distant cousins.

The twice-married Walker who died in December 2015, aged 78 (survived by second wife Iris and daughter Shelley from his first marriage, to Jackie) was a genius.

He of the craggy, deep-lined face, slate-grey pallor, comb-over hair and trio of teeth in lower jaw had no time for people who weren't as good as him. This made for a poor man-manager; the forerunner to Roy Keane.

One day Harper, sharp-witted but a stranger to irony, came over, face like the proverbial thunder.

"That bastard Walker just insulted me," he said.

"He was subbing my bowls, and called me semi-illiterate".

Me: "Semi-*illiterate*? Don't you mean semi-*literate*?"

Ronnie: "Are YOU taking the piss too? It's semi-*ILLITERATE!*"

Shortly afterwards, I suggested to Walker that he lay off Ronnie. His reply: "Bollocks. This is a man who'd forget his twin brother's birthday..."

He took delight in torturing Jim Gracey. Routinely, incessantly.

Every time Jim returned from a Northern Ireland squad training session, Walker would ask: "So, what's the mood in the camp like?"

He'd no interest in the answer, but knew the inquiry would irritate the testy, volatile Jim.

Then: "Have you finished that piece, Jim?"

"Five more minutes, Jimmy."

Four minutes, 50 seconds later: "Five minutes are up, Jim. Where's your piece?"

Jim: "Look, Jimmy, two more minutes, right?"

One minute, 50 seconds later: "Jim, get that fucking piece over, RIGHT NOW."

Jim, slamming his fist down on the desk: "For Christ's sake, give me a fucking break, will you?"

44

Malky: "What in God's name is goin' on here?"

Walker: "Not sure, Malcolm. I think Jim's a bit stressed out with all this pre-match stuff."

Malky: "Right, that's it. Calm down Jim, and let's get this paper away."

Walker would then wink at me: "Gracey takes it all too seriously, you know..."

It was a collective bugbear that Malky always backed Walker, even when he knew his psychotic deputy could make waterboarding feel desirable. Those two went back a long way. Malky told me about interviewing Walker (who cut his teeth on the Whig) back in 1959 – four years before the Whig went out of business following a disastrous dispute between its owners, the Cunningham family, and the NUJ.

"He was twitchy as hell. Couldnae wait for it tae be over. When MB inquired if there was anythin' he wanted tae ask, all he said was: 'can you smoke in here?'

"Ah didnae have anythin' for him except shifts on the Pink. But after a couple o' weeks, Brian Munn said: 'This guy's incredible. He's like lightning, he never stops. He's making the rest of us look bad'.

"Those early 60s were exciting times; Thomson had just bought us from the Baird family, were investin' heavily, and we were puttin' out 18 pages a day – as many as the Irish News and News Letter {which still had an ads-only front page} combined."

Walker, who succeeded Derek Murray as deputy sports editor in 1964, was still making everyone look bad in 1987. Officially, he covered racing and motorcycling, but often knew more about other sports than so-called experts.

Sammy Hamill tells of the time Walker was a contestant on Hughie Green's popular quiz 'Double Your Money' in the 60s. "His specialist subject was to have been boxing, but at the last minute he was told someone else had taken that," said Sammy.

"And so Walker, calm as you like – well, by his standards, anyway – said he'd switch to jazz. He'd no time at all to prepare, but still walked it."

Walker's finest moment came on Sunday, July 2, 2000 – the day Joey Dunlop died.

I was with him, (Irish Derby at The Curragh), when word came through that the iconic Armoy biker had been killed while racing in Estonia. Jimmy must have filed 10,000 words for over a dozen media outlets that day – again, without a note in front of him. And even under that incredible pressure, he delivered different pieces every time. Standing beside me was Clare Balding, then 29 years old, her face a fusion of

45

admiration and astonishment.

I'd more than a few run-ins with Walker, like the day I criticised one of Malky's 'groin strain' stories as not being worthy of a back-page lead.

"Well, John, it was either Malky's or yours – and as you didn't bother your fucking arse doing anything, we're going with his. Any other pearls of wisdom you wish to share?"

Recently I was giving off about someone's shortcomings when a colleague remarked: "You don't rate many people, do you?"

Reply? "You're right. But how can you describe a Google-and-Wikipedia, cut-and-paste, can't-do-colour-or-context, 100-words-an-hour merchant as 'good' when you've worked with Jimmy Walker..."

His fiery reputation, however, meant nothing to pipe-smoking Tom Selleck lookalike Jim Stokes the morning our tall, athletic rugby correspondent – who played alongside Bestie and Big Pat in junior internationals – failed to arrive at the expected time.

Walker – a stickler for punctuality (although he made an exception for Bob) – rang Stoker's wife, Rosemary, demanding to know where her husband was.

Minutes later – after Stoker had got in and taken a call from the frantic, upset Rosemary – he stood up, calmly approached Walker and said: "a word, Jimmy, in Malky's office".

There was no inkling of what was to follow – Walker being lifted off the ground by his lapels, pinned against the wall and told: "If you ever, EVER call my wife again you're going out that fucking window. Do you understand?"

An ashen-faced Walker replied: "Yes, Stoker, I can see where you're coming from..."

Stoker later told me: "I'd slept in, which was unusual for me, and Walker rang after I'd left. After Rosemary rang to say how unpleasant he'd been, I called him into Malky's room.

"He was smiling, but that changed when he was up against the wall. I eventually released him and he sank slowly into Malky's chair. I walked out, to a deathly silence. Walker emerged a minute later, humming. He always hummed after someone stood up to him..."

Jack made no attempt to disguise his disdain for Walker. The pair regularly traded insults...

"Jimmy, why don't you go take a bath?"

"I will, Jack – as soon as you stop writing letters to yourself."

That barb referred to correspondence that occasionally came in, backing a particular stance Jack had taken: "Sir, your correspondent Mr Magowan is absolutely right about Barney Eastwood..."

The problem was that Jack possessed a unique punctuation style (space, exclamation mark, space, full-point) at the end of certain sentences; that style was also used by the 'letter writer'.

Jimmy needed Jack to know that *he* knew.

Jack, in turn, loved driving very slowly past Walker at the bus-stop on cold, wet mornings.

"I wanted the bastard to see that it was me..."

Genial Jack, who left us in April 2009, aged 79 (no doubt delighted at living a year longer than Walker), was one of the founder members of the desk.

Like Walker, he started in the Whig. Unlike Walker, he was polite, encouraging, generous in word and deed.

If Jack, who was forever taking off, then putting back on, those trademark large, dark-rimmed glasses, liked something you'd done, he'd not only compliment you in public but via a hand-written note.

Praise from Jack – devoted husband to Betty and father to Simon and Jane – was *praise indeed ! .*

In those days our main golf stars were Ronan Rafferty, David Feherty and Jimmy Hegarty.

Jack would try to acquire the trio's scores, no matter where they were in the world.

"Magowan, Ireland here," he'd bellow, phone voice assuming a mid-Atlantic twang.

"I'm enquiring about Rafferty, Feherty, Hegarty..."

His brusque attitude to foreigners wasn't in keeping with his normal demeanour; 'xenophobic' is perhaps the kindest way of describing it. He became apoplectic the day he believed he was calling directory enquiries in Bophuthatswana, in apartheid-era South Africa.

Unbeknownst to him, the international operator put him through to Botswana instead.

"Magowan Ireland here. I'm looking for the number of Sun City Country Club... what do you mean, you don't know? How can you not know? Repeat it? I've already said it, you damned fool... Sun City... it's a white man's paradise – somewhere YOU'LL never be..."

There was an affectionate innocence about Jack. One day he'd quoted the winner of a women's golf tournament describing how she'd overcome the inclement weather to land the first prize, adding: "Now I need something hot and hard inside me – and I don't mean tea..."

Like Sammy, Jack was a fan of expressive and innovative page design. The rapidly advancing technology, allied to the huge, eye-wateringly expensive Goss Metroliner colour presses that had been installed by the paper (then owned by Thomson Regional Newspapers) in 1985, were welcomed as wonderful new tools of the trade. Reading one of Jack's pieces was like being immersed a warm bath; you wallowed in the words as they lapped gently around you.

Pedroza, warmly embraced by an elated McGuigan, left the ring to thunderous acclaim, the genie gone from a nine-stone bottle that must be ready to join boxing's empties...

Meanwhile, I was churning out shite about junior football and cricket.

Learn to write like Jack...

CHAPTER 8

Seated one morn in the phone room
I was weary and ill at ease
My hands were still a-tremblin
I thought it was the DTs
The buzzer broke the silence
In a really urgent tone
There was naught to do but answer
So I lifted up the phone
Gruffily I said: 'Who's speaking?'
Though I bore them no ill-will
Back came the answer ringing:
'Malcolm Brodie from Brazil!'
(Poem written by Bob Young, chief
copytaker and 'in-house laureate', 1957)

 The desk phone started ringing shortly after 9am that Saturday.
"Malcolm Brodie's secretary, please."
The caller sounded not unlike Malky; slurred Glaswegian. Perhaps he was
a relative from the oul' sod.
"She's not here at the moment. Can I help?"
A short pause, then: "Well, yes, if you can get me the number of
Malcolm's hotel in Stuttgart."
No problem there; I had it on a yellow Post-it note stuck to my screen.
Then: "Sorry, who exactly am I speaking to? We're not really supposed to
give out..."
Another pause. The caller seemed hesitant.
"It's Alec. Alec Ferguson. Tell Malcolm I called. Thanks, bye." Click.
The call was clearly finished, yet I held onto the receiver as if it wasn't.
"Colly, you'll never guess who just called."
Colly's eyes remained fixed on the screen.
"Oh, let me guess, John... Alec Ferguson? He rings all the time..."
Well, at least that's another 'interesting thing' we could talk about the
following day.
This was the morning of June 11 – the day before England played the
Republic of Ireland in the Euro 1988 championships. It was the Republic's
first game in any major tournament – and look who the opposition were!
Added spice for the showdown at the Neckarstadion in Stuttgart, West

49

Germany, was the presence of 1966 World Cup winner, the late Jack Charlton, in the Irish dugout and a smattering of English-born players wearing emerald green shirts on the pitch.

But the match itself was of only passing interest. The significance was, I'd be watching it with Colly and several of his close friends, including Jim, at the Ivanhoe Inn.

It was the first time Colly had invited me to spend 'quality time' with him. Prior to that, I'd join him in the Ink Spot on Friday evenings, or in the Blackthorn on Saturday afternoons – but he'd be frequenting those places whether I existed or not.

One time I quietly asked Malky why Colly wore the same clothes every day; could he not afford a decent wardrobe?

"Colly has more dough that most of his colleagues put together," said Malky, adding: "He's the only person I know who got a call from his bank manager because he had too MUCH in his current account. He throws all his statements in the bin, unopened.

"And he DOES change his clothes. It's just that, when he sees a shirt he likes, he buys a dozen o' them. Same thing wi' trousers; normally four or five pairs at a time. And two or three jackets..."

Colly's invite felt like a watershed; he wanted 'close friends' like Clem McIlhatton (one of the Ink Spot barmen) and Raymond 'Fordy' Wilson and Malachy Proctor – from 'downstairs' (i.e. production) – with him. I was now one, or at least I hoped I was.

I may have been awestruck by Walker, impressed and appreciative of Jack, indebted to and eager to please Malky, but I idolised Colly.

I was envious, too, of how popular he was, despite him being a grumpy bastard. He may not have been the most high-profile of the 'stars' of that era, but he was the one, above all others, whom people wanted to spend time with.

History shows that Ray Houghton headed a shock winner; it was somewhat surreal to see loyalists in the bar wildly cheering a Republic of Ireland goal.

This was, after all, 1988, a tense, bloody year that had already seen, among other gruesome incidents, the shooting dead of three IRA members in Gibraltar, the indiscriminate murder of three mourners by loyalist Michael Stone during the subsequent funerals at Milltown cemetery – and then the third phase of that horrific domino-effect, the beating and shooting dead of two army corporals who had unaccountably driven into the funeral procession of one of Stone's victims.

Dark days indeed... but I guess those loyalist punters' hatred of the

50

perennially over-hyped England football team transcended all that, at least for a couple of hours.

After the game we settled down to the delights of the Ivanhoe kitchen. I told the guys I'd taken a call from 'Alex Ferguson', and that Colly had been distinctly unimpressed. He wasn't alone.

"Who the fuck is he anyway?" asked Fordy.

"Another jumped-up Scot who thinks he can go south and show them how to 'win the weeg title'. He doesn't even know how to pronounce it! Sure, look at Billy McNeill; didn't he take City AND Aston Villa down last season? How many managers can say *that*?

He added: "Ferguson will be gone by Christmas, mark my words. Did you hear he's trying to get shot of McGrath and Whiteside, just because they go for a couple of jars with Robbo in the afternoons? For fuck sake, did he not just see McGrath against England – with 'super striker' Lineker in his back pocket? Best defender on the fucking planet, and this Scottish clown's trying to sell him..."

"Wow, who rattled HIS cage?" asked Jim.

Malachy replied: "Ach, it's all this talk about the new Sunday paper. We're going to be hit with a lot more Saturday night shifts when it comes out, and wee Fordy's been acting like Oscar the Grouch ever since it they announced it."

To which Fordy interjected: "Oi, am I the fucking invisible man or what?" The Fordy and Malachy sideshow gave me time to think of a story to tell.

"Wait to you hear this. When I was away in Newcastle-upon-Tyne for that newspaper law course this week, a lecturer told us that Jimmy Savile was a serial paedophile, and that all the national papers have known this for years but it's as if he's being protected by the establishment or something."

"Jimmy Savile?" asked Clem. "THE Jimmy Savile from Jim'll Fix It, that white-haired ponce that's going to be knighted? I can't believe that. If everyone really knew, they'd have nailed him by now. Did you tell Malky?"

I nodded.

"He rang from Germany on Friday. Said the papers over there are still full of the Inga Maria Hauser story. She's the wee girl who..."

"We know who she is," interrupted Clem, adding: "That's the thing about this place. I'll bet no-one here can name any of Stone's victims, but we'll always remember a young German backpacker who some sick bastard killed near Ballycastle."

Colly: "What did Malky say about Jim'll Fix It?"

51

Me: "When I told him, he said 'whaaa? Ah was at a function wi' him two year ago.' He didn't believe it".

Colly laughed as he rose to get another round in.

"That's Brodie logic for you. So Malky knows Savile, ergo Savile's a sound bloke; 'He can't be a monster – he bought me a Johnnie Walker Black and water at the Savoy".

Cue the Brodie stories.

It would often happen like that; someone would tell theirs, and start a chain reaction. We got through a lot – pints and Brodie stories – that day.

Jim brought up a little-known one from Paris in 1982 (prior to a pre-World Cup friendly with France), when Malky was having lunch with Jeekie in a swish restaurant just off the Champs-Elysees and some well-oiled locals at a nearby table become a little boisterous.

"The problem with these people," said Malky, eyes darting furtively from side to side and whispering (as if French people could understand slurred Glaswegian), "is that they have no class".

And with that – in a classic, irony-free moment – the doyen of sports writing lifted half a bowl of tomato soup to his lips and slurped it right down.

"Jeekie told me he didn't know where to look; you could hear the slurping all across the restaurant," said Jim.

That Ivanhoe Sunday also marked the first time I'd hear the 'magnifico' story – where Malky dictates "magnifico, magnifico, magnifico" to revered copytaker Bob Young.

Bob, who died in 1987, aged 71, then uttered the immortal line... "I heard you the first time, Malcolm..."

But which match did it refer to?

When Malky died in January 2013, many obituary writers attributed the triple 'magnifico' to Northern Ireland's 1-0 defeat of Spain in 1982. But, as you already know, the report didn't contain those words.

Most popular alternative suggestions: Brazil winning the World Cup in 1958, Brazil successfully defending their trophy in 1962, Brazil beating Italy in Mexico, 1970.

Wrong, wrong, wrong – and you heard me the first time.

Thursday, October 15, 1958...

Uprichard is the hero

From Malcolm Brodie in Madrid

52

Ireland goalkeeper Norman Uprichard was simply superb in last night's 6-2 defeat by Spain under the floodlights of the Santiago Bernabeu stadium. "Magnifico! Magnifico! Magnifico!" cried the Spaniards as Uprichard gave them 90 minutes of spectacular goalkeeping.
Didn't he let in six goals? True, but he must have saved dozens.

Many of the obituary writers also assumed that the copytaker was female. That's understandable, but also wrong.

Malky once told me that Betty McCaw was the Belfast Telegraph's first female copytaker – and that was in 1958.

"Up until then," Malky said, "It was all blokes. If ye came in as a junior reporter in our place, they made ye serve the first year as a copytaker. Ah had tae do it mahself..."

And on that point, who needs copytakers now? When I started, they were crucial – and you fought over the best ones. 'Pre-booking' revered, full-time professionals such as Betty McCaw, Julie Mullan or Joyce Traynor was a privilege you earned.

Those priceless ladies were artisans of a now sadly extinct craft, finishing your sentences before you'd properly formed them in your own mind. Full point, end par, new sentence.

The other side of that coin? Part-timers who came in to take match reports on Saturdays; decent typists, but: "Teddy Dogleash crossed for Eeen Rutch to score" or "Glasgow Waingers are back on top the Scottish Weeg after an easy win at Eye Drops Park". Just type what you hear...

Future Ivanhoe get-together material: The day I sent a profuse, written apology to the distraught mother of a young goalkeeper we'd described as "hopeless" rather than "hapless".

My big 'copytaker' moment: just before the 1993 Scottish Cup final between Rangers and Aberdeen at Celtic Park, which I attended with Jim. 'Paradise' is traditionally very noisy, so dictating the line-ups via mobile phone was always going to be challenging.

It started well enough... Goram, Brown, Gough, McPherson, Robertson; names Joyce was familiar with from taking Rangers reports every Saturday.

Aberdeen was going well too; we'd got over the first 'minefield' names such as Theo Snelders, moved onto the likes of McKimmie, Wright, Irvine, McLeish... but then came the Dons' number 11.

Me: "Paatelainen. P, A, A, T...

Joyce: "Whaa? Stop, stop. 'Pat O'Lineon'? There's only *one* 'A' in Pat..."

At this point, I raced down the back steps where it was quieter, although I couldn't see the match, which was just starting.

"No, his name's not 'Pat O'Lineon', he's not Irish. *Paatelainen* is his surname. His first name's Mixu..."

Joyce: "Mixu? What sort of weird name is that?"

Me: "It's Finnish, Joyce."

Joyce: "Finished, my backside. You haven't given me the substitutes yet..."

I was mentally drained by the time I got back to the press box.

"Well, that was a nightmare; anything happening on the pitch?"

Jim: "Aberdeen have made a decent start. Paatelainen just hit the post..."

Back in the Ivanhoe in 1988, Jim was still debating the origin of the 'magnifico' story. His reasoning was that it couldn't have happened in Spain '82...

When Billy Hamilton and room-mate Tommy Cassidy finally hit the hay in Valencia's Sida Saler Hotel, they initially couldn't sleep because of what sounded like raindrops on the window.

"We were lying there wondering what event had the greater odds – us beating Spain or it raining in Valencia in late June," Billy told Jim.

"Then we started thinking it sounded more like a tappity-tap than a pitter-patter – and, when we looked out, there was Malcolm Brodie, sitting on the balcony of a nearby room, rattling out his match report on a wee portable typewriter..."

It is almost dawn. Seven hours have passed since Northern Ireland last night defeated Spain to top Group 5 of the World Cup and qualify for the second phase. Yet, in the stillness of the room, with the Mediterranean only a few yards away...

Big Billy was less enamoured with 'MB' a few days later, after Northern Ireland's World Cup odyssey ended courtesy of a 4-1 defeat by France in Atletico Madrid's Estadio Vicente Calderon.

"We were 4-0 down and Gerry has a late shot at goal, which hits my ankle and is deflected into the net," he said.

"Afterwards Billy Bingham, accompanied by Malcolm, asked: 'Who got the goal?'

"I said it came off me so it was mine, but then Malcolm says: 'You can't claim it. I've already filed my report and it says Gerry scored. It's *his* goal.'

"I was too shattered to say anything at the time, but later it dawned on me: that goal was the difference between Gerry or me being top British scorer at a World Cup. He then had three goals and I had two..."

Pat Jennings famously failed to see the funny side of a Brodie match report after West Germany hammered our boys in Cologne on April 27, 1977.

The following day's banner headline...

AUF WIEDERSEHEN, PAT

I know what you're thinking; the ITV comedy-drama Auf Wiedersehen, Pet. But this was six years before that show was made, and Big Pat wasn't amused.

Ironically, Malky had nothing to do with the headline, although was clearly unimpressed by the performance of softly-spoken, shovel-handed Pat, who was only a few weeks short of his 32nd birthday. It's the stuff of legend that the Newry man played on for another nine years, ultimately setting what was then a goalkeeper's world record (119) for international appearances. Oops.

Big Pat's huge hands carried Malky's coffin in 2013; he must have forgiven him.

I was racked with jealously after listening to Jim shooting the breeze about Billy, Gerry, Pat and Tommy as if they were his best mates.

The most famous person I knew was Dundela boss Mervyn Bell.

(Tommy Cassidy would later have a role in an episode that threatened to destroy my relationship with Malky.)

The cup now runneth over with 'Brodie stories'.

Colly recalled Malky's short-lived sojourn into live radio reporting. First day, first post-match report, first words: "Linfield are back on top of the Irish League following a comfortable 2-0 win over Distillery at Windsor Park today; full point, end par..."

Then there was the day security staff directed a man nobody recognised up to Malky's office.

"Can Ah help ye?" asked a bemused Malky.

"I hope you can, Mr Brodie," said the man, who was reasonably well dressed and had one of those thick, overtly nasal Belfast accents the comedian James Young used to parody.

"The wife's left me, Mr Brodie. Said I'd knocked her around a bit when I was pissed, like, but I honestly don't remember..."

Malky: "You whaaa?"

Man: "But I'm on the straight and narrow now, Mr Brodie, swear to God.

Haven't touched a drop in weeks. But I need a deposit on a flat so the kids can visit... you're a man of means, Mr Brodie; the sort of decent man who would see it within himself to help someone..."

Malky: "OUT, OUT! Get OUT! Fer fuck sake, who let that hobo in? Is someone takin' the piss here? Call security! Heads will roll for this, mark ma words..."

"The funny thing is," said Colly, "Malky was the most generous man I've ever met, but he'd NEVER lend to anyone, not even his closest pals. It was anathema to him. He'd give it to you before he'd lend it."

Later Colly visibly cringed when recounting the time Ronnie answered a phone call for Malky, looked around the office and then said: "Where the fuck is that dumpy wee Scottish git?"

Malky, emerging from seemingly nowhere, shouted across: "Is that for me, Ronnie?"

It was the blind leading the blind when Shore Road native Ronnie and Malky left Belfast one wintry evening, bound for a bowls association function in the north west. All was well until they reached the unforgiving Glenshane Pass – and Malky's car got stuck in the snow.

"Ronnie, jump out like a fella and push ma car."

Ronnie: "Are you serious, Malky? I've got a hired monkey suit on."

Malky: "Well, Ah've got mine on too and someone has tae push ... here, put these two mats under the back wheels tae get some traction..."

One minute later: the wheels spun, propelling both mats over a nearby fence and drenching Ronnie in a cocktail of snow and mud. Somehow, Malky's car made it onto a piece of the road where the tyres could get sufficient purchase. A dishevelled but relieved Ronnie jumped back in.

"For a minute, I thought we were gonna be stuck here all night," he said, adding: "boot to the floor, Malky, and I'll get cleaned up when we get there."

Malky: "What are ye talkin' about, 'boot to the floor?' Get over that fence right now and bring those mats back..."

Chain-smoking, Crues diehard Ronnie, who lived in Bangor with wife Helen, sons Darren and Gareth and daughter Ann, was often the butt of office jokes but was an incorrigible wind-up merchant himself.

On one occasion, before Jim's predecessor Billy Ireland left on a European trip, prankster Ronnie sneaked into his suitcase and stapled the legs of his pyjamas together.

On another – and cognisant of the strict Troubles-era security at Aldergrove airport – Ronnie slipped pornographic magazines underneath Billy's clothes.

"Let's see the big tub of lard talk his way out of this..."
Malky was fond of a joke, but not when he was the butt of one.
Like when he returned from abroad to be informed by Jack that Stoker had circulated a poster of a Sumo wrestler with the speech bubble: "Oi, Jimmy, look after the place like a fella while I'm away."
Jack inadvertently shopped Stoker: "It was so funny, Malcolm; I haven't laughed as much in ages."
By the time Stoker got to the office, a memo was sitting on his desk.

To: Jim Stokes.
From: Malcolm Brodie, Sports Editor.
Message: See me, re Sumo wrestler.

I wondered that day if I'd ever feature in a 'Malky story'. Probably not. I'm too inconsequential.
I wasn't aware then that 'Sliding Doors Moment 3' was imminent.

CHAPTER 9

After A levels I want to see the Belfast Telegraph's then editor, Jack Sayers, to ask for a job.
"What's your ambition?" he enquired.
Being the sports fanatic I was, and with all the brashness and naive confidence of youth, I replied confidently: "To succeed Malcolm Brodie."
I can see Sayers now, rocking back in his seat, laughing loudly...
(Gordon Burns, former host of The Krypton Factor)

Colly read the note just once, then casually handed it over.

"I have went. Watch out for the knives. JG"

"Where'd you get this, Colly – and what the hell does it mean?"
Colly was relishing the intrigue.
"It's a Mid-Ulster thing. People from that neck of the woods tend to say 'I have went' when they mean 'I have gone'. Quite simple, really..."
"Stop arsing around, Colly. You know exactly what I'm asking."
"Well, John, I guess it means that DisGracey is leaving for pastures new..."
"What new pastures?"
"Oh, I'd say a certain Sunday paper, wouldn't you?"
"No."
"Yes."
I felt faint. Jim leaving... for Sunday Life? Why? Who'd want to leave the job he already has? And what does "watch out for the knives" mean?
"He probably means Walker," said Colly.
"I can't imagine any tearful hugs between those two when he goes..."
"Does Malky know?"
"He knows. Jim will have told him before anyone else. I'd say I'm the second person he's told. He must have left that note on my desk last night."
"God. I can't believe it, Colly. Honestly, I'm stunned."
"What, stunned that he's going – or stunned that you'll be replacing him?"

Three months earlier...

58

Belfast Telegraph Newspapers Ltd is planning a new Sunday newspaper this year. Mr RC Crane, managing director, said today: "This exciting new development will mean increased opportunities for employment in the newspaper business in Northern Ireland. The necessary journalists and advertising staff will be recruited shortly. The Editor will be Edmund Curran, currently deputy editor of the Belfast Telegraph.

A fortnight after the Ivanhoe gathering, I got a call from Ed asking me to meet him in an office upstairs.

Upstairs? All very cloak and dagger, this.

"I'll come straight to the point," said Ed.

"As you know, I'm the launch editor for Sunday Life, and I think you should apply for one of the jobs in sport."

Me? I was flabbergasted. Or flattered. Maybe both.

"Ed, let me get this straight; are you... actually offering me a job?"

He smiled.

"No, I'm just saying I think you'd be a very strong candidate if you applied. Maybe you'd like to go away and think about it."

"I will Ed, I will."

"Oh, and one other thing, John... not a word to anyone downstairs."

Five minutes later: "Malky, Ed Curran has just offered me a job in Sunday Life."

Malky: "Whaaa? Ye serious?"

Me: "Deadly serious. I'm to mull it over, but I think I know the answer already."

Malky: "Well, if that's the case we'll be sorry tae lose ye. Ah must say, ye've been an invaluable member of ma team o'er the past..."

Me: "Woaah! Hold your horses, Malky. What I mean is, I'm not going to take it. I've always wanted to work for the Tele sports desk and I'm not quitting after less than a year."

Malky: "Oh, that's all right then. Ah wasnae pushin' ye out the door, mind; just thought this would be an opportunity for ye to become a front-line football man, and that's unlikely to happen here wi' big Gracey in front of you."

Well, thanks for stating the obvious.

But what would happen in three years' time, when Malky retired? Jim would presumably take over as the main footy man – and, hopefully, I'd have done enough to step in as his number two.

We got on well, could carve up the football duties between us... yep, that sounded like a plan.

But here's what Jim hadn't disclosed: he'd also been sounded out by 'the Life'.

To this day, I've no idea if Ed turned to Jim after me, before me, or wanted both of us.

Jim later admitted that his decision to leave was uncharacteristically spontaneous.

Was I glad he was going? Well, no – because we'd become close friends and comfortable colleagues.

On the other hand, his unexpected departure had opened the door to me getting his old job.

And surely I'd then be the main football man when Malky retired – only three years hence. Then again, who knew if Malky even wanted me?

As I'd never thought Jim would leave, equally I'd never considered the possibility of being the great man's new leg man.

Yet now it was within my grasp... or was it? Malky's response to the Sunday Life approach came across as insultingly indifferent.

When I told Colly about this, he looked a little sheepish.

"What? Out with it, Colly."

He was like a politician weighing up a measured, non-incriminating response.

"Well, it might have had something to do with me repeatedly calling him 'Shelley' the other night. I was a bit pissed, like..."

"Why Shelley?" I asked; something to do with the popular ITV drama series starring Hywel Bennett, perhaps?

Colly: "As in Mary Shelley, creator of Frankenstein."

The penny dropped.

"You didn't really... did you?"

Then, in hope rather than expectation: "I take it Malky hadn't a clue what you were on about?"

"Um, well, he sort of got it after I suggested that he'd finally created someone capable of dethroning him..."

"No, Colly, NO! Please, please tell me you didn't say that. And do you really think I'm that good?"

"Fuck no! What I mean is, well, maybe... look, you're getting me all flustered here. And it doesn't matter anyway; we were both hammered. Malky won't remember a thing about it."

Jim left just before the start of the 1988-89 season. The talk was that Malky fancied Gordon Hanna as his new leg man.

This wasn't well received on the desk; although Gordon was extremely popular with the lads, he wasn't the sort of bloke likely to muck in with them when it came to the hard yards; page design and subbing duties. The tension was unbearable; why wasn't Malky saying anything?

Finally – on Jim's last day – the boss man called me into his office.

"So ye'll help me wi' the senior football from now on, like a fella?"

"Malky, I'd be delighted to."

"Good. Right, that's it."

As I turned to leave: "John, one other thing."

"Yes, Malky?"

"Just remember this… there's plenty o' life left in oul' Shelley…"

CHAPTER 10

I was desperate not to disappoint Malky when the first "right, what have ye got?" came, and quickly realised why Jim said so little in the mornings. The man was up to his eyes in phone calls; waste-of-time ones with well-meaning gougers, non-returned ones, occasional strike-it-lucky ones. He was like a gold prospector, ploughing through a mountain of crap for precious nuggets.

I didn't have to dig too much that July.

Two items were monopolising the sports pages; the Seoul Olympics ("they'll be talkin' aboot that 100m final for years," said Malky) and George Best's testimonial at 'The Shrine', scheduled for early August. MB, who'd co-written a book about Bestie, was "behind the eight ball" with that.

Incidentally, one myth debunked by Malky was that Bestie had signed for United in his poky wee office.

That apocryphal tale emanated from an oft-used black and white picture of the teenage Best and Eric McMordie visiting Royal Avenue prior to departing for Old Trafford.

"The truth is, Ah don't even remember them bein' there," confessed Malky.

"In those days we published loads o' pictures of young hopefuls going off for trials, and most o' them came back disillusioned.

"But then during an end-of-season tour of America with Ireland {Malky hailed from a time when the 'Northern' prefix was rarely used} in 1962 Ah met up with Matt Busby and he mentioned that the boy Best was something special.

"Ah told the boys when Ah got back, and of course Walker remembered Best in the Tele, with his Lisnasharragh blazer on. It took us hours tae find that bloody photograph."

A benefit for Bestie had been mooted since Big Pat's two years earlier and organisers of that one, such as Linfield's Billy Kennedy and David Crawford, and Crusaders chairman Derek Wade, wanted something similar for the wayward son.

The Irish FA initially said no but the organising committee, Best's agent Bill McMurdo – and Malky – kept pressurising them.

Eventually the mandarins of 20 Windsor Avenue – former home of Thomas Andrews, the man who built the Titanic – relented, and superstars such as Johan Neeskens, Roy Aitken, Ossie Ardiles, Trevor Francis, Johnny Rep, Paul Breitner, Ruud Krol, Emlyn Hughes, Liam Brady

and 'Wee Willie' Henderson breezed into Belfast on August 8, 1988.
There were nearly 25,000 at the game – remarkably, it was only Bestie's
19th appearance at Windsor. He was handed a cheque for £75,000.

I could write a book about the greatest footballer I've ever seen – and one
of the most intriguing, captivating, charming and, yes, utterly
exasperating, people I've ever met – but this isn't it.

What I will say is, the last time I spoke to Bestie, he still harboured mixed
feelings about that testimonial.

"Yes, I was grateful so many had come, but I won't forget the nastiness
leading up to it," he said.

"People were saying Big Pat deserved his benefit but me – a low-life
waster, money-grabbing drunk who'd brought shame on his country –
didn't.

"I hadn't even asked for a fucking testimonial in the first place. I told
Brodie that I wasn't going to beg so if people want to vote with their feet,
let them. And they did. It was a great night."

Unlike the night he told me that.

I was sitting with Bestie at the Belfast Telegraph Sports Stars of the Year
Awards in the Europa, nine months after he'd been diagnosed in March
2000 with liver damage so severe, it required a transplant. Consequently.
the now Portavogie-based fallen idol was on orange juice – and bored out
of his mind.

It didn't help that Alex, his missus (although not for much longer, it
transpired), was downing white wine like nobody's business and cadging
countless Marlboro Lights off me.

I remember asking Bestie about the 1968 European Cup final – surely the
highlight of his career – in an effort to cheer him up with a pleasant
memory.

"That was actually one of my worst games for United," he said.

"I'll never forget how distraught I felt as we were standing around waiting
for extra time. The whole world was watching, and I'd served up a load of
shit."

Other Bestie revelations: he "couldn't stand" Alex Higgins (with the
greatest respect to the folk behind hit musical Dancing Shoes which had,
as its showstopper, the two hellraisers meeting up in hospital). He was
"horrified" when The Hurricane breezed into his ward.

Also: the time a pissed-out-of-his-skull Bestie spent an hour in Malky's car
outside the Culloden Hotel, "crying my lamps out about the monumental
fuck-up I'd made of my life" and then fretting for a week that his
confidant would sell the story of their emotional encounter to the

tabloids. "He never printed a word of it, bless him."

Bestie was devastated, too, at being pipped to the 1971 BBC Sports Personality of the Year award by Princess Anne, who'd won the European Eventing Championship at Burghley.

"Are you seriously telling me that more people voted for her?" asked Bestie.

"That was the year I made a tit out of Banksie at Windsor; maybe the establishment didn't want to honour a bloke who'd embarrassed the World Cup-winning keeper. At least Mary P brought it home the following year."

Jeekie was co-presenter that night in the Europa, and helped me lie to Bestie about why he'd been invited. He thought he'd be presenting an award; instead, he was inducted into our Hall of Fame.

I think he smelt a rat, though, when he saw Denis Law lurking nearby. When Bestie returned to the table after receiving the award from Denis, his missus noticed that the impressive bronze trophy was based on a Tele front page from five years earlier – the day after Alexandra Macadam Pursey took George Best to be her lawfully wedded husband. A pure, hitherto un-noticed coincidence, but another excuse for Alex to shriek "more vino!"

Prior to the Bests' arrival, Jeekie had asked diners to kindly desist from bothering the guest of honour for autographs – a request that brought rapturous applause.

One of the most energetic applauders – a rotund businessman at the next table – was the first person to approach Bestie after the meal started.

"I know I'm not supposed to be doing this, George, but my wife will kill me if I don't get you to sign this..."

Within minutes, a queue of over 100 had formed. Jeekie just shook his head in disgust.

It didn't surprise me that Bestie fell off the wagon within a few weeks. Less than five years after that Europa bash, we'd be lining the rain-soaked streets of Belfast for his funeral.

I'd built up a few numbers for Irish League managers and players and it helped that I'd been at Ballymena United and that my best friend was Davy Smyth, then at Larne.

Davy, who died from cancer aged 53 on Christmas Day 2016, was easily the most charismatic person I've ever met. It's a cliché I know, but women really did want to be with him, while men just wanted to be like him.

The Eric Clapton lookalike enjoyed holding court in the bar after matches, but he loved socialising with journalists too, and much quality time was spent in 'Frames', across the road from the Tele, or in the Inkspot.

Jim and Malky – who affectionately referred to him as 'The Gypsy' – grew very fond of my long-haired, bearded, self-effacing, dry-witted soulmate. (A brief aside: Benalmadena, southern Spain, and a barely-dressed, exotic young lady approached myself and Jim in a crowded beach bar. Her: "That half-canned mate of yours over there, Davy what's-his-name, is a fucking liar. Says he's slept with 200 women." Jim: "You're right, love; he IS a fucking liar. It's far, FAR more than that...")

Mingling with contemporary Irish League players was nothing new; I was of a similar age to most of them.

I could talk their language; scoring important goals at Shamrock Park? Yep, done that. And ask Glens keeper Ricky Adair about the diving header AND dipping volley that flew past him in that floodlit tournament final. I'd also got to know a young Michael O'Neill, who lived next door to my then girlfriend in Brigadie, Ballymena and whose older sisters, Maura and Una, I knew from the St Louis days.

Managers were a different proposition. The only ones I was already acquainted with were Larne's Paul Malone and Ballymena's Alec McKee, who'd managed me in the youth team.

'Maloney', an irrepressible 'raker', regularly had me in stitches after Larne training sessions – often inadvertently.

He was a classic "whatchamacallit" merchant: "This'll have to be my last pint; my whatchamacallit – my wife – is coming to get me..."

Maloney was riding high with hitherto 'lowly Larne' when I started working in Belfast.

They'd won the whatchamacallit, the Ulster Cup, in 1987, beating Coleraine 2-1 in the final at the Oval, and had reached the final of the same competition a year later, losing 5-2 to Glentoran at Windsor. They'd also make it to the 1989 Irish Cup final.

They had a really good squad of players with Catweasel-lookalike Vinny Magee in goal, fast-raiding full-backs Trevor McMullan and Tommy Huston, reliable central defenders Paul Carland and Eddie Spiers, my boy Davy in midfield alongside Harry Kernohan, Bryan McLoughlin and Ian Bustard (Alex Higgins doppelganger Tommy Sloan was there too) and the likes of Paul Hardy (who'd move to Ballymena and break his home-town hearts with the Irish Cup winner at the Oval) and Francis Smith annoying opposing defences.

It feels strange typing out their full names; as a regular attendee of Inver with Davy, it was Husty, Carless, Spiersy, Smicker, McLocks, Busty, Argey – and of course Maloney – who joined you for a post-match libation. Ultimately, it all turned sour for hot-headed Lurgan man Maloney; in March 1991, eleven Larne players went on strike after he withheld their wages following a dismal 4-0 defeat by Cliftonville.

An 'anonymous' spokesman for the rebelling players rang Jim Gracey that Saturday night to outline their position.

"We ju-ju-just wa-wa-want what's rightfully ow-ow-owed to us," the spokesman informed Jim, who replied: "It's great hearing from you, Spiersy."

Spiersy: "How di-di-did you know it wa-wa-was me?"

Jim: "Oh, just a lucky guess..."

(I'm not making fun of Spiersy, by the way; I had a stammer when I was younger, which still makes an unwelcome return when I'm nervous or wound up. But, really, if you're going to elect an 'incognito' spokesperson...)

I didn't bother much with Coyler; the Irish League's only full-time professional manager was Malky's bailiwick.

Morning ritual would include calls to Ronnie McFall and Terry Nicholson, respective managers of Portadown and Glenavon who were very much in the ascendancy back then.

Today, we might have referred to it as the 'Mid-Ulster spring'. Suddenly, after years of predictable Belfast Big Two dominance – 12 of the previous 13 league titles had been won by either Linfield or Glentoran – two other sleeping giants were finally beginning to stir.

These were the days before mobile phones, and when footballers spoke to each other on buses.

It was best to contact people before they left for work or, if office based, just after they arrived.

I bonded almost instantly with 'Big Ronnie' – the only manager who remained in situ the entire time I worked in sport. It was to our mutual benefit; he used me for information and vice versa.

Having learned from John Dinsmore that you don't end a phone call until you have a story, I'd grill the Ports boss until he coughed up something about his own club, or palmed me off with a juicy titbit about a rival.

Some of my biggest local football scoops came from an exasperated Big Ronnie desperate to get shot of me.

Serves him right for bringing that wonderful Glens team to the Showgrounds during their 'invincibles' championship-winning season of 1980-81 and sinking the Braidmen's own title dreams courtesy of a Ron

Manley brace.

Ronnie, a devout disciple of the legendary Ports manager of the 60s, Gibby McKenzie, had just turned 40 but was already vastly experienced and busy ransacking his former club for quality youngsters such as Philip Major, Brian Strain and Alfie Stewart, and building a team he believed was capable of taking home-town Portadown to an historic first title.

He even made a cheeky bid to Dundalk for their promising young striker Dessie Gorman – a move that was reported in a down-page snippet in late 1988.

Malky's piece quoted Ronnie thus: "I asked Dundalk if they would agree to a transfer but they just weren't interested. We are only one or two players away from the team I want."

For the next quarter of a century, Portadown, despite their unprecedented success, would remain "one or two players short" of the team he wanted.

Fledgling managers who called Big Ronnie for advice were told: "Spend every penny you get your hands on – the bastards will sack you anyway..."

One man who found that out, early in my career as the Tele's 'football correspondent', was Carrick's Jim Hume.

I'd got a tip-off one morning that Jim had got the high jump at Taylor's Avenue.

I thought this would be an excellent opportunity to use the fabled 'second question technique.'

What you do is, instead of asking the obvious first question – "did you guys sack Hume last night?" (and be screwed if they say "no comment" or "where'd you hear that?") – you skip immediately to the second: "When are you going to appoint a successor to Jim Hume?"

Geordie Wright, the Carrick secretary, immediately answered: "I don't know. We'll probably advertise the post, see who's interested..."

Bingo!

HUME AXED BY CARRICK

By John Laverty

Carrick Rangers today sacked Jim Hume after two and a half years as manager at Taylor's Avenue. The decision to terminate Hume's employment at the club, taken after a board meeting late last night, is perhaps not really surprising when the cold statistic of only one win this season is taken into consideration.

Date: November 2, 1988.
Significance: Malky was later than usual that morning, but already had a story in the basket about QPR showing interest in Lee Doherty.
Bob Fenton, who was in charge of designing that day's back page, decreed that mine was the better story. Who was I to argue?
According to Colly, this was the first time he'd ever seen football copy from a Brodie 'leg man' lead the back page ahead of a story from the great man himself.
Malky didn't utter a word, one way or the other, when he read it.
Ergo, I couldn't read him.

Derek Brooks, the Linfield secretary, was a sharp-witted man and a big help. Club secretaries – George Ruddell at Glenavon, George Wright at Carrick, Freddie Anderson at Bangor, Don Stirling at Ballymena, Gordon Scott at the Oval – were invaluable when you couldn't reach a manager. My first call to Derek was an awkward one, though; the Sunday News had just splashed their front page with this...

Twelfth of July shock for Linfield supporters...

YOUR NEW SIGNING IS A CATHOLIC

They were referring to 23-year-old Antoine 'Tony' Coly, a skilful Senegalese who, along with Abdeli 'Sam' Khammal, a 20-year-old Moroccan, had arrived at Windsor Park on loan from Belgian side Club Brugge.
"Is this true, Derek?"
"I have no idea," he said, "and if you ask me again in a year's time, I'll still have no idea. I'm not going to dignify a question like that by attempting to answer it."
Nevertheless...
"Okay, Derek, but if he IS a Catholic, this would be an historic signing; I'm sure you appreciate that."
A brief pause, then: "And John, you'll also appreciate how incredibly popular Davy Walsh was... A-ha! You don't know who he was, do you? Look it up, and stop asking stupid questions about Catholics at Linfield."
Decades later, I still don't know if Coly was Catholic, but after seeing him and Khammal, a Muslim, pose for a photoshoot alongside other 'new'

68

Linfield signings Darrin Coyle (the boss's son, brought back from Everton) and George O'Boyle (repatriated from Bordeaux on loan), it was clear that religion would be the least of their worries.

July 25, 1988...

BLUES SHOW OFF BIG GUNS

By Malcolm Brodie

Dethroned Irish League champions Linfield, determined to win a major trophy in the coming season, today paraded their four big-name signings – including coloured pair Antoine Coly and Abdeli Khammal.
O'Boyle, just back from a prolonged holiday in Spain, looked like a coloured player himself.
"You would think they were The Three Degrees," quipped manager Roy Coyle.

CHAPTER 11

"It must be war – Kate Adie's here"
(Graffiti on the Falls Road)

No one warned me about The Disappointed Look.
That's what the 'leg man' inevitably got on arrival at an Irish League match.
The Look was followed by The Rhetorical Question: "Is Malcolm not here today?"
Well, not unless he's suddenly shed 40 years and eight stone.
Linfield committee men often came across as the most dismayed, followed by Glenavon. Ports suits could be, too.
Glentoran, however, seemed pragmatic even though, under the guidance of Tommy Jackson, they were reigning champions and Irish Cup winners: "I see Brodie's away with his beloved 'dethroned Irish League champions' again..."
It was easy for this ersatz Brodie to empathise with livid BBC hacks when the corporation's 'Chief News Correspondent' Kate Adie was parachuted into their patch for the 'big' stories.
But covering those games was fun.
Ards home matches were particularly enjoyable, illuminated by local reporter Jim Palmer's arid commentary on the travails of the Castlereagh Park faithful, 'still misty eyed about the time Billy McAvoy, Dennis Guy, Ronnie McAteer and Dessie Cathcart brought home the bacon for Billy Humphries' trophy-winning outfit.'
("Our striker's first touch reminds me of a dog with a balloon...")
Ditto the triumvirate of Dougie Sloane (father of ITV Sport head honcho Niall), Brian Courtney and Vicky Gordon at Portadown, Gordon and Billy at Glenavon, the permanently tired and emotional Paddy Toner (brother of Alec) at Distillery, Grant Cameron at Coleraine, my old pal Billy Spence at Ballymena and the fluent Russian-speaking Roy Kitson at Bangor's Clandeboye Park, home of the best half time tea.
A match didn't have to be lousy for Downtown Radio's Ivan Martin to fall asleep in the press box.
'Greedy' was always nodding off; probably knackered from those early morning radio stints with sidekick Richard Young.
He may have missed out on shut-eye, but was rarely short of food. Like when he took me to a Republic v Northern Ireland afternoon game at

70

Lansdowne Road.

First stop: petrol station just before the M1. He emerged with a plethora of crisps, nuts and chocolate bars. Oh, and two cans of Diet Coke.

"This'll keep us going until Drogheda," he said.

"I know a good place for lunch..."

The local media's very own Waldorf and Statler – John McAnulty and Jimmy Davis – helped make the long trips to Newry worthwhile.

The John boy almost got us into terrible trouble with his report of a highly volatile Newry v Crusaders Irish Cup game on February 20, 1988, which alleged that the Hatchetmen's terrifying midfielder Kirk Hunter had attacked Newry's Joey Cunningham.

I say 'alleged'...

After the sending-off, Kirk Hunter got hold of Joey Cunningham inside the tunnel and proceeded to beat him to a pulp...

The gifted Cunningham, then 22, sustained a fractured cheekbone which sidelined him for the rest of the season. He'd later become a lynchpin of Big Ronnie's all-conquering Ports.

Hunter got a lengthy ban and suspended prison sentence for beating his opposing midfielder "to a pulp"; the fabled Shankill Road hardman was still under suspension when the 1988-89 season got under way.

One Monday, after yet another attempted maiming, I quoted a rival player as saying Hunter was "an animal and a thug" who should be banned for life.

It appeared on the back page, along with an update on the victim (Larne's Paul Murnin, hospitalised with a fractured leg) and a picture of the assailant, looking suitably fearsome.

Later that evening, I was at a black-tie function in the Europa. Hunter clocked me, and immediately propelled himself in my direction with that trademark gangly gait.

I felt my bowels loosen.

A beaming smile emerged, however, as Hunter reached out to shake/crush my hand.

"Great photo of me on the back page tonight, mate," he said, "the wife loved it; can you get me a copy?"

(Speaking of assault, we once splashed the front page with Newry referee Frank McDonald getting beaten up after officiating at a junior gaelic match – which had been reported in the Pink, with no mention of what happened to Frank. Reason? The man entrusted to deliver the report was one of the assailants...)

One Saturday, following a Glens game, I was berated by a completely naked Tommy Jackson, who'd objected to something I'd written.
As chubby Jacko, who always showered after a match, began jabbing his finger into my chest, every bit of his bare body started to wobble; yes, that bit too.
Jim Gracey was pissing himself by this stage, as were the Glens players.
"What the fuck are you laughing at, Gracey?" spat an incandescent Jacko.
"Nothing, Tommy – honestly," squeaked Jim.
A favourite Solitude memory was of Ballymena's late, daft-as-a-brush winger Gregory Kearney 'crossing himself' in front of bemused Cliftonville fans after scoring a terrific goal.
A few of the lads on 'Hamburger Hill' (the stand that reeked of fumes from the fast-food van parked below) looked around at the press box as if to say: "will you tell him, or shall we?"

One drawback to ad libbing your Pink copy was forgetting what you'd just dictated, but I never described a team as "booking their place" in the next round, or "claiming" victory.
Claiming? Cue Coyler filling in application forms after Linfield got the better of Bangor.
And *mainland*. Avoid.
To me, it was merely another way of saying "cross-channel", but nasty letters from nationalist readers suggested otherwise. One began thus: "Dear Linfield-loving cunt". And ended with "Yours in Sport, C Doherty..."

A phone call on Monday morning, October 10, 1988 was particularly memorable.
Why so certain about the date? I knew it was two days after Linfield had 'claimed victory' against Coleraine in a TNT Gold Cup match, courtesy of a hat-trick from the prolific Martin 'Buckets' McGaughey (and the day before Paisley heckled John Paul II in Strasbourg: "I renounce you, antichrist...").
Main headline that Saturday night...

MARTIN'S DAY

One problem: Newry Town's Eamonn Hawkins – a full-back – scored FIVE against Carrick that same afternoon.

Unprecedented, phenomenal, history making – but not, seemingly, worthy of a decent billing in the ISN.

It didn't help that there was more "tension on the streets".

A few weeks earlier, eight young soldiers had been killed by an IRA bomb at Ballygawley in Co Tyrone. And in late September, an inquest held in Gibraltar decreed that SAS men who shot dead three Provisionals on the rock earlier in the year had 'acted lawfully'.

A time for cool heads, but the bloke on the blower hadn't been briefed.

"Why was it 'Martin's day' and not Eamonn's?" he asked.

I tried to explain that we'd gone by the importance of the game and not the achievement of an individual. He wasn't buying it.

"No, what you're saying is that a hat-trick by a Prod means more than five goals from a Catholic..."

By this time Walker was repeatedly yelling across: "Tell that clown to fuck away off." Ad nauseum.

After I hung up, Walker guldered: "Don't waste time with wankers like that. Get back to work right now – and, next time, tell whoever it is to go fuck himself."

"Why don't YOU go and fuck yourself," I uttered under my breath. At least I THOUGHT I did.

"What did you just say?"

Then: "Colly, did YOU hear what he just said? He told me to go and fuck myself."

Colly: "I didn't hear anything, Jimmy. I doubt if John would have said that."

Walker: "But he DID, Colly, He did. You did, didn't you?"

Me: "Yeah, I suppose I did."

Walker: "See, see? Right, I'm going to the editor's office, and you can start looking for a new job."

Off he went, Brillo-pad hair flopping. He returned six minutes later.

"The editor wants to see you, right now."

I tapped gingerly on the door of Roy Lilley's office, trying desperately – and fruitlessly – to think of a plausible excuse.

Steeple-fingered Roy: "John, did you just tell the deputy sports editor to go fuck himself?"

Me: "I did, Roy, but..."

Roy: "Look, I don't need to hear any more."

So this is it, then. What would I tell my folks?

Roy: "Here's what you're going to do. You're going to trudge slowly back to your desk, head bowed as if you've just got the biggest bollocking of your life. Then you're going to apologise to Jimmy. Say it was inexcusable, that it won't happen again. Got that?"

Me: "Yes, Roy. Thanks, Roy, I really appreciate this."

Roy: "It's one thing wanting Jimmy to go fuck himself – which, admittedly, is a tempting thought for us all on occasion – and actually saying it. Bear this in mind: if you're back in this office for a similar outburst there will be a vastly different outcome. Now get out."

IT'S HAWKEYE HAWKINS!

By Malcolm Brodie

Statisticians were today trying to work out if Newry Town's Eamonn Hawkins merits a place in the Guinness Book of Records.

There's no doubt, however, that Hawkins' one-man, five-goal destruction of Carrick Rangers has earned the 27-year-old an eternal place in soccer history.

Hawkins, a bank clerk, was back counting money today but could be forgiven for losing count of his weekend goals tally.

"I still can't believe it," he said.

"The first goal was a penalty, but four more goals from open play after that was just incredible. How people will be expecting me to do this every week!"

Walker didn't tell Malky about our altercation. Instead, he borrowed a tenner off me at lunchtime.

He may have lived in a King's Road mansion, but Walker never seemed to have any money on him. The 'lunchtime tap' became a frequent occurrence.

"Tell him to go fuck himself," said Colly.

CHAPTER 12

"They died with their boots on." Click.

Malky's reports normally ran to between 600 and 800 words. This one amounted to a mere six.

Still, it gave a flavour of what happened to Coleraine when they visited Ukraine for the second leg of a European Cup Winners' Cup tie against Dynamo Kiev in 1965.

Already trailing 6-1 from the first leg at Ballycastle Road, the Bannsiders feared another mauling in front of 60,000 screaming Soviets.

In the end, they did well to keep the score down to 4-0; died with their boots on, indeed.

This was one of the perils of 'behind the Iron Curtain' trips. You were always bricking it that the pre-war Russian phone would pack up or, as happened Malky in '65, lull you into a false sense of security before cutting you off; the dreaded dull *click*.

Something similar happened on my first Euro trip – Linfield away to Turun Palloseura (better known as TPS, thank goodness) in early September, 1988.

Copytaker Joyce Traynor had come into work specifically to take my copy from Turku, Finland at midnight but it looked like a wasted journey.

The TPS chairman, however, said his friend – a distinguished looking gentleman – would let me use the car phone in his big Volvo.

Car phone, eh? This was a first. It worked perfectly too, but those long Finnish names – a chilling forerunner to the 'Paatelainen' experience – meant I was on yer man's fancy blower for over an hour.

"Can I pay you? It took a lot longer than expected..."

The gentleman replied: "Think nothing of it. Just glad I could help."

As he drove away, the TPS chairman said: "Don't worry about the long call; that man is vice-president of Nokia. They have a factory here."

"*Nokia*? Sorry, never heard of them."

I got the Turku gig because, as was tradition, Malky accompanied the champions. Spoiler alert: our lot usually lost.

So the boss jetted off with the Glens to a European Cup tie with Spartak Moscow and I travelled with the Blues for their their Uefa Cup foray to the mouth of the Aura river in southwest Finland.

First mistake: not bringing sufficient 'advance expenses'. Three days away? Methought £50 should be enough. Not when a round of drinks for four was nearly £30.

Second mistake: writing about the 'tiring' three-hop journey: Belfast to London, then Helsinki and onto Turku, prompting narky letters pointing out that I was getting paid to be there – not taking time off work, fighting with the missus and blowing the family income in an exorbitant Nordic country.

After the first 'hop' we bumped into Scottish actress Dee Hepburn, who played a female football star in hit movie Gregory's Girl and was waiting by the luggage carousel. A couple of the Linfield lads challenged me to 'say something clever'.

Upshot: "Oi, Dee, if you've brought your boots you can come with us to Finland. We've a bit of an injury crisis …"

(What was it with famous females? In 1994 I was strolling down a New York street when I spotted Barbra Streisand walking towards me. She was 100 yards away; sufficient time for me to come up with a Trademark Witty Remark. As our eyes finally met, I blurted out: "you're Barbra Steisand...")

While checking out Turku's spotlessly clean boulevards, I bumped into Bryan Butterfield from Ballymena.

Not a Blues fan who'd travelled, but a man who'd been working in a Finnish art gallery, and who'd recognised me as a fellow native of The City of the Seven Towers.

"The last time I saw Linfield was at the Showgrounds in the 70s," he recalled.

"Jimmy Hill was manager and they had Eric Bowyer, Alan Fraser, Eric Magee and Paul Malone in the team. They were keek that day..."

The Blues, minus injured midfield pair Lee Doherty and Tony Coly (who remained in Belfast for treatment), battled to an encouraging goalless draw in the Kupittaa Stadium, largely thanks to first-rate performances from goalkeeper George Dunlop, defenders Alan Dornan, Lindsay McKeown and David Jeffrey, and midfielders Sam Khammal and Philip Knell.

Third mistake: Meeting up with the manager and his coaching staff in the lobby bar after filing my copy.

"So, what did you write about us?" asked Coyler, who was downing champagne – his favourite tipple, btw, not a premature celebration.

"Well, I still have the notes with me," says I: "I'll read you a bit..."

Before last night's match in Turku, a Finnish journalist asked me for a
translation of Linfield's motto, Fortuna Audaci Juvat.
"Fortune favours the brave," I told him, and the Finn smiled.
"We'll see," he said.
Ninety nerve-jangling minutes later, we did see. We saw a weakened
Linfield side, minus Lee Doherty and Tony Coly, shrug off their recent
domestic disappointments with the sort of display...

The Thin-lipped One's demeanour darkened.

"What the fuck is THAT?" he said, adding: "Are you winding me up?"

Startled by the abrupt mood swing, I spluttered: "But Roy, it's very
positive..."

His reply: "That's not the issue. Why the fuck are you writing about
Doherty and Coly? What part did THEY play tonight? THEY'RE not Linfield
Football Club. Linfield Football Club are the guys out there on the pitch,
not two blokes sitting at home scratching their arses. We come up with a
performance like that tonight, and the first people you namecheck aren't
even in this fucking country."

He was fucking right.

That was the last time I'd mention injured players in a match report – and
definitely the last time I'd read out copy prior to publication.

The smile only returned to Coyler's face when I told him the Glens had
lost 2-0.

Here's what wasn't read out after the second leg in Wrexham a month
later:

Roy Coyle's team did everything expected of them last night. They were
asked to keep things tight at the back and flood the midfield. They did
that. They were urged to get further forward, create chances and score;
they did that too. But what they didn't do was prevent TPS scoring.
George O'Boyle grabbed an 'equaliser', if you could call it that, late in the
game, but this was one away goal that wasn't going to count as double.

The second leg was played in Wales because some idiots had thrown four
items – a stone, two bottles and a golf-ball – onto the Windsor pitch
during the European Cup tie with Lillestrom (drew 1-1 in Norway, lost 4-2
at home) a year earlier.

On the eve of the Wrexham game, Billy Bingham and his second wife
Rebecca van Strang (whom he married at St Albans in 1986; Gerry

Armstrong was best man, Malky a witness) turned up at the elegant Vale of Llangollen hotel.

(He met his first wife, Eunice – a Sunderland girl – in the 50s; the pair were married for 26 years and had two children, Sharon and David).

I'd spoken to Billy while gauging the 'mood in the camp' prior to a dull 0-0 draw with the Republic at Windsor a few weeks earlier; first impressions were of a rather aloof character.

But on this occasion Southport-based Bingy, who had just turned 57, was positively gregarious; clearly a different animal away from the tension of a World Cup qualifier.

"John, would you care to join myself and Rebecca for dinner?"

"I'd be both flattered and delighted to accept your kind invitation, Mr Bingham."

"Oh please, John, call me Billy."

He was great company; reminiscing about the tiny Woodstock Road terrace this shipyard worker's son grew up in during the thrifty 30s, of getting into scrapes with 'Fenians' from Short Strand, and about the strange sense of loss the Elmgrove Primary schoolboy felt when "Mrs Simpson stole our King".

"All I'd heard about 'Fenians' was that their eyes were closer together and that they bred like rabbits; hardly enough reason to stone them, but everyone else was doing it."

When the Glens told young William Laurie Bingham he was too scrawny to make it as a "top plure" in the late 40s, he hired Robert 'Buster' McShane to beef him up.

"They always mention Buster when talking about Mary P, but he looked upon me, a fellow east Belfast native, as his most accomplished prodigy."

A man not unaware of how good his football CV is, Bingy spoke fondly of the glory days as a "plure" with Sunderland (where he continued his shipyard apprenticeship "just in case"), Luton, Everton and the legendary Northern Ireland 1958 team.

Peter Doherty was one of his all-time heroes, along with ex-Man United and Republic of Ireland star Johnny Carey, who signed him for Everton.

"Did you know I wrote a book about football?" Bingy asked. I didn't.

"It was back in 1962. 'Soccer with the Stars', it was called; I got a tidy advance from the publisher, Stanley Paul. Nearly 200 pages about my career, and how I saw the game shaping up over the next decade. Ahead of its time, that book..."

His biggest regret was the Toffees blowing their big chance of winning the First Division title in 1975 (Bingy, then manager, had done it as an Everton player 12 years earlier).

"We'd the best squad of plures for years, but lost home and away to a hopeless Carlisle team and ended up three points behind champions Derby," he said.

"I still can't believe we threw those Carlisle games away; mind you, if we'd won them, I'd never have ended up back with Northern Ireland, and talking to you..."

He told of the "torrent of hate mail" after appointing ex-GAA player Martin O'Neill as Northern Ireland captain.

"Some people thought the timing wasn't great, with IRA men starving themselves to death and Paisley's 'Third Force' on the streets, but I disagreed," he said.

"Martin was not only a terrific plure, but a natural leader. I kept all the 'fan mail' about that. It makes me laugh when you think about what we went on to achieve."

As we consumed chef's special butterfly fillet steaks with pepper sauce and lyonnaise potatoes, I began wondering if those stories about Bingy being a shameless tight-arse were apocryphal.

Malky told me that during the 1980 tour of Australia, Bingy brought him along to a jewellery shop in Sydney he'd visited 10 years earlier. On arrival, he produced a rather modest-looking watch.

"I bought this here in 1970; it had a lifetime guarantee but stopped after three years," Bingy told them.

"If I can't get it mended quickly, I'll accept a full refund. Here's the receipt..."

I declined the offer of a postprandial brandy; "Gotta do my preview stuff, but thanks all the same, Billy; see you real soon."

Two days later, at checkout, the 'extras' bill came to over £100. What the fuck?

"That £83.50 item was Tuesday night's dinner, Mr Laverty. Your guests said the full amount was to be charged to your room..."

In the early 90s, Glenavon captain Duncan Lowry was suspended by the club when he suggested, following a home European defeat, that the away leg would be just a 'holiday'.

Perhaps 'Duncan Disorderly' was thinking back to Glenavon's notorious 1991 'Sodom and Gomorrah' excursion' to Tampere, Finland, when the playing staff seemingly forgot they were actually leading 3-2 from the Mourneview leg and had an historic Cup Winners Cup victory within their grasp. The Tampere debacle – and other tales of inebriation and debauchery – later.

I accompanied Glentoran, Portadown, Crusaders, Coleraine – and an impeccably behaved Glenavon – on enjoyable, if predictably unsuccessful, Euro ventures but, for sheer drama, nothing usurps Linfield in the autumn of 1993.

Then managed by Trevor Anderson, they'd been paired with Dinamo Tbilisi of newly independent Georgia in what was now known as the Uefa Champions League, although the 'league' bit of it wouldn't kick in until after the second round proper.

To save costs for this 'first preliminary tie', the Blues shared a charter to the former Soviet republic with Dublin side Shelbourne, who'd been drawn against Ukrainian opposition and would be dropped off in Lviv.

Four hours into the flight from Dublin – and seconds before it was due to touch down at Danylo Halytskyi International Airport – the Georgian Airlines Tupelov TU154, carrying just over 100 people, suddenly swooped back up into the night sky.

None of the Russian-speaking cabin crew could articulate what had happened but we ascertained a cockpit warning light had suggested the landing gear hadn't locked down properly. Oh great!

The plane circled above the airport, dumping fuel, while engineers on the ground used binoculars to see if the wheels could carry an emergency landing.

At this point, Blues chairman David Campbell asked me to teach him the Hail Mary.

All I could think of as we descended for a second – it would be final, one way or the other – time was: if we survived, this would be a great yarn for the next day's Tele. It was already too late for the morning papers, ha!

That abstract thought helped keep me sane as fire trucks raced towards the slowly descending aircraft. As we hit the runway, the plane lurched to the right before shuddering to a halt.

I thought we'd all get sliding down the emergency chutes but, as far as the cabin crew were concerned, it was drama over. We decamped to the terminal for two hours while the starboard landing gear was repaired. We were getting back onto the same bloody plane! Lucky Shels; their nightmare was over.

That night, people who never touched alcohol were downing whisky and brandy like there was no tomorrow – which was what many were thinking at the time.

Fortunately, the 'midnight plane to Georgia' flight was incident-free. The squad finally got to bed a 5am, just as I was starting to 'etch'.

Monday, August 16, 1993, page 1...

BLUES IN AIR DRAMA

By John Laverty in Tbilisi

The aircraft carrying Linfield players to a European game was involved in an emergency landing drama early today.
More than 100 passengers and crew – including the Irish League champions and Dublin side Shelbourne – were on board the Tupelov TU154 which was forced to abort its initial landing attempt.
Linfield midfielder Lee Doherty said: "This was one of the worst things I have ever experienced."

I didn't surface until lunch time but wasn't missing much; with the exception of one training session, we weren't allowed to leave the hotel. "Too dangerous" barked one of the armed security men.

The civil war that paralysed Georgia after it declared independence from Moscow in April 1991 had escalated; just before we arrived, American CIA agent Fred Woodruff had been shot dead just outside Tbilisi and, according to our man Oleg with the AK-47, the streets were full of "crazy armed bandits."

Mind you, the £50m Metechi Palace which looked down on what was, in peace times, one of the world's most beautiful cities, was a more than adequate prison.

We were the only guests occupying the majestic building, which opened amid a wave of euphoria and optimism just weeks after Independence Day. With its glass lifts gliding up and down the empty floors – and a cheerful chappie playing grand piano in the cavernous, polished marble lobby – you couldn't fault our hosts for wanting us to feel 'at home'.

They even stocked the bar with cans of Guinness – a welcome gesture; there were no other alcoholic drinks available. It ran out after less than a day.

Oh, and a sign in the lobby read, in English: "For the comfort and safety of all guests kindly deposit all firearms with security. Thank You."
Predictably, some started calling our new residence, some 2,200 miles from Belfast, Hotel California but it felt more like The Shining.

They had a receptionist – a lovely looking but rather dour Georgian girl – working a full shift, even though no other guests were allowed in.

She watched TV most of the day, and got rather excited when the Linfield squad appeared in a news clip arriving at the hotel.

"Come, see," she shrieked to a couple of us sucking on empty stout tins.

We missed the 'VT' of the lads getting off the bus, but could see a distinguished-looking bloke being interviewed. The Dinamo manager, I suggested.

"No, no no!" she laughed. "It's President Shevardnadze."

Of course. Eduard Shevardnadze, former Soviet foreign minister – and the man tasked with trying to bring peace to this hell-hole after the violent ousting of predecessor Zviad Gamsakhurdia. But why was he on telly, just after a clip about little Linfield?

"He said this is more than a game of football," said Valeriya (we were on first name terms by now).

"He said this is the first sign of the reconstruction of our country."

Holy shit!

"But it's only football, Valeriya..."

"Yes, but it's the first match with foreign visitors since independence," she explained, adding: "It's also the first night-time event in two years. The curfew has been lifted for one night; all the politicians, army generals and diplomats will be there."

Another whoop of astonishment. And one more question.

"Tell me this, Valeriya... how many are they expecting at this game?"

She conversed with one of the guards in Russian.

"The stadium should be full... at least 50,000."

Holy shit!

A crowd of 50,000-plus in the Vladimir Ilyich Lenin Stadium (later rechristened the Boris Paichadze National Stadium) – the largest any Linfield player had ever performed in front of – settled down on a balmy late summer evening in the Caucasus, expecting the visitors to get tanked.

But keeper Wes Lamont had the game of his life and, after going behind early on to Shota Arveladze (who'd later play for Rangers), Linfield equalised through Ritchie Johnston, eventually falling to a John McConnell own goal.

I was later told that Linfield had declined the opportunity to sign Dinamo's highly rated young midfielder Georgi Kinkladze for £100,000. Whatever happened to him? Oh yes... Man City shelled out over £2m for him a couple of years later.

Arveladze, meanwhile, scored again in the second leg at Windsor, with Garry Haylock grabbing a late consolation.

Why did it have to be the same old story? Once again, this page will be devoted to hard luck stories from local clubs in Europe.

Then:

Linfield are about to be sensationally reinstated to the European Cup – because opponents Dinamo Tbilisi allegedly bribed match officials during the first leg in Georgia. Uefa are investigating and have immediately suspended Georgian champions Dinamo, who defeated the Blues 3-2 on aggregate after Wednesday's 1-1 draw at Windsor Park.

We held the late Friday edition back (in the Tele, being 'late for the early' or 'early for the late' was often the same thing) to get that story in. It was worth it, though. Worth hearing Malky, too.

"Whaaa? Are ye sure this isnae a wind-up?"

"Honestly, Malky, it isn't. Uefa have just announced it. Looks like the Blues are heading to *vunderful, vunderful Kovenhavn* after all..."

"But why in the name o' God would a big club like that feel they had tae bribe a ref? It doesnae make any sense."

We later discovered that the Turkish referee, Erman Torughu (whose performance, funnily enough, had been described as 'jittery' in The Independent's match report) was handed an envelope containing 5,000 American dollars by a Tbilisi official a few hours before the game; Mr Torughu reported the corruption attempt to Uefa the following morning. My mind returned to that Tuesday afternoon chin-wag with Valeriya translating the Georgian president's comments: "He said this is more than a game of football..."

Dinamo's appeal failed, inspiring one of the best-ever displays by a local club in continental competition – the reinstated Blues' 3-0 epic hammering of FC Copenhagen (managed by Richard Moller Nielsen, who'd guided Denmark to that astonishing Euro 92 win) in mid-September.

Haylock and a delirious McConnell put the home side 2-0 up by half-time, with Johnston propelling them into dreamland after the break; Linfield's first European victory in 11 years, and first clean sheet in 13 continental games. Surely they wouldn't blow a three-goal lead?

September 30, 1993...

Time-warped Blues crash out of Europe

By John Laverty in Copenhagen

I don't normally criticise match officials but I'll make an exception here. Never have I witnessed a display as appalling as this one. Mr Roman Steindl works as a travel agent in Austria. Maybe he'll sort out FC Copenhagen's flights for the next round of the European Cup. After all, he helped them get there. Ninety minutes of an enthralling game in the magnificent Parken Stadium had elapsed. The Danes were 2-0 ahead on the night but losing 3-2 on aggregate.

Just one little peep on that whistle would have done it, Mr Steindl. But 91 minutes passed, 92, 93, 94... instead of putting the Blues out of their misery, he plunged them into it. On 94 minutes 10 seconds, Copenhagen were awarded a free-kick on the edge of the box. Lars Hoger buried an absolute screamer past Wes Lamont from 22 yards. NOW the whistle was blown, plunging Linfield into that ill-fated extra time. But where did the 'extra' time at the end of 90 minutes come from? There had been no injuries, no time-wasting from the visitors. Where did it come from, Mr Steindl?

It was substitute Kim Mikklesen who applied the bitter *coup de grâce* with a fourth goal against a deflated, demoralised Blues in 'real' extra time; insult was added to already grievous injury when the Danes were drawn against the best team in the world, AC Milan (yes, Baresi, Costacurta, Maldini, Albertini, Boban, Donadoni, Gullit, Rijkaard, van Basten, Savicevic, Papin *et al*). FC Copenhagen made over £1.2m from that glamour tie.

Now THAT'S a hard-luck story, and here's another one: Linfield again, en route home from another demoralising result in Denmark, almost exactly a year after the Copenhagen torment.

84

This time they were hammered 5-0 by Odense BK in the second leg of a Uefa Cup tie after an encouraging 1-1 draw at Windsor.

I may have empathised with the anguish of 12 months earlier, but this was a pathetic display and I wasn't going to sugar-coat it.

September 28, 1994…

Linfield's Danish pasting

By John Laverty in Odense

The story of the Irish League club in Europe: it begins with the concession of an early goal, continues with the concession of a few more and ends with elimination. Sadly, we revert to type on occasions like this. Simple things like finding a team-mate 10 yards away – bread and butter things – are forgotten. Long, aimless balls from the back, things you wouldn't dream of doing against Distillery or Ballyclare, become par for the course in places like this. Why?

(Continues in this vein for another 600 words)

I'd no qualms about it – what I hadn't envisaged was free copies of the Tele being handed out on the Belfast-bound plane.

I'd no idea such a hard-hitting headline had been written, accompanied by a 'picture byline' of me grinning like The Joker, as if mocking the battle-weary troops.

Chairman David Campbell buttonholed me at the Aldergrove luggage carousel.

"What you wrote was disrespectful, an utter disgrace," he thundered.

Then, the *pièce de résistance*: "Brodie would NEVER have written anything like that…"

Perhaps I should have said "they died with their boots on".

CHAPTER 13

An incredible late goal by goalkeeper Alan Paterson won Glentoran the Roadferry League Cup at the Oval last night.

Arch rivals Linfield just couldn't believe it, the freak goal ending their 21-game unbeaten run in front of 10,000 spectators.

Paterson's goal – the first scored by a keeper in a cup final – just four minutes from time was a carbon copy of the goal scored by Cliftonville keeper Andy McClean against the Blues in the opening game of the season.

Paterson punted the ball from his hands down the centre of the pitch. It bounced once and Linfield sweeper Lindsay McKeown appeared to leave it. But to his horror the ball bounced over George Dunlop, leaving the keeper with egg all over his face.

(News Letter, December 1, 1988)

Veteran Glentoran goalkeeper Alan Paterson could hardly have dreamt he would score the winning goal in a cup final, but that's exactly what happened at the Oval last night.

With only four minutes left on the clock and extra time looming, Paterson sent a long clearance from his own 18-yard line. As his international goalkeeping counterpart George Dunlop came off his line the ball shot up off the turf and over his despairing reach for an amazing climax to this Roadferry Cup final.

(Irish News, December 1, 1988)

"Best wishes and good luck to Alan." The match ball inscription was hardly a contender for great quotes of our time but in the context of last night's memorable Roadferry League Cup final at the Oval, it was a sporting gesture supreme.

Dunlop had just helped Glentoran goalkeeper Alan Paterson rewrite British soccer's history books with a freak goal to beat all freak goals.

(Belfast Telegraph December 1, 1988)

With a knick knack Paddy whack
Paddy scores a goal
Geordie Dunlop is on his hole
(Glentoran supporters, November 30, 1988)

Have you guessed the missing word yet? Clue: a curved yellow fruit, rich in potassium.

Unfortunately for the horrified sponsors, the 1988 Roadferry League Cup final will forever be remembered as the 'Banana Match'.

The shameful night Linfield's Sam Khammal and Tony Coly were repeatedly pelted with bananas by monkey-chanting tossers who'd forgotten, or were unaware in the first place, that the Irish League's first black player, Alan Gracey, had proudly worn a Glens shirt less than 10 years earlier.

Like 10,000 others, I'd braved the cold, damp late November evening to take in the first 'Big Two' meeting of the season.

The Blues had come good after an inauspicious start and were enjoying a long unbeaten run. They were highly fancied to win their second trophy of the campaign – and Coyler's 30th as manager.

Number 29 came courtesy of a 2-0 win over Portadown – who, presumably, were still two players short of the finished article – in a replayed TNT Gold Cup decider at the same stadium.

But the Cock n' Hens could match the old enemy for early season silverware, having seen off Larne in the Lombard Ulster Cup, and they had home advantage here.

The barrage of bananas, oranges and obscene chants as the teams emerged from the tunnel was no real surprise in the 80s, when a 'Morgan day' meant nothing more than switching to dark rum after the Smirnoff ran out.

We were just three-and-a-bit years on from the notorious 'Blue Pig (Irish Cup) Final' (which I attended as a neutral spectator), when a blue-painted piglet raced around the Oval pitch, evading incensed stewards, while a cockerel proudly strutted its stuff on the sidelines during a 'Pig of a game' (Jim Gracey's inspired ISN headline that night) which finished 1-1, with the Glens winning the replay 1-0.

Similar stunts were *de rigueur* at another powderkeg derby – the Buenos Aires Superclasico between River Plate (unaffectionately referred to as Gallinas, i.e. Chickens) and bitter rivals Boca Juniors (*Los Chanchitos*, or Little Pigs). This was the first time, however, that anyone could recall Belfast's finest (who'd also rioted at Windsor two years earlier) resorting to live farm animals.

Linesman Jackie Poucher was also felled by a brick (Malky described that as a chilling echo of the 1966 Big Two showpiece final, when Glens keeper Albert Finlay got poleaxed), and psychotic arseholes dropped burning wooden planks on rival fans from the rafters of the railway stand.

Quite a challenge for the young BBC commentator, Mike Nesbitt. The replay, settled by Paul Mooney's own goal, fell on the future Ulster Unionist Party leader's 28th birthday.

The disgraceful abuse meted out to Coly and Khammal (one godsend: another three days, and they'd probably have been pelted with unwanted eggs as well, following health minister Edwina Currie's sensational salmonella claims) was every bit as shocking.

So too was the apparent reluctance of local hacks to report it.

To be fair to the News Letter's Brian 'Skipper' Millar (who regularly shared a room with Malky on Northern Ireland away matches), he did refer to the pitch being "littered with banana skins" further down his copy (although there'd be no follow-up in the next day's edition), but that was the only fleeting mention the three local papers could muster between them.

Having already seen how the two mornings had handled the disgraceful episode – rather poorly, to be brutally frank – I was eager to read what Malky had phoned over.

Like the others, it was all about 'Paddy' Paterson's freak goal (after Gary Macartney had equalised Paul Mooney's first half strike) and no mention of bananas. What the hell was going on here?

I thought better of mentioning this when he came in; discretion the better part of valour and all that. And it wasn't that long since the "go fuck yourself" incident with Walker.

But then my boss began dictating his back page piece to Angela:

Linfield manager Roy Coyle today dismissed suggestions that his Northern Ireland international goalkeeper George Dunlop would quit after conceding a freak goal from his Glentoran counterpart Alan Patterson...

"What's going on, Malky?"

"Whaa? Whaddye mean?"

Me: "What I mean is, why are we still banging on about Paddy's goal, when everybody's talking about how Coly and Khammal were treated?"

Him: "Ah'm gonna get tae that. Ah've already spoken tae Coyler and Campbell about it. If ye'd listened a bit longer, ye'd have heard me dictatin' it."

Me: "That may be so, but why aren't we leading off with the bananas? You guys were yakking about it enough in the press box last night..."

Then: "Right, that's it. John, Ah'll see ye in ma office, right away."

Twenty seconds later: "Right, I'm gonna tell ye this, absolutely straight. Don't ye EVER question ma authority in front o' folk again. Who'd ye think ye are? MB is the boss-man here, and don't ye ever forget it. Ye might get away wi' that sort o' backchat wi' Walker, but ye won't wi' me. And Ah'll write ma piece whatever the fuck way Ah want, *capisce*? Right, that's it. Get out o' ma sight."

It felt like my whole body was still quivering when *Don Brodi* retook his place alongside Angela.

"Listen, Angie, on second thoughts Ah think we'll start that copy another way..."

LINFIELD FURY OVER BANANA INCIDENT

Taunting of Khammal and Coly an 'absolute disgrace'

By Malcolm Brodie

Linfield's management committee will meet shortly to discuss the jeering and taunting of their black players Sammy Khammal and Tony Coly, and a virtual 90-minute banana throwing onslaught, at last night's Roadferry Cup final with Glentoran at the Oval.

"This was an utter disgrace," said Linfield chairman David Campbell. "To throw bananas for the entire game was entirely unacceptable. The ball boys, stewards – and even our goalkeeper – spent a lot of the time lifting bananas."

Roy Lilley strode across to the sports desk with a broad smile on his face. "Well done today, Malcolm; you certainly didn't miss those idiots and hit the wall."

A beaming Malky replied: "Cheers, Roy. Sometimes ye have tae tell it like it is: completely, absolutely straight and no bullshit."

He glanced across the room and winked.

"Ain't that right, John?"

CHAPTER 14

The upshot of the Banana Match? Sweet (Irish) FA.

This was the year Liverpool's John Barnes famously back-heeled a banana that had been thrown at him by a moron at Goodison Park.

Like Alan Gracey, the abused players had found a way of blocking out the bile with dignity and restraint.

(Poor 'Graz' faced additional terrace torment about his criminal past; as a wayward youth he'd raided a local post office and got collared by the boys in blue after the postmistress pointed out that, although the robber wore a mask, he didn't have gloves – and his hands appeared "blacker than a normal person's...")

'Bravery of Linfield boss' admired

Dear Sir,

When I played for Glenavon I had to put up with racist taunts which seemed to come from from every other team's supporters, with probably the worst coming from the small minority of Bluemen who took great delight in calling me all the names of the day, along with being a "black Fenian b*****d", which still makes me laugh.

When I moved to Glentoran I knew that a minority of their fans had also taunted me in the past but I never let it worry me because I was now a Glenman.

Any Glenmen whom I met welcomed me with open arms and made my time there very enjoyable.

All supporters will back their own players no matter what colour or religion they may be.

Roy Coyle signed those two players with the intention of doing the best for Linfield and has to be admired for his bravery which has paid off with a trophy in the cabinet already.

He probably knew what these two players would come up against, but these things never deterred him.

It seems the incidents at the Glentoran match have had no effect on these players as they are still playing great football.

Meanwhile, some Linfield fans should think back to what they have been putting other teams' players through because they are Catholic or black.

What would the reaction have been of the Linfield supporters if Tommy Jackson or Billy Sinclair had signed the two coloured players?

Yours sincerely,

Alan Gracey

Other Glenmen wrote in, pointing out that offended Bluemen, who were so fond of being "up to their knees in Fenian blood", arrived at the Oval bearing 'LINFIELD' banners with the 'N' and 'F' intentionally fused together.

For Coly, the more gifted of the two imports – but also an infuriating luxury player who rarely tackled back – revenge was served cold.

The silky midfielder scored a crucial goal in the subsequent (and relatively banana-less) Irish League encounter at the Oval, a 3-2 victory that sent the Blues six points clear at the summit and well on their way to wresting the title back. He's best remembered for the majestic, sweeping 30-yard 'goal of the season' contender, again at the Oval – that put the final nail in Glentoran's hopes of lifting the Irish Cup for a fifth successive season.

Khammal, an inconsistent winger who wasn't a patch on homegrown talent such as Coleraine's Raymie McCoy, faded after a promising start (he was 'Guinness Player of the Month' in September; "the first foreigner to achieve the honour", Malky wrote) although, if the scuttlebutt is to be believed, he and Coly were more regular scorers at Pips International nightclub.

The other *soi-disant* member of Windsor Park's Three Degrees, George O'Boyle, saw his summer tan fade but not his talent, weighing in with 19 goals, and Stephen Baxter, with 28, even managed to outscore established strike partner 'Buckets' McGaughey.

The Gibson Cup title trophy, Coyler's 10th in 12 seasons, was secured courtesy of a solitary Buckets goal at Mourneview Park on April 15, 1989 – a date forever synonymous with what happened in another stadium that afternoon.

In sports journalism, you tended to have more lucid recall of the big news that broke on a Saturday; the murder of Army corporals Derek Wood and David Howes in Andersonstown, the Shankill and Omagh bombs and Paisley's "never, never, never" rant in front of 100,000 at the City Hall. When those came, we'd convert the ISN into a newspaper; it was, de facto, an 'edition' of the Tele.

And by the time we went to print on the day of the Hillsborough Disaster, 79 Liverpool fans had been confirmed dead.

Malky, who'd been etching about the Blues' title-clinching win over Glenavon, 'recast' his copy to account for the sudden solemnity of the occasion; Linfield players muted hitherto raucous celebrations after news about the tragedy enveloping the Liverpool v Forest FA Cup semi-final filtered through.

The wily old pro was brilliant at that; Walker, who rarely praised Malky, told me of a remarkable response to the previous worst disaster in British football history: Saturday, January 2, 1971.

"We'd just put the Pink to bed when Malky rang from Ibrox to say that part of a stand had collapsed, with multiple casualties. I told him it was too late to do anything – unless we produced a second edition on the hoof. 'If you rustle up enough staff, I'll produce the copy,' he said.

"Finding the printers wouldn't be a problem – they were either in McGlades or across the road in the 'Malcolm Brodie Lounge' of the Brown Horse – the hardest thing would be persuading them to get back in.

"But when they heard what had happened, they'd no qualms. Malky dictated the copy to me – and we were the first paper in the world with the story."

Malky later told me he only went to Ibrox because of the significance of the date; he'd thought of doing a nostalgic piece about a previous visit decades earlier.

"On the second day o' January, 1939, Ah was at Ibrox for the record-breaking Old Firm game, which was played a day late because Ne'erday had fallen on a Sunday..."

Depending on which account you read, the crowd that day was 118,567, 118,730 or 118,561. It was certainly the largest ever recorded for a league match in Britain.

Exactly 32 years later, aged 44, Malky would report on how 66 people perished on Stairway 13.

Never will I forget the nightmarish scene as over 40 bodies were laid out on the white frost cover, stretching from the corner flag to the goalpost at the Copland Road end. Ibrox had become a mortuary, a tomb encircled in the swirling fog rolling in from the Clyde, a hospital for the stricken.
Never will I forget the hundreds of weeping women waiting in the dark outside, hoping for news of their menfolk, their children.
Never will I forget the sight of a young St Andrews Association nurse who was herself assisted to an ambulance, overcome with emotion and exhaustion.

(As Malky dictated his ISN copy to Walker, traumatised teenager Kenny Dalglish – the only person present at the Ibrox, Heysel *and* Hillsborough disasters – was fleeing the carnage with other Gers fans.)

Belfast's Big Two held a minute's silence at Windsor for the Hillsborough victims a week later.

The game was of little consequence to the Blues, save for giving a lithe, blond-maned, jubilant David Jeffrey the hubris of parading the Gibson Cup in front of their dethroned rivals.

It finished 2-1 to Glentoran; a hollow victory for visitors who could still call upon the likes of Jim Cleary, Billy 'Casko' Caskey, Barney Bowers, Raymond 'Nuts' Morrison, Johnny Jameson and lethal front-man 'G-Force' Macartney.

No one that day realised that this would be the first gig by 'Roy Coyle and his Easybeats'. Almost exactly a year later, the Irish League's most successful manager – and future most trophy-laden Glentoran boss – was out of a job.

CHAPTER 15

April 25, 1989...

Linfield to nip Glenavon in the Bud

By John Laverty

*A Linfield defeat is, more often than not, followed by a Linfield win.
And that could be bad news for Glenavon in tonight's Budweiser Cup final
replay at the Oval...*

A further 300 words of preview bumph, then...

*...Supporters will recall that Glenavon conceded a lot of midfield
possession to the Blues in the first match but looked dangerous on the
break, with in-form Geoff Ferris and Gary Blackledge always ready to
snap up the half chance.
Another good evening of football is in prospect, but I don't go along with
the view that Glenavon's late equaliser in the first game was the turning
point for them.
Prediction: Linfield to win inside the 90 minutes.*

It was going to be a busy week, kicking off with a Sunday trip to see Derry
City, Irish League champions in 1965, make history by winning titles on
both sides of the border. They followed up the previous October's League
Cup final rout of Dundalk at Oriel Park (Paul Doolin 2, Jonathan Speak and
Noel Larkin) with a routine 2-0 victory over Cobh Ramblers (another
double from Doolin) at the Brandywell which secured the second leg of
an historic, unprecedented treble.
A week later, Malky, Jurgen from Lurgan and myself would clamber into
the boss's 'variable speed Honda' bound for a heaving, red-and-white
bedecked Dalymount Park and a turgid, scoreless FAI Cup final against
Cork City (Felix Healy's goal in the replay ultimately got the three-time
Irish Cup winners over the line.)
That would be my second round-trip to Dublin in five days, following an
epic Republic of Ireland v Spain World Cup qualifier (1-0 to Jack's boys,
courtesy of an own-goal from Real Madrid's Michel – then the world's
highest-paid player).
But before that, the Budweiser Cup final replay, which I'd be covering

because Malky had jetted off to Malta with Northern Ireland.

I'd no doubt that Linfield would win, and said so in my preview piece.

It grated when Malky's 'predictions' often amounted to "you pays your money and takes your choice" or "your guess is as good as mine". What was the point?

Instead, the good readers got my well-reasoned argument, complete with forecast that Glenavon's long barren run, stretching back to their City Cup victory of 1966, would continue.

Result: Linfield 1 Glenavon 6.

One of the most dramatic games in local football history, one of the most humiliating results of Roy Coyle's career – certainly on a par with losing the 1976 Irish Cup final to B Division Carrick – and the proverbial fairytale for Terry Nicholson's Lurgan Blues in their centenary year.

Linfield defender Lindsay McKeown was red-carded but rampant Glenavon were already 3-0 up by then, through a Ferris brace and Gary Blackledge. Stevie McBride made it 4-0, with Philip Knell's superb overhead kick for Linfield no more than a spectacular irrelevance as Duncan Lowry and man of the match Ferris twisted the knife.

To be fair to ashen-faced Coyler, he admitted afterwards that his team – who'd won 40 of their previous 55 games – had been "paralysed" by Nicky's men. I didn't feel sorry for him, but made sure to laugh heartily after he attempted a lame joke that "this wouldn't have happened if Brodie had been here."

An astonishing result, but my intro didn't live up to it: "If you're going to end a barren run of 23 years without a trophy then, my goodness, this is the way to do it". Yuk!

Lurgan mafioso Billy Ireland did it right: "Glenavon ended the famine with a feast". Simple, effective, poignant, wonderfully apt.

One abiding memory was Billy, who'd started dictating his copy at 4-1, slamming the phone back into its cradle when Lowry bagged the fifth, grabbing me by the lapels and, eyes bulging, screaming "5-1, 5-1! Stick THAT in your paper tomorrow!"

Later, on TV, a reticent, tongue-tied Ferris could only answer "billiant, billiant" (sic) when asked about his sensational performance.

'Billiant'? What sort of inarticulate idiot is this... and him in the police?

It was the softly-spoken striker's finest hour as a player – but, a quarter of a century later, PSNI 'Detective Sergeant Geoffrey Ferris' would emerge as the shrewd, astute officer who 'broke' notorious double-killer

95

and *femme fatale* Hazel Stewart, ultimately compelling her to own up to her involvement in the murders of husband Trevor Buchanan and Lesley Howell, wife of her lover Colin Howell.

I met up with Geoff at Davy Smyth's funeral in 2016, and as we walked back into Ballymena town centre afterwards, we talked about his now legendary encounter with Stewart. What he told me must remain confidential.

Suffice to say, though, it was a *billiant* interrogation.

CHAPTER 16

July 10, 1989.

"Fuck me, you are one smug-looking wee shit."

"Come on Colly, give us a break here. It's not every day you stick a headline like THAT on the back page."

Then the phone rang.

"John, Adrian Taggart from security. What's your plans for lunchtime? Are you heading out of the building?"

"Gee, I dunno, Adrian. But you're wasting your time if you're asking me on a date. You just ain't my type, mate."

"Ha-bloody-ha. You'll be laughing on the other side of your face when you hear who's at the back gate."

"Who? Do tell, kind sir."

"A crowd of rather large, hairy-arsed Shankill gentlemen. And, trust me, they'll be more than happy to take you to lunch."

"Holy shit! How many?"

"Oh, about a dozen. Apparently you've deliberately ruined The Twelfth for their lot with your disgusting lies, so they'd like to 'talk things over' with you.

"Oh, and by the way, the switchboard is going nuts as well..."

"Christ, Adrian, how do we get out of this?"

"What do you mean *we*, Kemosabe?"

Four hours earlier, first call of the day: "Is that you, John? MB here. Ye get ma stuff okay?"

"Yes, Malky, have it right here on the screen."

"Aha-aha. Anythin' happenin' over there?"

"Nah. Sure it's two days before The Twelfth, Malky. Quiet. What time is it in Boston?

"Nah, not Boston, we're in Connecticut now. A town called New Britain. It's the middle o' the night over here. Ye'll give that piece o' mine a good show, like a fella? Right, that's it, ciao."

Five minutes later: "John, it's your old mucker from Giffnock."

"Malcolm?"

"Duh, yeah. How many fucking Glaswegians called Malcolm do you know?"

"You'd be surprised. Don't tell me; you're inviting me over for another evening of debauchery in Victoria's."

"A pleasant thought, pal, but the fair ladies of Souchiehall Street will have to tarry a little longer. No, I'm ringing to tip you off about the story of the century."

"I'm all ears, Malcolm. Shoot."

"Mo Johnston is signing for Rangers today."

"Get the fuck outta here!"

"John, how many times: that Eddie Murphy skit just doesn't work with an Ulster accent."

"*The* Mo Johnston? Signing for *Rangers*?"

"Yep, *that* Mo Johnston. Although us Huns know him better as 'Dirty Fenian Bastard'. I guess we'll have to think of another term of affection now, or perhaps not. There was a line in the Scottish Sun this morning, saying Rangers were gonna make a move for him."

"The Scottish Sun. How'd *they* hear that?"

"Apparently a work experience bairn tipped them off."

"A work experience bairn tipped them off?"

"Christ, are you just going to repeat everything I say? Yes, John. A work experience kid. He was in his little sweetheart's house when he spotted a fax from Rangers with 'Maurice John Giblin Johnston' writ large."

"He saw a... sorry, I'm doing it again. Okay, let me get my head around this. Mo supposedly re-signed for Celtic three weeks ago. So I still don't see..."

"He signed a *pre-contract* form, which ain't worth a fuck. He'll be fined a couple of grand for backing out of it. From what I hear, Rangers are sorting out his French tax problem and trebling what the Tims were gonna pay him."

"I was going to ask how you know this, but of course; your oul' boy's a club director."

"Not my dad, John, my uncle. He rang very late last night. Let's just say he was pissed in more ways than one."

"But how come nobody's following up on this? There wasn't a cheep about it on the radio."

"That's because nobody believes it. There's a press conference at Ibrox today. Everyone thinks they're going to 'break the mould' by signing John Sheridan. But our wee Mo's the man, trust me."

"Malcolm, have you any idea what'll happen if we run this and I'm wrong? The Twelfth is on Wednesday, for fuck sake. My credibility will be..."

"*What* 'credibility'? Look John, if it's right – and it is – folk will be talking about this for years. And it'll be the Belfast Belly Laugh that'll have told everyone Mo's put pen to paper for the Bluenoses."

"But our first edition will hit the streets before it's confirmed."

"Yep, but the presser's just for the cameras. He's already signed. That fax the wee lad saw – the one you failed to ask me anything more about, tut, tut – his lassie's oul' boy deals with all the insurance for Gers players. Sometimes when you put two and two together, you really do get four. Now you want me off the phone."

"Bye, Malcolm. Love you to bits. Owe you a least a hundred pints of heavy for this, pal."

"We need to re-do the backer," I shrieked over at Sammy.

"Mo Johnston has just signed for Rangers."

The assistant sports editor didn't flinch, just took an extra-long drag of his Benson & Hedges and said: "Okay let's do this – but God help you if you're wrong."

JOHNSTON SIGNS FOR RANGERS!

By John Laverty

Glasgow Rangers today shocked the soccer world by signing Scottish World Cup striker Mo Johnston from French club Nantes! Johnston, a life-long Celtic fan, will become the first Roman Catholic to play for the Ibrox club, and the £1.5 move is bound to stun Rangers fans – and their fierce rivals from across the city, who believed he was rejoining them.

I wince when I see how hideous that intro is – and I see it a lot, because my brother Gerry has that back page framed and proudly mounted on a wall in his house.

Glasgow Rangers? What was I thinking, and s*occer*? Really, John? And what's the '*Scottish* World Cup?' Not to mention that other bugbear: *Roman* Catholic.

None of this irked at the time. I couldn't wait to see the Tele hit the streets, with my ballbreaker on the back page.

Oh, and that 'Scottish Sun work experience kid' yarn? Completely kosher: take a bow Keith Jackson, who was then just 16 and who, ironically, would grow up to be a renowned hack with the Currant Bun's big Caledonian rivals, the Daily Record.

After the Radio Ulster lunchtime bulletin reported that the unthinkable had actually happened – and our security man imparted the news to those gentlemen in Library Street – the phone calls stopped and my prospective lynch mob departed, presumably to toss their Rangers scarves onto the nearest bonfire site.

2pm: "Is that ye, John? MB here. Ah've just had ma breakfast... eggs benedict, first class. Tell me, is it still as quiet as a mouse back hame?"

"Token Taig," said Malky, quickly adding: "No offence".
I hated it when he did that.
"There was no offence taken, Malky, until you said 'no offence'. You've now offended me by assuming offence in the first place."
"Aye, ye've said that afore, now that Ah think of it. Sorry."
"You've just done it AGAIN, Malky!"
The former Belfast Telegraph sports editor was calling from Malmo; we were having what you'd now call 'bantz'.
June 8, 1992; seven months after his 'retirement', MB was in Sweden to cover the European Championships – and I wasn't. But that's a tale for another time.
He wasn't referring to Mo either; rather a lad called Chris Cullen, whom Linfield had just signed from Cliftonville.
"So, Ah take it ye went big wi' that one?"
"Well, actually we didn't. It's in a small panel down the side."
"Whaa? Yer pullin' ma leg. How come?"
"Because it was decreed that we shouldn't mention his religion."
"Whaa?"

January 5 that year; front page headline in the Sunday Life...

NO-GO FOR CATHOLICS
Linfield boss spells out why he won't be signing RC players

Had the thoughtful, intelligent, articulate Eric Bowyer taken leave of his senses?

Ulster's Catholic soccer stars have been told they have almost no chance of playing for the province's biggest football club.
In a frank admission, the manager of Linfield admitted it would be "virtually impossible" for him to sign a Catholic – even if he wanted to.

Similar views had been expressed in an interview Bowyer gave to a Blues fanzine, but the you-know-what really hit the fan when the successor to

Roy Coyle (who used to joke that he was "the only 'RC' at Windsor Park") repeated his views to the big-circulation Life.

That set off a chain reaction: the influential US-based Irish National Caucus reiterated their demand that the Irish FA sever its "cosy links" with the Blues, and threatened to boycott Coca-Cola unless they withdrew their advertising billboards from Windsor – that so-called bastion of Protestantism and, ergo, a 'cold house for Catholics'.

The INC – led by Fermanagh-born priest Fr Sean McManus – accused Linfield of failing to field 'a local Catholic' since 1950 and promised further demonstrations should Northern Ireland qualify for the 1994 World Cup in America.

Bowyer, who wasn't a full-time manager like his predecessor – his 'day job' was chief executive of the Newry and Mourne Health and Social Services Trust – was stunned by the reaction to his verisimilitude, but later declared he was glad he spoke out.

It was borne of frustration; Bowyer, a popular former Blues captain, had attempted to bring Jim McFadden to Windsor but (and despite a "megabucks" offer) the move fell through because of the flak the Cliftonville midfielder believed he'd get from his own community.

"At no time did anyone at Windsor tell me I couldn't sign a Catholic," Eric told me after the Sunday Life story broke.

"They wanted to be top dogs again, didn't care how it was done and I wouldn't have had it any other way; there isn't a sectarian bone in my body."

In those days, the Blues were lagging behind two-time Irish League champions Portadown (Big Ronnie obviously got the two players he needed), while across the city, Wee Jacko, rejuvenated by the likes of Raymond 'Soupy' Campbell and Justin McBride and with 'Nuts' Morrison playing out of his proverbial skin, was coasting to the 1991-92 title (Glentoran would finish 12 points ahead of Ports and 17 clear of third-placed Linfield).

Bowyer was also suffering in comparison to the trophy-machine he'd replaced – although Coyler himself didn't pull up many trees in his first 18 months.

So, a dozen years after Big Ronnie convinced a dubious Glens board that recruiting the likes of Jim Cleary and Gerry Mullan was the only way to compete with rampant Linfield – and almost three years on from Mo Johnston – the Blues finally got Fr McManus off their backs by signing Cullen.

Not that you'd get the significance of that by reading the Tele...

"Sammy, Linfield have just signed a Catholic."

"Who is it?"

"Chris Cullen."

"Never heard of him."

"He's a young squad player with Cliftonville."

"Is this some sort of token thing?"

"Undoubtedly."

"So, what do you propose we do about it?"

"DO about it? We lead the back page with it! This is huge. This is Mo Johnston, part II."

"Has he actually signed?"

"No, but Bowyer's confirmed he's coming. He knows Cullen from his time at Cliftonville."

"Okay, sounds good. But I'll have to run it past Roy Lilley."

"Why?"

Sammy's patience was starting to fray.

"Because, John, young Cullen is about to become very famous and I'd just like to see how we proceed with this. Who knows, they might even want it as front-page lead."

Wow! Front AND back-page leads. By 1992 – and unlike Malky, who never lost it – the thrill of seeing my name in the paper had evaporated, but there's always a *soupcon* of excitement when a big yarn is taking shape.

And this was big – certainly big enough to lead the paper at both ends; I hadn't had a sniff of that since the day 'By David Lavery' and 'By Malcolm Brodie' ruined the 'dream double'.

Sammy emerged from the editor's office after ten minutes.

"We can run the story, but not mention Cullen's religion."

"Are you winding me up? His religion IS the story! Without that, it's just the Blues signing some unknown grunt."

"John, the decision's been made. You still want to write it?"

"Well, you're the sports editor – it's your call. But it can't be a lead now. We'd look stupid if we splashed the back page with Chris Who from Cliftonville reserves. We're going to look stupid anyway; it's as if we don't 'get' it."

"Okay then – and thanks for reminding me of what my job title is. It's only been a few months and I'm still getting used to it."

Linfield move for Cliftonville kid Cullen

102

Linfield have made a surprise move for Cliftonville's young utility player Chris Cullen, writes John Laverty.

Cullen, an amateur, played against the Blues in the Bass Irish Cup quarter-final and his agreement with the Solitude ends later in the summer.

Linfield manager Eric Bowyer said today: "Chris would be a useful addition to the squad and can play in a number of positions."

Cullen, 21, was signed by Cliftonville from Kilmore Rec last year and has made only a handful of first team appearances."

Bowyer has also beat Glenavon in the race for Ards winger Robert Campbell, with former Blues skipper David Jeffrey moving to Castlereagh.

And that was it. A few measly pars.

"MB wouldnae have stood for that malarkey. MB would have told them, absolutely straight, 'Ah want THAT-and-that-and-THAT-and that, full point, end par…'"

The following day, page one of the Irish News:

LINFIELD BID TO SIGN CATHOLIC CONFIRMED

By Stephen O'Reilly

A Co Down soccer player last night said there was a "strong possibility" he would become the first Catholic to play for Linfield in decades.

Cliftonville defender and midfielder Chris Cullen said he was waiting for a formal offer from the Belfast club, but had already held talks with Linfield manager Eric Bowyer.

The Downpatrick man said he had met Mr Bowyer in Ballynahinch and that he was "surprised" at the interest in him.

Asked about the prospect of being the first Northern Ireland-born Catholic to play for Linfield in over 30 years, he said: "It doesn't worry me in the slightest, I only want to play football".

He agreed that some Linfield fans might not welcome him, but that he was "prepared to take it" and prove himself on the pitch.

"This is a sprat tae catch a whale," said Malky.

Or maybe a Hawk…

CHAPTER 17

George Ace felt abnormally leaden as he trudged up Royal Avenue.
The place seemed noisier than usual; probably last-minute work on the
£20m CastleCourt shopping centre, which Belfast Lord Mayor Reg Empey
would be officially opening for business in the morning.
Wednesday, April 18, 1990 brought a lovely spring day, but the foul-
mouthed former News Letter sports editor didn't look full of the joys
when I bumped into him at Bank Buildings.
"What's up with you, George? Did somebody demand a refund?"
(Since retiring, George had become the go-to guy for hand-stitched shoes
and dinner suits. With end-of-season gala dinners, this was a lucrative
month. I'd been one of the wily old spiv's many ask-no-questions
customers: "John, toss me another fucking tenner and I'll throw in a
waistcoat AND cummerbund, and that's me cutting my fucking throat
here...")
"Coyler."
"Oh. Is he in Thompson's?"
"Grouchy bastard rang an hour ago. You wanna join us?"
"Funnily enough... nah, George, he's your mate and clearly needs your
soothing voice. Have you seen the Tele?"
"I have, and you can tell that no-arsed wee fucker Brodie it's his fault my
day's been royally fucked."

LINFIELD FAITHFUL RISE UP IN ANGER

By Malcolm Brodie

*As Linfield crashed to their sixth defeat by Glentoran this season, their
supporters protested vehemently near the end of last night's Smirnoff
Irish League match at Windsor Park – a defeat which ended any hopes of
the Blues qualifying for Europe next season.*
*"Sack the board", "Coyle out", "what a load of rubbish" they chanted.
Scarves were thrown in disgust and later a crowd gathered outside the
official entrance demanding to meet officials, and eventually a deputation
was received.*
*Earlier, supporters had begun streaming out of the stadium, leaving in
utter disappointment at yet another downfall. During the game one irate
supporter climbed the perimeter rails and hurled his scarf at the Linfield
dugout.*

This defeat was the final straw for the Linfield faithful, who have been brought up on a constant diet of success.

To be an also-ran, as has happened at the club this season, is a stigma to them.

The verbal abuse hurled at manager Roy Coyle as he walked to the sanctuary of the dressing-room was quite incredible.

A surprise awaited George at the Arthur Street hostelry – a relaxed, contented, convivial Robert Irvine Coyle, sipping a flute of his favourite champagne.

"What the fuck?"

"You feeling okay, George?"

"I'm fine, but what in Christ's name is up with you? Where's the fucking coiled-spring Coyler we all know and don't particularly love?"

"You know, George, there's more to life than football. Or in your case, rugby."

"Really? There's something weird going on here, and I'll fucking find out what it is."

"Calm down, George. Those ultra-thick lenses of yours are steaming up. The usual, I presume?"

George spent two hours with this alien who'd surreptitiously replaced the "disagreeable shite" he normally drank with.

They discussed topical issues; political reaction to the murder of four UDR men in an IRA explosion near Downpatrick, Charles Haughey making the first official visit to 'the north' by a Taoiseach since 1965, 'political prisoners' at The Crum rioting over the lack of segregation and of course the soon-to-open CastleCourt.

"I'm told it'll revolutionise shopping in central Belfast," said George's newly-philosophical pal.

Who IS this fucking imposter?

Veteran hack George's fair-haired drinking partner then talked about the summer holiday he and heroic wife Abbie (they married when old misery-guts was 16) were planning.

"It'll be good to get away from this place and not think about football..."

"Well," replied George, who freelanced for The Times, "It's a fucking pity you still have to think about it. Some of the deadwood will be fucked out on their arses, no doubt?"

"No doubt, George – but I won't be making the decision..."

"Fuck off, Coyler! You haven't thrown in the fucking towel, have you?"

"I have. As from this morning, I am no longer manager of Linfield Football Club. So let's have another drink and raise our glasses to 15 years, 31 trophies and the end of an era. Abbie will be collecting me soon, so set 'em up..."

Later: "Coyler, is it okay if I tell the News Letter about this? It's a big fucker of a story."

"Tell whoever you want, George. See you tomorrow..."

In the end, *the end* of Coyler's stint as Linfield's record-breaking boss was more amicable than you'd imagine.

He later told me he'd spoken with the Blues chairman, ostensibly to discuss the unseemly protest after the demoralising 3-1 defeat by those *bêtes noires* from across the river.

"David Campbell looked at me and said: 'Roy, do you really *need* all this shit?' to which I replied: 'you know what, Mr Chairman, I *don't'*. And that was it. No raised voices, no acrimony. I think, in the end, myself and the club had just grown sick of each other. Fifteen years is a long time."

The departure of the most successful manager in Irish League history was a gargantuan story, the most seismic in 40 years – but it was the Tele, not George Ace's old pals round the corner in Donegall Street, who were first to run it.

Legend has it that the boul' George, who was slurring his expletives by the time Abbie Coyle collected her unemployed husband, rang with the "fuck me" news – and nobody believed him.

Apparently he was told: "You're a week old with that, George. Coyler talked to Campbell about quitting last week, and was talked out of it. If he'd had resigned, we'd know all about it. But thanks for the call, mate. You take it easy, now..."

Next day:

COYLE QUITS AS LINFIELD BOSS

15-year reign at Windsor Park comes to an end

By Malcolm Brodie

Roy Coyle today resigned as manager of Linfield – a post which he held for almost 15 years during which the club have had incredible success. A glorious era ended around mid-day with the announcement that he had quit.

Coyle was subjected, along with members of the management committee, to a torrent of verbal abuse after Tuesday's defeat by Glentoran. He has had enough. He could take no more.

Ten league championships, three Irish Cups, seven Gold Cups, four Ulster Cups, five Co Antrim Shields, one All-Ireland Cup, one League Cup, a few other near misses and six times Manager of the Year... some haul since November 17, 1975, especially when you consider the barren 18-month start made by the young, inexperienced player-boss.

Cynics might say 'yes, but it's *Linfield,* who trouser 15% of every penny the IFA make from internationals. Who *wouldn't* be successful?'

True, but it still takes a special person to deliver the goods so consistently, and under such constant pressure. If managing a rich club was so easy, Real Madrid wouldn't change their head coach every two or three years.

And Coyler bagged all those trophies – a third of which were the holy grail itself, the league title – with one hand tied behind his back... a 'Prods-only' playing staff.

How much more domination might there have been, had the Troubles-fuelled political stasis been different and he'd been able to recruit, say, Jim Cleary, Felix Healy, Peter Murray, Damien Byrne, Paul Doolin, Ray McGuigan, Liam Coyle... or Dessie Gorman?

As successor Eric Bowyer would later point out, there was no impediment from the board... but would any of those Catholics have wanted to come?

Again, a cynic may argue that, with their tradition and conveyor belt of silverware (Coyle's 10th title was the club's 40th), the Belfast giants could always attract the best youngsters, albeit mined from one particular seam.

By the end of the 80s, though, even that lustrous carrot was fading; who'd have thought the outrageously gifted Raymie McCoy, whom we all thought for years was Windsor-bound, would instead opt for Glenavon?

I'm not sure Coyle's achievements will ever be fully appreciated – even by Bluemen themselves, many of whom couldn't warm to a former Glentoran player and Beersbridge Road native who cut his teeth alongside Oval legends Jim 'Bimbo' Weatherup, Walter Bruce and Billy McKeag in the late 60s.

The ultra-intense Coyler came across to many as a cold fish anyway. He once confided that, in the early days, he'd keep his media comments to an absolute minimum in a bid to come across as sagacious and enigmatic, rather than 'thick as champ' (which he was anything but).

The man whose trophy haul would reach an unparalleled half ton (including 16 with the Glens), wasn't one for sentimentality; son Darren and son-in-law Paul Mooney, who married Coyler's daughter Jacqueline, got no special treatment from a boss some petrified playing staff likened to The Terminator: "Can't be bargained with, can't be reasoned with, doesn't feel pity, or remorse..."

"Ruthless bastard" was another description, as was "the world's only living heart donor".

Listen to this from marauding left-back Colin Crawford, who got the gimlet-eyed stare even after helping Coyler win six league titles:

"I was subbed at the Oval – the Glens beat us. No problem with the decision; it was only through sheer disappointment that I walked straight down the tunnel into the dressing room.

"There was no disrespect meant. It didn't occur to me that I'd done something upsetting. Coyler came in afterwards to say that he didn't like my actions, and that I'd never kick a ball for Linfield again. Soon afterwards I was told the club had decided to release me.

"I was stunned and asked Coyler: 'did the last six years mean nothing?' His reply: 'You were lucky'. After that, I couldn't get away quickly enough."

Crawford also told the Sunday Life about his own brief managerial stint with Carrick: "I wasn't ruthless enough. I felt guilty leaving players out. You need a nasty streak; I wasn't cut out for it..."

Notorious sore loser Coyle found it impossible to be sanguine or pragmatic about defeats, maybe because they brought disgusting spittle showers and attempted assaults.

He's well aware of how fortunate he was to keep his job after disastrous Irish Cup final reverses to Carrick (2-1) in 1976 ("the lowest point of my career") and Coleraine (4-1) a year later; it's the stuff of legend that beating the Glens 3-1 in the Co Antrim Shield final at the tail end of 1976-77 granted the rookie a reprieve he fully embraced.

(The 'Lurgan Mafia' claimed that, at one stage during those difficult early days, Coyle actually shook hands on taking the Glenavon job – then reneged. As a Scottish judge might say: 'not proven'.)

Linfield were on the slide in 1990. Their manager tried, and failed, to recreate the Coly-Khammal magic with Algerian duo Hocine Yahi and Abdi Dehnoun.

That didn't help, but the fatal blow was administered by those seven successive defeats by Glentoran, including the Irish Cup semi-final at Windsor on April 7 when Soupy Campbell's Maradona-style wonder goal (ironically, only three days after world champions Argentina, minus the Hand of God, had played the Blues in a glamour friendly in the same stadium) was followed by the by-now inevitable G-Force dagger to the heart.

(To be fair, the second of Glentoran's 'magnificent seven' against Roy Coyle and his Easybeats – Ulster Cup, 3-1 at the Oval in late August – was highly fortuitous, ref Alan Snoddy disallowing a perfectly good Paul Mooney goal which would have made it 2-0 and then awarding a joke penalty to the Glens after the ball struck Lindsay McKeown's ankle; from that day on, prankster Lindsay would offer his foot, rather than his hand, to Snoddy before kick-off.)

Coyler's final silverware with Linfield came via a 2-0 Gold Cup final replay win over Portadown at the Oval on November 2, 1989, David McCallan and Philip Knell getting the decisive goals.

But the 'Mid-Ulster spring' was in full bloom and, despite Glentoran's hex over *Lin-failed*, it would be Portadown and Glenavon going at it hammer and tongs for the 1989-90 title.

Glenavon's catastrophic scoreless draw at Bangor in the penultimate game – former Seagull Gerry Armstrong, then 35, missed an absolute sitter in the second half – opened the door for Big Ronnie's home town team to squeak the title by a single point, beating Linfield 2-0 in a heaving, jubilant Shamrock Park, ten days after Coyler and Ace drained Thompson's champagne stocks.

After 66 years, Ports could finally hoist the Gibson Cup and exorcise the infamous 'gypsy curse' hanging over them since 1940, when fans brought a coffin into the ground proclaiming the 'death' of their hopes of beating Belfast Celtic to the title – this apparently infuriated a gypsy woman who damned the club never to finish first.

That old gypsy was no match for Portadown's principal benefactor, late Golden Cow Dairies owner Ted Clarke, who poured tranches of a multi-million-pound fortune into both his local club and local church.

(Malky once quipped: "Old Ted was told there were two things money couldnae buy – a Gibson Cup for the Ports and a ticket tae the Kingdom of Heaven. He was clearly determined tae prove everyone wrong...")

Big Ronnie's men were feeling cursed earlier that season when striker Marty Magee was banned for six months for possibly headbutting linesman Andy Marno after being sent off at Carrick's Taylor's Avenue. Note 'possibly', because the alleged offence was never proven, and there was no TV footage to verify Marno's claims.

109

Magee, a former all-Ireland amateur boxing champion, maintained his innocence.

"We had a throw-in and I went to challenge the Carrick full-back," Magee told our paper.

"Next thing, the ref called me over and said he was sending me off for throwing an elbow."

"I went over to the linesman, but I never touched him. He fell to the ground and I was in shock".

Marno, however, insisted Magee had decked him.

What does the Irish FA do in a situation like this? For most observers it was simple enough; if Magee was found guilty of such a serious offence, he should be banned for life, never mind six months.

If not; well, if you're not guilty then you're innocent, yes?

Upshot: in a shameful fudge, the Windsor Avenue mandarins rescinded the red card but decreed that Magee should nevertheless be banned for the rest of the season – for something he may, or may not, have done.

But what began with an alleged Glasgow kiss ended with Scotsman Stevie Cowan – Magee's inspired, prolific replacement – getting the party started by burying a neat header past Linfield keeper George Dunlop for his 14th goal of the season. Substitute Gregg Davidson's first of the campaign banished any doubts that the title trophy (which had been sitting in a car halfway between Portadown and Coleraine, where Glenavon were beating the home side 3-0) would be heading for the Brownstown Road.

What a team Big Ronnie had built in less than four years: the reliable, experienced Mickey Keenan in goal, a brilliant back four of Philip Major, skipper Brian Strain, Alfie Stewart and Ian Curliss, tough-as-teak Roy McCreadie alongside the silky Joey Cunningham, David Mills and Kevin McKeever in midfield and, up front, Sandy Fraser forging a formidable 'Little & Large' partnership with compatriot Cowan.

Meanwhile, we'll probably never know what exactly George Ace told the News Letter that April evening.

We do know this: the day after Coyle's resignation was officially announced to a breathless press posse who'd gathered at Windsor, the back-page lead headline in the 'Linfield bible' was...

WHELAN A DOUBT FOR LIVERPOOL

Oh, the irony: the Irish League's biggest bombshell since Belfast Celtic's withdrawal in the late 40s – and a story of intense personal interest to the vast majority of the News Letter's true-blue Protestant readers – had just broken... yet a minor ankle injury sustained by a Dublin-born Catholic playing for an English team was deemed more important.

Not only that, but the only reference to Coyle's departure came halfway through an inside, downpage filler: "Linfield team affairs will be handled by caretaker manager Billy Rodgers following the resignation of Roy Coyle".

Fifteen years, 31 trophies... seventeen words.

Earlier in the week, their back-page splash (on the morning of what turned out to be Coyle's last day in charge) wasn't a preview of the pivotal Big Two encounter, but a report on little-known West German cyclist Roland Schelter winning a stage of the Northern Ireland Milk Race. And on Saturday, April 21, the day after an emotional, grey-suited former Linfield manager addressed a packed press conference in Belfast – and the dawn of a new era at Windsor – the only reference to Coyle was at the bottom of an inside page, tucked into a story about Bangor's visit to Windsor: "It will be an eerie place, a team rudderless for the first time in almost 15 years now that Roy Coyle has had to resign from the full time post."

A grand total of 47 words over two days.

I wasn't sure about what was the more shocking: Coyle's resignation or the News Letter's 'coverage' of it.

Just how good was Roy Coyle – one of the few people who can name all the actors in The Magnificent Seven and who used to hang out with one George Ivan Morrison at Orangefield Boys? Put it this way: even if you excised all Linfield achievements from his CV, the man who went on to boss Ards (twice), Derry, the Glens and Newry would STILL be up there as one of the greatest managers of all time.

CHAPTER 18

The wise man does not lay up his own treasures.
The more he gives to others, the more he has for his own.
(Lao Tzu)

Question: what do Steve Smyth, Don Ardmore, Mike Williams and Ian Stevenson have in common?

Answer: none of them exist. They were all pseudonyms of the late Dr Malcolm Brodie MBE.

It wasn't his Belfast Telegraph salary – generous though that was, augmented by 'Rivers of Gold' era expenses – that made him one of the richest journalists in Britain.

No, it was the man's legendary so-called 'cor empire' which ensured he'd never have to rattle a tin can outside CastleCourt.

Even back in 1990, with Malky a year away from 'retirement', he was pulling in over a grand a week from other outlets – before he'd written a single word.

In those halcyon days, national newspapers paid their regular stringers coveted 'retainer' fees; in Malky's case this was around £350 a week from each of the Daily Telegraph, Sun and News of the Screws. Filing actual stories was extra.

Earlier in his career, his empire included a national Canadian media group, to which he'd supply a daily digest of Ulster news for the Great White North's Ulster ex-pats. Then there were the books, including one on the history of the Irish League for which I wrote a couple of chapters for a not insubstantial fee.

I don't think he was obsessed with money though; in all the time we spent together, the only time he'd mention the filthy lucre was when advising me on pension contributions.

His earnings and investments were looked after by "folk Ah trust" – such as local hockey legend and financial expert Dixon Rose – although he did reveal, one boozy night in San Francisco, that he hadn't dipped into his Tele salary for 27 years.

A sports editor regularly gets calls from other newspapers and media outlets asking for help, guidance and commissioned stories.

Nowadays, if the query related to, say, boxing, you'd transfer the call to the boxing correspondent and forget all about it.

Malky wasn't like that. Wherever the call emanated from, it always ended with him and that immortal Brodieism "leave that with me".

If he couldn't do the work himself, he'd delegate – or subcontract – to the specialist, and subsequently pay them handsomely (I never heard anyone complain that they'd been poorly remunerated).

But as far as the initial requester was concerned, their go-to man from then on would be Malcolm Brodie, whose already considerable fame and reputation was further augmented.

When Malky died in 2013, some obituary writers used a humorous anecdote about him doing pieces for TASS, the Soviet news agency, in the 60s. Methinks that's apocryphal; an after-dinner joke that morphed into a non-contested fact.

It's true, however, that when Malky failed to file from the Dnepr Dnepropetrovsk v Linfield European Cup match in 1989, that old dog-eared address book came to the rescue.

Sammy Hamill, sitting at home that night, got a call from Moscow: Irish Times' Russia-based correspondent Conor O'Clery, whom wily old Brodie had managed to get through to from central Ukraine.

Conor was more than happy to take the great man's match report copy over the phone, then dictate it to a bemused Sammy who rattled it out on his typewriter. *That's* what you call contacts.

Resourcefulness, omnipresence and synonymity were the keys – as was the man's astonishing worth ethic. Fear of boredom was more of a driver than pounds and pence, as exemplified by the number of committees he volunteered to sit on.

He was the hardest working hack I've ever known; a genuine, seven-day-a-week, sleeves rolled up grafter.

When his sons were young, he'd book family holidays to Bangor and Millisle – so he could still get to 'Royal Avenue' while Margaret and the boys, and occasionally their maternal grandparents, were left to fend by themselves.

After putting up with a few years of this, Mrs Brodie read the riot act.

"We went tae Italy every year after that," recalled Malky, adding: "Margaret had a point. She said Ah was gettin' Madrid, she was gettin' Millisle – and even then Ah was nippin' tae the office at every turn. Ah wasnae seein' enough o' the kids as it was. Those Italian holidays were great, though, especially Sanremo."

Apart from being a workaholic, Malky was also the most generous of people – as long as you didn't actually ask him for money (as Colly pointed out earlier). Remember the brass neck who walked in off the street that memorable day? Malky had no time for cap-in-hand, hard-luck stories.

Colly would often reminisce about the sports desk's 'Day of Delight' summer outings to north coast hostelries organised by – and often paid for – by the boss man, and occasionally featuring stick-thin Ronnie Harper stripping off for a dip.

(One freezing day, Derek Murray shouted over at a blue-skinned Harper: "fuck me, Ronnie, you look like a biro refill".)

He wouldn't make an issue of it, but Malky would regularly pay for the Tele's British Legion representatives' annual Remembrance Day visit to the Cenotaph in London.

His Soccer Yearbook ("ma annual") brought an unenviable haul of tedium every year, yet all its considerable proceeds went to charity.

And, like countless others, I had to fight him just to get a round in.

Not only that, but his influential friends acted all Brodiesque on discovering who your illustrious colleague was.

I rarely had to pick up the tab in any Big Apple hostelry owned by wealthy Northern Ireland natives Jack Dorian or the late Gerry Toner, aka 'King of the New York Irish'.

"Put that wallet away, sonny. Any friend of Brodie is a friend of mine..."

How many people did Malky treat at the Ink Spot social club (of which he was president) over the course of a month? "Put it this way," confided one of the barmen, "his tab comes to a lot more than you earn."

Even the 1966 World Cup winning heroes were treated to the acclaimed Brodie hospitality in October of that year.

Sammy Hamill: "England were in town for a European Championship match and Malky had organised a reception in the Tele boardroom to celebrate their World Cup victory. I think he'd organised it with Alf Ramsey over a late drink in the Royal Garden Hotel in Kensington the night they won the thing.

"As a cub reporter, I was excited at the thought of seeing the England stars in our office. But then Malky handed me a list of addresses and said: 'I want you to pick up Harold Shepherdson at the Midland Hotel and take him round these places'.

"There was an even bigger shock when I turned up at the hotel to collect the England team trainer and found him waiting with ... Ramsey himself. Malcolm hadn't mentioned the big boss was coming too!

"Next thing, they'd climbed into my wee red Mini, Alf in the back and the lanky Shepherdson in the front. Off we went round Belfast, calling at a wholesale jeweller, an Irish linen emporium, a liquor distributor – all contacts of Malky's, naturally.

"As I was dropping them off, they asked if I'd like to join the team, who were having a light tea. I ended up sitting alongside Bobby Moore and Martin Peters, with Gordon Banks just across the table."

He added: "Even now, I find that whole episode hard to take in. It might have been a typical day in the life of MB, but for a young lad like me it was surreal, unforgettable."

When Sammy was incapacitated for four months with a major heart problem: "I don't think there was a day Malky didn't ring either myself or Shirley to ask how things were going. I also remember when we brought our first child, Gavin, home; Malky's card contained a substantial cheque, so we could open a bank account for him."

There are numerous examples of MB largesse, but those less conspicuous acts of kindness were also commonplace.

The death of my mother Mary after a long illness in November 1993 is a painful memory, not least because it later emerged that the so-called 'priest' who performed the funeral service, 'Father' Daniel Curran, was a predatory paedophile.

It's nauseating to recall that piece of shit with his faux piousness being anywhere near us during a period of great heartache.

After the funeral, Malky asked where refreshments would be served.

"The Fair Hill Bar. Why, you gonna come?"

"Nah, Ah'm drivin'. In any case, it's all about yer close family an' friends today. See ye anon."

A few hours later, having entertained over 50 people, myself and brothers Gerry and Paul steeled ourselves for the eye-watering tab.

"It's already been taken care of," said the barman.

"Your friend Mr Brodie rang earlier..."

May 1990. Malky asked me to help him compile a preview supplement for the World Cup in Italy.

"Come roon to the hoose," he said. "We'll have peace tae pool our ideas, and Margaret will get ye somethin' to eat."

Colly couldn't believe it.

"You hear that, lads? 'Ah've just invited ma illegitimate bairn to ma hame for neeps an' tatties'".

"So what, Colly? You and Harper used to go round there all the time."

"Yeah, but that was to wash his car and cut the grass; we never got anywhere near the fucking house, and now Lord Muck here's getting a guided tour. Make sure you get some photos for the plebs."

Having imagined Chez Brodie, I was shocked by what a modest dwelling it was.

Not familiar with 'Rochester Drive' in advance, I presumed it was in a commune of opulent mansions befitting the more affluent inhabitants of east Belfast.

Instead, the taxi pulled up outside an inconspicuous semi.

"You sure this is it, driver?"

"Absolutely. You're looking for Brodie, aren't you? Well, this is where he lives. I drop him off all the time."

It was a lovely place, which Margaret kept spotlessly clean and tidy. It's just that I was expecting... well, Malky was a millionaire.

Contemporaries such as Walker (Kings Road) Billy Clark (Helen's Bay) and Gordon Hanna (Hillsborough) had considerably larger houses; petrol-head Sammy had a better car.

But the country's richest hack kept the home bought for him and Bloomfield native Margaret Stevenson after they'd got married in 1949.

"Ah was never one o' them 'keep up wi' the Joneses' types," he told me. "Rochester Drive was comfortable, handy for the boys' schoolin', handy for ma work and close tae Allan, who'd settled on Stirling Avenue; we were happy there. Why move just because ye can afford a swankier place? Ah never saw the logic in that. If somethin' ain't broke..."

The only credit Malky craved was intangible – the by-product of what he achieved, not what it paid.

He loved his exclusive clubs – the Reform, the Caledonian in London for Scottish ex-pats, the Elysium at the Culloden (where he spent most of his time wearing a bath robe and reading the 'DT' beside the pool) and the Ink Spot.

Expensive holidays every January with Margaret in Barbados – where he'd stay in the plush Sandy Lane resort (owned by Irish tycoons Dermot Desmond and JP McManus), spending hours talking cricket with great pal Sir Everton Weekes – and, latterly, on cruises along the breathtaking Norwegian fjords, were the closest Malky came to ostentation.

Margaret, who worked at CE ('Charlie') Bourke's department store on the Newtownards Road, was 18 when she met her future husband.

The pair would sway to Glenn Millar and Tommy Dorsey tunes and hold hands in John Dossor's legendary Gala dance hall; "Ah knew from day one that Margaret was the girl for me," said Malky.

"Ah couldnae believe this beautiful creature was happy tae spend time wi' a dumpy wee kid from Glasgae. It didnae take me long tae pop the question – Ah was the happiest man in the world when she said aye –

then came the tricky bit."

As Margaret was only 19, Malky – then 22 – would need William Alexander Stevenson's written permission to wed.

"It was what ye had tae do when a bride was under 21," said Malky. "Waitin' for her father tae agree was the most nervous Ah've ever been."

The pair got married at Knock Methodist Church in east Belfast on September 14, 1949, and honeymooned in London and the south of France before settling into Rochester Drive.

Margaret – her sons called her "Maggie" but her husband never shortened her Christian name – was a delightful host that evening back in 1990; Malky played Sinatra on the hi-fi and presented me with a gold Parker pen.

That World Cup supplement was the closest I got to the tournament. It was Jim Gracey, representing the Sunday Life, who accompanied Malcolm – the first time two reporters from our building had gone out to a *Mundial.*

"Sicily was a complete basket case," Malky told me.

"Punters frae Ireland and Egypt mixin' wi' the Dutch and Sicilians; ye couldnae get a bite tae eat."

Jim remembers it differently: "The waiters and restaurant owners couldn't get enough of us.

"It didn't take them long to work out that the wee man with the big belly was a great tipper.

"And it didn't matter how late we got there or how long the queue was; Malky was always ushered straight in."

He added: "It must have cost him a fortune because they were ripping everyone off.

"Malky always seemed happy to pay it, but one night even he went spare after seeing our bill.

"He said 'explain this *billo* tae me, *garcon',* which wound them up anyway because we were in Don Corleone country, not Paris.

"The *cameriere* said: "This is for the use of the table, this is for the chairs, this is for the cutlery and this is for the tablecloth'. I kid you not.

"Then Malky says: 'no fuckin' way am Ah payin' that'. Next thing, *la polizia* arrive.

"One of them told us, in perfect English: 'This bill is correct, signori, and you must pay'.

"Funnily enough, we asked directions from the same cop the next day and he couldn't speak a word of *Inglese...*"

I remember Malky telling me that the football in that tournament, especially from the Republic, was "soporific", a word I had to look up in the dictionary. Jim agreed – up to a point.

"Big Jack was using an early form of *gegenpressing,* nearly 30 years before the likes of Jurgen Klopp made it fashionable," he said.

"The difference was, Jack didn't have world class players like Mane, Firmino and Salah up front."

Another thing Jim discovered about Malky on the islands of Sicily and Sardinia: his hatred of cats.

"We were always wearing shorts at the restaurants, and they kept coming round and rubbing themselves against his legs.

"Malky would spring up, plate in hand, and jump from one foot to the other, screaming at the waiter: 'cat, cat… get rid o' that fuckin' cat!'

"You know what, though… before Ireland's match with England in Cagliari, the press corps were in tee-shirts and we all laughed at Malky – and the Irish Press legend Con Houlihan – for bringing their parka coats to the stadium. Like, it hadn't rained in Sardinia at that time of the year for decades.

"Then… well, I've never witnessed a thunderstorm like the one that night…"

Jim's favourite 'Malky moment' from Italia 90: "I was on my way to the open-air press box in Palermo when a bloke in his late forties, wearing tee-shirt and slacks, stopped me. 'Could you tell Malcolm Brodie I'd like a word with him?' he said, in a polite Belfast accent.

"I said I would, and enquired as to his name. 'Tell him it's the Bishop of Down and Connor', he said, to which I replied something like 'yeah, right, and I'm Pope Jim from Lurgan. Pleased to meet you'.

"Two minutes later: 'Malky, see that idiot manically waving at us from four rows down? He says he's the Bishop of Down and Connor, and wants to meet you'.

"Malky looked down and went: 'Whaa? Hey, that's ma old pal Tony Farquhar. He sits wi' me every year at the GAA dinner in Bundoran. He really IS the {Auxiliary} Bishop of Down and Connor. Oi, Tony. Bout ye? Ah'll be doon wi' ye in a minute or two…'"

While we're reminiscing about all things 1990: three encounters with Old Trafford legends closer to home:

1. Alec Ferguson (August 8): Derry City had drawn 1-1 with FA Cup winners Manchester United in a pre-season friendly. Afterwards I walked

into the United dressing room – to find a grey-suited Fergie standing there, all on his lonesome.

"Does no one want to talk to you?" I asked.

"Apparently not," he replied, "and *you* are?"

"John Laverty, Belfast Telegraph. You won't remember, Alex, but we spoke on the phone a couple of years ago. You were looking for Malcolm Brodie's phone number."

"I remember rightly. A Saturday morning, wasn't it? Thanks for sorting that out."

We spoke for 10 minutes – mostly about Norman Whiteside ("a fantastic servant for the club; he was really happy with the deal he got at Everton, we're still friends") – then the locally-based reporters finally arrived *en masse*.

Me: "Where the hell were you guys?"

Them: "We were talking to Jim McLaughlin..."

Typical. They leave the Man U manager kicking his heels for someone they talk to every day. Who was it described Derry as having a village mentality?

2. Paul McGrath (October 17): Lansdowne Road, 40 minutes before the start of a Euro 92 qualifier with Turkey. I'd got caught up in the notorious Dublin traffic; a security man ushered me in through the gate behind the West Stand. While walking past the home team's bus, I spotted somebody slumped in a seat near the back – Paul McGrath, in full playing kit and tracksuit.

Stepping back a couple of paces to make sure it was him, I noticed the vehicle's door was open, and gingerly climbed on board.

"You okay, Paul?"

I'd met the 'Black Pearl of Inchicore' before, prior to the scoreless Northern Ireland v Republic World Cup qualifier in September 1988. I doubted if he'd remember; at that moment I'd have been shocked if he knew his own name.

He briefly looked up, muttered something, then waved his arm in a "go away" gesture, which I immediately complied with. The hitherto affable security guy went puce.

"Get the fuck away from here, or I'll throw you into the street..."

I retreated to the far end of the tiny car park and, a couple of minutes later, a stern-looking Jack Charlton clambered into the bus. Shortly afterwards, Big Jack alighted, accompanied by the Villa defender who walked slowly and unsteadily, head bowed, to the players' entrance.

He looked over, saw me watching and shook his head, as if to say 'the game's up'.

At half time, however, the new FAI chief executive, Sean Connolly, strode into the cramped press room and bellowed: "For those of you interested in Paul McGrath's absence, the player suffered a recurrence of a knee injury in the dressing room before the match and was withdrawn from the starting line-up..."

And at the press conference following a comfortable 5-0 victory (Aldridge hat-trick, O'Leary, Quinn), Charlton said: "Paul's knees were bothering him. He wasn't happy... Paul was embarrassed... he's had problems... look, can I go now? It's been a fucking long day."

Everybody knew the "dodgy knees" story was utter bollocks, but none of the southern boys were prepared to "do an Eamon Dunphy" and challenge the official version, which was printed as fact the following day. And the identity of 'unidentified man in the bus' the Independent referred to on October 18? Well, now you know.

3. Denis Law (November 2) 'The Lawman' was officially opening a video shop co-owned by a friend, and I was his chauffeur for the day. What a lovely, gregarious man, bereft of the airs and graces others of his stature might feel they're entitled to.

My only quibble: the car reeked of Benson & Hedges afterwards.

"You ever have a puff before a match, Denis?"

"Before, at half-time... the place was stinking. Bestie hated it."

"Any favourite Bestie moments?"

"Chelsea. At the Bridge. He was sticking the ball up this poor guy's arse and bringing it back down. Bobby didn't like him doing that, and I was pissed off too.

"Anyway, he got bored torturing just one of them and tried sending three or four for the same packet of fags. He was fucking about; I eventually cracked and screamed 'get it into the fucking box, you wee f...FUCK ME, WHAT A GOAL!'

"That was one they still talk about, but you'll never see it; there were no TV cameras."

I chanced reminding the charming Aberdonian, who'd just turned 50, about the day when he bagged a double hat-trick for City in an FA Cup fourth round tie against Luton at a rain-drenched Kenilworth Road – only for the match to be abandoned on 69 minutes after the pudding pitch became unplayable. Remarkably, City lost the replay 3-1.

"You had to bring that up, didn't you? It didn't bother me then {1961} because I was a cocky kid, convinced we'd beat them a few days later. Did you know I got City's goal in the replay as well?

"That Luton game was the only time I scored six – of course Bestie did it years later – and it was wiped off the record books."

I often contrast that day with a less convivial encounter a decade later, when I 'interviewed' one of the heirs to The King's throne – Paul Scholes. Scholesy's right up there with Keano, Sparky, Bestie, Eric The Red, Robbo, the Black Pearl and The Lawman on my list of all-time Manc favourites. I loved the time at United's Carrington training base when, after his team-mates drew up in Aston Martins, Porsches, Ferraris and Lamborghinis, devoted family man Scholesy arrived in a people carrier.

Then I met him, during a coaching course at Tillysburn.

I'd brought along a work experience kid who thought all his Christmases had come at once as we shook hands with the brilliant midfielder in a small pitch-side caravan.

The sponsor's special guest might has well have had 'I don't want to be here' tattooed on his forehead; he sat, unsmiling, feet up, delivering monosyllabic answers (the usual suspects: "yes", "no", "hopefully" and "obviously") to questions my young pal had drawn up earlier.

Ten torturous minutes, then: "Paul, I'm going to cut this short. It's clear you don't want to do it, but you could have made an effort for the kid."

Sometimes I wonder what became of that schoolboy. Hopefully he's watching hard-hitting, motormouth pundit Scholesy on telly and wondering if that really is the same person.

(Compare that episode to this: October 1993, an interview with Michael Laudrup in a deserted cafe at Denmark's Copenhagen training base. The Barcelona superstar – arguably the best player in the world at that time – asked if I'd like tea and toast. "That would be nice, Michael." I expected him to click his fingers and a waiter to come running. Instead, he went behind the counter and made it himself. Now *that's* class).

CHAPTER 19

Malcolm was famously generous with his hospitality. An invitation to Belfast was always an honour, an opportunity to hear him talk about every luminary from Best to Puskas, and a challenge for those not experienced in the ways of whiskey.
(Henry Winter, The Times)

I woke up with the hangover from Hades and the leader of the murderous Red Hand Commando lying beside me. We've all been there, right?

Three weeks earlier: "Right, Schemer. Ah hope ye've got yer passport up tae date. Ye're going tae Belgrade wi' Ireland."
This was a shock; Malky had never missed a Northern Ireland match.
"How come? Are *you* not going?"
"Oh, Ah'll get there for the game, but ye'll have tae do the preview stuff. Ah have tae be in London on the Tuesday; Ah'm being presented with the inaugural Doug Gardner Memorial Trophy at the British Sports Journalism Awards."
"Congratulations, Malky. But... aren't you one of the people who decides who wins these awards?"
"Aye, but Ah recused maself from the judgin' for that particular one."
"O... K. I get that..."
Malky shifted uncomfortably.
"Ah think they wanna honour me cos Ah'm retirin' in a few month. Sports Minister Robert Atkins will be there. Right, that's it. Don't forget tae ring the travel people with yer passport details, pronto."
Belfast Telegraph back page headline, Wednesday, March 27, 1991:

Bingham's boys have a mountain to climb against classy Yugoslavia
From John Laverty in Belgrade

Below that:

National award for Telegraph Sports Editor

Beograd wasn't a desirable destination back then. I'd harboured hopes of hopping onto the spectacular Belgrade-Bar railway, or checking out the Wander Kalemegdan fortress. Even a riverside bar along the Danube or Sava would have been nice.

But we arrived during the immediate aftermath of the Serbian/Yugoslav capital's largest anti-communist protest since World War II, which resulted in thousands of protesters being shot at and tear-gassed by police and soldiers loyal to the country's detested Marxist president Slobodan Milosevic.

Two people were killed and more than 100 badly injured during a period of worsening political crisis in the patchwork Balkan collective of six volatile republics, whose failing economy had led to an uprise in nationalism and increased ethnic and religious tension.

The four-day-long protest ended after despot Milosevic promised to make the state media (which, like virtually everything else in Yugoslavia, was controlled by the authoritarian, Serbia-centric Socialist Party) more "objective", and release incarcerated politicians who'd been critical of the volatile country's largest, most authoritarian republic.

His alternative solution to insurrection – mass genocide – was on its way. A basket-case country, with Catholics and Orthodox Christians fighting each other, 100,000 protesting in the city centre against an undemocratic, unholy alliance, sectarian murder in the badlands border area, soldiers and armoured cars on every street corner; no wonder we felt at home.

And, like Northern Ireland, our hosts had a 'mixed' football team to cheer – but there the comparisons ended.

Whereas our boys were an honest, motley crew who regularly punched above their weight, Yugoslavia were, at that time, threatening to become the best team on the planet.

Their kids had won the 1987 FIFA World Youth Championship in Chile, while Red Star Belgrade were on their way to beating Marseille in the 1991 European Cup final in Bari.

(Earlier that season the 'other Scottish Malcolm' – my Mo Johnston informant – told me about Rangers assistant boss Walter Smith's priceless post-Belgrade 'scouting report' to Graeme Souness after the Teddy Bears had been drawn Red Star in the second round: "We're fucked").

At one time, the Yugoslav national team could call on Croatians Robert Prosinecki, Zvonimir Boban, Robert Jarni, Igor Stimac, Alen Boksic and Davor Suker; Serbs Dragan Stojkovic, Predrag Mijatovic, Sinisa Mihajlovic

123

and Vladimir Jugovic; Montenegrin Dejan Savicevic, Macedonian Darko Pancev and Slovenian Srecko Katanec; all genuine world class 'plures', as Bingy would say.

It was Dinamo Zagreb skipper Boban, however, who is credited with – literally – kicking off the Balkan conflict when he launched a Cantona-style kung-fu attack on a police officer who was beating up a home supporter during fierce rioting between Dinamo and Red Star fans at the Croatia capital's Maksimir Stadium in May 1990.

With a large number of Dinamo fans having joined the Croatian military, and Red Star supporters bolstered by members of the Serbian armed forces, a powderkeg exploded into what history has deemed the unofficial start of the 'Homeland War'.

Boban, who was handed a lengthy ban, dropped from Yugoslavia's 1990 World Cup squad (which reached the quarter finals) and who clearly had the freedom of Belgrade withdrawn, was missing when Northern Ireland took to the field at a sparsely populated, 55,000-capacity Marakana Stadium. Why support a 'country' your own president claims no longer exists?

Ironically, the blue-shirted home side that day contained just two Serbians, alongside four Croatians, three Bosnia-Herzegovinians, one Montenegrin and one Macedonian – Darko 'the Dark Destroyer' Pancev, who bagged a hat-trick in an inevitable, comprehensive 4-1 win over our patched-up lot who were missing first-choice regulars Alan McDonald, Gerry Taggart, Danny Wilson and Nigel Worthington.

I had to guess the line-up for my preview piece because Bingy was in one of his more uncooperative moods: "...but John, if I tell you the team then you'll know it before the plures, and that can't be right..."

{So how come the Beeb guys already have it, then?}

It wasn't difficult to predict anyway; at training, Bingy would call each plure over individually; if you were starting, you got a handshake, if not, you had to make do with an apologetic pat on the backside as you ran off.

Paul Kee was in goal, with Mal Donaghy, Gary Fleming, Colin Hill and Anton Rogan in defence, Steve Morrow, Kingsley Black, Robbie Dennison and Jim Magilton in midfield and Iain Dowie up front alongside Kevin Wilson.

Dragisa Binic rewarded the hosts' early pressure, but then big Hill headed in a completely unexpected equaliser just before half time to give us a semblance of hope.

Ultimately, however, the super-slick Slavs, inspired by the brilliant young

Prosinecki in midfield, could have bagged eight or nine.

Afterwards Bingy said: "This is definitely one of the best teams ever. I'm sure they'll top Group 4 and could even win the Euros next summer..."

The night before the ironic dismantling of our wee country in Belgrade, Portadown were clinching their second successive Irish League title back in Belfast – the first provincial club to achieve such a feat. Glentoran's surprise home loss to Bangor got the party started for Big Ronnie and Co across the lough at Seaview.

The Ports' reward for retaining the Gibson Cup with five matches to spare – an all-red glamour European Cup date with the newly-crowned champions, but not in war-ravaged Belgrade. Instead, the match would be played 140 miles away in Szeged, Hungary.

With Malky 'etching' upstairs, I was feeling at a loose end when we got back to the heavily fortified hotel (Milosevic's idea, bless him).

In the near-empty lobby bar stood a fully-regaled Northern Ireland supporter whom I recognised from news bulletins back home... Winston Churchill 'Winkie' Rea, boss of the notorious Red Hand Commando, son-in-law of veteran UVF legend Augustus 'Gusty' Spence (Gusty was temporarily released from the Maze to attend the happy couple's wedding and promptly 'absconded' for a few months) and a one-time detainee at Her Majesty's pleasure.

The future Progressive Unionist Party peace advocate (who visited Tyrone GAA boss Mickey Harte's home after the shocking honeymoon murder of his daughter Michaela in 2011) stubbed out his cigarette and reached out a hand.

"Winkie Rea, chairman of the Shankill Supporters Club."

Among other things.

"John Laverty, Belfast Telegraph."

"I know who you are, John. Good to meet you."

Touche.

"Oh, okay. You too, Winkie. If you don't mind me saying, you're looking rather lonely."

"That's because other Shankill guys are in the air already. I missed the fucking flight. Don't ask."

No fear of that, pal.

He used his gravelly, nasal McCooey voice (pronouncing 'chance' as *chunks;* "Oi, mate, any chunks of guttin' us a drink here?") to stand me a pint of Kabinet.

"So, Winkie, I take it you're staying here."

"Not sure yet, mate. I'm flying back with you guys in the morning. Got booted out of the other place. Still waiting to hear if I've got a room. There's always the lobby floor; I've had worse."

Despite early reservations, I found the chain-smoking, wheezing Winkie rather disarming (if that's the right word) and endearing company.

He'd just turned 40, was of average height like me, had unkempt hair, was overweight and clearly unfit, wore a genial expression on his puffy, blotchy face and wasn't scary looking like contemporaries Johnny 'Mad Dog' Adair and Billy 'King Rat' Wright.

After half an hour I heard myself say: "Listen, Winkie, you can bunk in with me if you like. There are twin beds in my room; plenty of space. As long as you don't snore."

"John, you're a life saver."

Now that it was established that we'd be spending the night together, Winkie and me could relax, set up a table and wait for Malky.

If my boss was annoyed at "a punter" being there, he didn't show it. Quite the reverse; it was clear from early on that the diehard Norn Iron supporter was also a big fan of the legendary sports editor.

"So, Malcolm, what was your biggest ever scoop?"

I thought he'd need time to think about that. Instead, he answered immediately.

"Jackie Milburn joining the Blues in 1957 was the most sensational football story the Tele has ever broken."

He was undoubtedly right. 'Wor Jackie' quitting his beloved Newcastle United (for whom he'd bagged 177 goals in 353 appearances, helped the Magpies to three FA Cups and ultimately had a statue erected and the main stand named after him at St James Park) for an Irish League club was incredible, even though the former England centre-forward was, by that time, approaching his mid-thirties.

Linfield's marquee recruit was still a fabulous player though, as he'd prove by topping the local game's scoring list in his first two seasons (55 and 56 goals respectively).

The Ashington-born former pitman was a decent manager too, guiding the Blues to nine trophies in four seasons, including the league title and Irish Cup, scoring at every away ground except Mourneview and being named Ulster Footballer of the Year in his first season.

His shock move to Windsor ultimately benefited everyone; the gates swelled exponentially when John Edward Thompson Milburn, second cousin to those up and coming Charlton boys, Bobby and Jackie, was one of the visitors. Wor Jackie's Ulster love affair faded, however, after he received a letter threatening to disfigure his wife with acid if the Milburns continued to employ a 'Fenian gardener'.

"Ah'll tell you this, absolutely straight: Jackie Milburn was the best footballer ever tae play in the Irish League. Ye couldn't exaggerate how big a thing this was."

Winkie: "How'd it come about?"

"Money, Winkie; what else? Linfield offered him use of a four-bedroom detached house near the sea in Holywood, a £1,000 signin' on fee and 25 quid a week, which was half again what Newcastle were payin'.

"Not only that, but his wife Laura fell in love wi' the place after the pair o' them came over for Billy Neill and Sammy Hughes' benefit match at Glentoran."

Winkie: "But how'd *you* get the story?"

"In 1956, Jackie scored a screamer for Newcastle against Linfield in a friendly tae celebrate the new Windsor floodlights gettin' their big switch-on.

"Ah remember the Linfield secretary, Joe Mackey, saying something like 'Christ, if only we could get someone like him'.

"Jokingly, Ah said tae Joe 'well, if ye ever do sign him, sure let me know."

"Ah thought nothing more o' it but then, in May 1957, Joe asked me tae meet him behind Ormeau Swimming Baths."

Winkie: "Christ, *that* sounds a bit dodgy."

Malky delivered the sort of withering look a man of Winkie's *stature* wasn't used to.

"In *a bar* behind the swimming baths, okay? And he just came straight out wi' it – 'we're signin' Milburn, but ye can't release the story for four days.'

"Ma first thought was, 'this is gonna be the biggest scoop o' ma career', but then anxiety set in. Four days? The longest four days of ma life, let me tell ye.

"Ah kept listenin' tae the radio bulletins, fully expectin' the whole thing tae break from the Newcastle end. Then Joe finally rang at lunch-time on the Saturday, tellin' me it was all systems go and tae blast it on the front o' the Pink.

"The headline said 'Milburn signs for Linfield', but he didnae put pen tae paper until early July. It was around the Twelfth, and Jackie thought all the Union Jacks on the Donegall Road were for him.

"In the meantime, Ah'd got pelters from Linfield committee men, who said that Ah couldn't possibly know something that important ahead of them."

He looked across the table at me: "Now, where've we heard THAT before?"

My cue to take over as emcee.

"Surely Willie Johnston must have been one of your biggest scoops?"

"Och aye, that was a big one.

"It was a slice o' luck, really; Ah was havin' a wee dram wi' Harry Cavan {FIFA vice-president} in his hotel suite when a fax came through from FIFA HQ in Buenos Aires about Johnston failin' the drug test.

"It made front page headlines all over the world."

(Briefly: after Scotland lost 3-1 to Peru in their 1978 World Cup opener, midfielder Archie Gemmill was asked to supply a urine sample but was too dehydrated so Johnston took his place, subsequently testing positive for the banned stimulant Fencamfamin. Johnson was sent home in disgrace from Argentina as a drugs cheat; it later emerged – too late to save his career and reputation – that the Femcamfamin had been innocently taken as a constituent of Reactivan, an over-the-counter medicine used to combat daytime fatigue.)

"The joke goin' round the Scottish camp was that Johnston should have shown FIFA a video of his crap display against Peru tae prove that whatever he took certainly wasnae performance enhancin'," said Malky.

At this point, Bingy strode in and gave me a playful shoulder massage.

"Right, young John, who's getting them in?"

Well, clearly not you, you tight bastard.

"Hey, Billy, great to see you. You've arrived at the right moment. We're just talking about Malky's greatest scoops."

Bingy: "Did you mention the one I tipped you off about in '86?"

Malky: "Oh aye, that one. Ah'd just finished an interview wi' Billy before the game against Brazil in Guadalajara when he said {spoiler alert: Malky's attempts at doing a Bingy accent were always terrible} 'by the way, Mel-cem, I'm going out to men-ege in Seedy Areebia'. Just like that..."

The next hour became a classic Malky-Bingy nostalgia fest. Naturally, it majored on Sweden 1958, when we beat Czechoslovakia 1-0, lost 3-1 to Argentina, drew 2-2 with the mighty West Germans and then saw off the Czechs again, 2-1 after extra time in a play-off, to reach the quarter-finals where they fell 4-0 to France.

All in all, a particularly memorable experience, on and off the pitch.

"Church in Halmstad in the morning, training in the afternoon then off to the Norre Kat club at night; well, it worked for us," said Bingy.

Malky: "Do you remember the wee boy who translated for us? He kept calling Gerry Morgan {the team trainer} 'Uncle Gerry' and we later found out his da was a millionaire."

Bingy: "Bengt Johansson. Lovely lad. Didn't Norman Uprichard teach him to sing The Sash?"

Malky: "And he thought Jimmy McIlroy's name was 'Smoothie', cos that's what Gregg kept callin' him."

Bingy: "The wee Halmstad girls were round him like flies. I remember shouting: 'Oi, there's a few other Irish boys over here, if you lassies would care to look."

Malky: "What about Malmo, when Morgan found out the Germany game was live on TV and asked {Peter} McParland tae fake an injury so that the folks back home would see him and his magic sponge on the box?"

Bingy: "Yeah, but then when McParland was *really* crocked, Morgan didn't believe him and stayed sitting on his arse beside Peter Doherty."

Malky: "Ah couldnae believe it during the second Czech match when Morgan used up all the whiskey try'na stop the swellin' on Uprichard's knee."

Bingy: "I have a lovely photo of us celebrating getting through to the quarter-finals. It looked like whiskey in those glasses, but Morgan had filled the empty bottles with cold black tea."

I asked Bingy which team was the best he'd ever seen.

"Yugoslavia, earlier today. No, it has to be Brazil, 1970, although the 1982 team was tasty too. With plures like Zico, Falcao, Oscar, Eder and Socrates all at their peak, they should have won."

Malky: "For me, it has tae be the Real Madrid team that beat Eintracht Frankfurt 7-3 in the 1960 European Cup final. Ah was at Hampden that day; Puskas and Di Stefano were unbelievable."

Bingy: "I bet you guys didn't know that myself and Puskas scored in the same match. Aha, silence! Would you believe it was in a fundraising friendly at the old South Liverpool FC ground in 1967?

"The local Bankfield House community centre was in danger of closing and they asked myself, Billy Liddell, Dave Hickson, Malcolm Allison and John Charles to take part. They also sent invites to Pele and Puskas – and Puskas accepted, as long as they paid his flight over from Spain.

"Puskas had never played at Anfield or Goodison, but when people heard he was coming to Holly Park all hell broke loose. In the end, they had to restrict the gate to 10,000. My team won, naturally, 5-3, but Puskas got all the goals for the other lot. He must have been 40 years old then, and still a brilliant plure."

He was less complimentary about his 1982-86 World Cup captain Martin O'Neill ("good going forward, but not too clever when it came to defending") and the goalscoring hero of *that night* in Valencia ("Gerry was pretty ordinary as centre-forwards go; hard working but ponderous. Did you know, he only started playing 'soccer' after being banned for lamping some guy at a GAA match?").

"That was something I learned from the great Peter Doherty; getting ordinary plures to do extraordinary things. But Peter also had some diamonds too in '58, not that I'm blowing my own trumpet, you understand..."

This was Malky's penultimate trip with 'Ireland' as sports editor; his last would be the Faroe Islands tie in Landskrona, Sweden, in September (5-0, Clarke hat-trick, K Wilson, McDonald).

Belgrade was also the first of many foreign excursions with him; I remember thinking, as the glasses were lifted for the final time, that Malky really did have The Best Job In The World.

It was time for Winkie and me to hit the hay.

First night nerves kicked in: do we disrobe together, which side does he prefer – and what does one discuss at awkward moments like these?

So tell me, Winkie, what does the boss of a ruthless paramilitary organisation actually do? Describe a typical day...

In the end, we had a nightcap, a couple of ciggies and nodded off while rambling, by this time incoherently, about football and movies. Sweet dreams.

The following day, as squad and media boarded the buses for Surcin Airport, Yugoslav army tanks began blocking the main routes into the city.

CHAPTER 20

We didn't need the police to confirm it was a bomb.

There was that horrible, all-too-familiar dull sound, then the whole Belfast Telegraph building seemed to shake. Definitely close by.

Within a few minutes myself and reporter Gail Walker – a future Tele editor – were on our way up the Shankill.

Saturday lunchtime, October 23, 1993. I'd written about atrocities before, but this was the first time I'd been to the scene of one, so soon after it happened.

A fortnight earlier I'd been watching, on television, the aftermath of the devastating Latur earthquake in India.

This was a similar, chilling, surreal scene; shocked, distraught people clambering over the dusty rubble of what had been Frizzell's fish shop, trying desperately to rescue those who were still alive, uncovering parts of those who hadn't survived the carnage, unaware, terrified, of just how many there were, as the fish eyes strewn throughout the debris augmented the ghoulish horror.

Journalists are meant to have an air of detachment but all I could do was stand there, numbed, in an altered state of consciousness, as Gail spoke to traumatised witnesses nearby. Even for someone not directly affected, it was already clear this apocalyptic, haunting vision would be seared into future nightmares.

"John... JOHN? A quick word."

It was Denis Cunningham, a local man whom I knew in a social capacity. His clothes were covered in dust and other matter from the explosion. I thought he was coming over to provide some detail about how this heinous event had come about.

Instead: "John, get out of this place, quick. There are a lot of very angry people not far away. They'll want someone to pay for this, the sooner the better. And if I know what you are, I'm not the only one."

That brought mixed emotions; I knew what Denis meant by 'what you are' and was grateful for him pointing me in the right direction – out of the Shankill, asap. But I couldn't help feeling angry too; what had I got to do with this abominable evil, how could anyone associate me with it?

He was right, though; revenge for the IRA killing nine innocent people – and one of the bombers, as well as maiming scores of others – was swift and merciless. Within hours two men were shot, one of whom later died, and over the next eight days a total of 12 Catholic civilians were killed by loyalist gunmen, including six of the eight people murdered in the 'trick or treat' Greysteel massacre.

Just over a fortnight later, Windsor Park would host that notorious, seething 'Night in November' sectarian hate fest – the Northern Ireland v Republic World Cup qualifier – which would mark the end of Billy Bingham's second spell as manager. More on that later.

(Malky was on his way home from the Liverpool v Crusaders European Cup tie at Anfield when a 150lb IRA bomb ripped through the Belfast Telegraph building on Wednesday afternoon, September 15, 1976. Joe Patton, a 64-year-old from the stereo department, lost a foot in the blast and died in hospital four days later. Fourteen others were injured, including 70-year-old part-time security man Andy Kennedy who challenged the bombers in the loading bay and was shot in the arm. Some 800 people were in the building at the time. "No one expected us tae get a paper oot the next day, but we did," Malky told me. "It was only four pages, cost 1p – we called it the Penny Marvel – and was very late, but it got ontae the streets. Ah think poor Joe would have been proud o' us." The 'Penny Marvel became a collector's item but also a source of regret for editor Roy Lilley. "He led the emergency paper with a nothin' story aboot the UDA – when the biggest story o' the day was, literally, staring him in the face," said Malky. "Fer years afterwards Roy kept sayin' tae me: 'what was I thinking?' But Ah dinnae think anyone was thinkin' straight back then").

In early December, I took a call from Winkie Rea.

"We're having a do at the Shankill club to mark Bingy's retirement. He's going to make a speech, and it would be great if you said a few words. Hey, it'll be like a Belgrade reunion."

"I'd be delighted, Winkie. When did you say it was?"

It didn't take long for anxiety to creep in.

"Malky, I've been invited to speak at the Shankill Supporters Club dinner for Bingy's retirement. Are you going?"

Malky: "Whaaa? Ye must be jokin'. Ah wouldn't go up there if ye paid me, and Ah'm a true-blue Prod."

An hour later: "Winkie, I'm afraid I'm not gonna be able to make it to Bingy's do."

Winkie sounded distraught.

"What do you mean, you're not going? I've already put you on the fucking poster."

"Okay, Winkie, here goes: I've no interest whatsoever in religion or politics, and I abhor sectarianism. But I was brought up as a Catholic, and this is maybe not the best time to visit the upper Shankill."

Winkie: "Wow, a *Catholic*, eh? Who knew?"

He added: "So the rumours are *true*, then; altar boy at All Saints and former gaelic footballer with – yes, that's it: Glenravel. Your folks were so devout they had their honeymoon in Lourdes. You've been going steady with a Prod for years, and you once dabbled with the Broadway Boot Boys in Ballymena – tut, tut – but saw sense after being taken for a diving lesson at Harryville Bridge. Oh, and you nearly went for an early bath at the Great Eastern too, only one of the lads recognised your mate {Tony McCall} as a pal of Rab McCreery..."

"Stop, STOP! Jesus Christ, Winkie. I'm bricking it even more now. I didn't even *know* there was a thing at the Great Eastern {the lower Newtownards Road establishment myself and Tony, a former team-mate of the well-connected Glens legend Rab, had visited for a quick pint before the 'Blue Pig' Irish Cup final} until now. And, by the way, I actually escaped from that so-called diving lesson in Harryville."

"John, you'll be perfectly safe in our club, okay? Have you forgotten the craic in Bremen, when you changed the words of Deutschland Uber Alles and nearly started a riot with the krauts? The boys are looking forward to seeing you again."

"Mmmm. Didn't Michael Corleone give a similar assurance to Carlo? What was it: 'Don't be afraid, Carlo. You think I'd make my sister a widow?' And then Clemenza garotted him."

Winkie expelled one of his trademark wheezy chuckles.

"True, but Carlo was a piece of shit who deliberately beat up his missus in order to set Sonny up. And while we're referencing The Godfather, don't forget what Sollozzo said to Tom Hagen after they cornered him: 'Relax, Tom. If we were here to kill you, you'd be dead already.' *Capisce*?"

"That's funny; Malky also says *capisce*. You *Dons* all talk the same."

"In that case, *capisce* THIS, John: I'll fucking kill you if you DON'T turn up."

"Now *there's* an offer I can't refuse."

A hugely enjoyable evening with Winkie and the Shankill boys in early January 1994 would be the last time I'd spend quality time with Bingy. He told me that the 'Night in November' wasn't the first time he'd wound Big Jack up.

"I'll never forget nutmegging Jackie at Elland Road," he said.

"It was back in '58 when I was playing for Luton.

"The big bastard was furious, especially with me doing it in front of the Leeds fans.

"He came straight across after that passage of play broke down and said, 'You try that stunt again, little man, and I'll knock your fucking teeth down your throat'.

"I just laughed – rather nervously, as I recall – but I didn't risk trying it a second time.

"Afterwards, however, Jackie shook my hand and said, 'Well played, kid'. That left me rather bemused as I was four years older than him and had played in a World Cup; something he hadn't done..."

But what was Bingy thinking that night at Windsor, when he whipped up an already feral home crowd? (*See Chapter 25*). Was he entering a second 'Billy Boy' childhood?

"No, I knew exactly what I was doing. I knew Jackie would be nervous as hell, so I thought, 'Okay, let's make the bastard angry too'. Anxiety and anger aren't good bedfellows."

He added: "In hindsight maybe it wasn't too clever. But it was my last game and I desperately wanted to win. It didn't matter who the opponents were."

Yeah, right...

"Okay, I wasn't too happy either with the way they'd behaved in Dublin last March," he said.

That was the 3-0 tanking at Lansdowne when raucous home fans – 33,000 of them – relentlessly sang "There's only one team in Ireland", to the tune of Cuban folk song Guantanamera, after goals from Andy Townsend, Niall Quinn and Steve Staunton had sunk our boys in the space of 10 shattering first-half minutes.

It was humiliating for proud Ulstermen Bingy and Jimmy Nick sitting in the 'northern' dugout.

He didn't quite get his revenge at Windsor but, knowing Bingy, he'll be delighted that he outlived 'Jackie'.

We'd speak on the phone occasionally, but that correspondence evaporated with the onset of his dementia.

The last time I met him – in Belfast city centre, accompanied by his son David – Northern Ireland's most successful manager hadn't a clue who I was.

134

CHAPTER 21

Raise your glass to the legendary Scot who is everybody's Freeman of Ulster.

With the retirement of Malcolm Brodie MBE, for 40 years sports editor of the Belfast Telegraph and Ireland's Saturday Night, a million souls have marked the date as they would a Royal abdication.

But hasten slowly. This is no final whistle. No social milestone can switch off such a high capacity journalist.

He'll retain a relationship with the Telegraph and, of course, with the network of international agencies, broadcasting stations and newspapers who, for years, have taken any material he sends them.

'Hasten slowly.' I'd never heard that oxymoronic phrase before. Apparently, it's from the Latin *festina lente* and is more commonly translated as 'more haste, less speed'.

I walked past 'hasten slowly' a lot because the piece that contained it, written for the paper by the late Derek Murray and illustrated with a brilliant caricature of the retiring sports editor by acclaimed Holywood cartoonist Rowel Friers, was framed and mounted beside the Ink Spot door in September 1991.

It freaked me out. What did Derek mean by 'hasten slowly'? And why isn't it a 'final whistle'?

Suddenly, the doubts that had flowed like rivulets through my psyche three years earlier came flooding back.

I remembered how long it took for Malky to confirm that I really *was* going to be his new 'leg man' in 1988 and, although nothing had been said to the contrary, there had been no official confirmation either that the sports editor elect, Sammy Hamill, definitely had me in mind as number one football writer.

That gushing eulogy from Derek, better known then as a manager at UTV but who'd been Malky's right hand man for four years in the early 60s, appeared to suggest that, although the paper was definitely appointing only its second sports editor, it could well be 'as you were' with the football coverage.

After a few nights of progressively unsteady walks past 'hasten slowly' and getting myself worked up – and with the 'end of an era' only days away – I finally called Sammy at home.

"Here's what's happening, John. You WILL be the main football man. You'll be going to the big match every week, and all the Northern Ireland games. Malky will cover for you on your day off. Understood?"

It wasn't just the 'hasten slowly' thing that had put me in bad form close to the date of abdication – Friday, September 27, 1991; Malky's 65th birthday.

Earlier that month I'd travelled to the Hungarian border city of Szeged with Double winners Portadown, who'd landed what should have been a glamour European Cup tie with defending champions Red Star Belgrade. But with the Balkan conflict escalating into all-out civil war and Belgrade one of the most dangerous places on earth, Serbia's pride and joy, *Crvena Zvezda,* were forced to play their matches outside disintegrating Yugoslavia.

It was a pleasant trip though, with a predictable outcome – 4-0 to the nomads who'd lost, among others, Prosinecki, Pancev, Mihajlovic and Savicevic to Spanish and Italian giants in the summer.

The next morning, Ports chairman Marshall Beattie told me this: Red Star would be having an extraordinary general meeting with 'potential withdrawal from the European Cup' the sole item on the agenda.

Their president, Svetozar Mijailovic, had told Marshall that many of Red Star's players faced being drafted into the Serbian military, and that the club couldn't guarantee making the trip to Shamrock Park a fortnight hence – thus handing the tie to Portadown.

What a story! One of those yarns that had national and international interest; UEFA didn't even know about this, but the BelTel did.

I couldn't get to the news stand quick enough after landing in Belfast. Obviously the Tele will have splashed the back, and maybe the news desk will have trailed a bit on the front too. The European champions about to withdraw – with Portadown taking their place; *get in!*

My piece, originally 600 words long, had been cut to 250 and placed at the very bottom of the back page – even lower than a story about Crystal Palace chairman Ron Noades apologising for ill-advised remarks about black footballers.

Back-page lead that day...

BANGOR 'CZECH' IN FOR DEBUT

By Malcolm Brodie

... A preview of the Seasiders' UEFA Cup tie with those behemoths of European football, Sigma Olomouc (despite their undoubted fame, we'd referred, wrongly, to them as *Olomouc Sigma*).

I was raging, and not just because the headline's pun had inverted commas; as if the reader was too stupid to work out that *Czech* was a play on 'check'.

No, this was beyond the pale – and unprofessional; which sports desk would put the country's UEFA Cup representatives ahead of the champions, especially when the latter was a much bigger club?

And this wasn't your run-of-the-mill follow-up piece about how much the trip cost, or who'd picked up a calf strain.

My story was followed up by the UK nationals, who obviously didn't have staff judging the merit of stories by who wrote them.

Although my revelation of Red Star's imminent demise was correct, the timeline wasn't. Serbia's biggest club made it to Shamrock Park (another 4-0 drubbing) and, like the similarly homeless, conflict-suffering Derry City back in 1972, hobbled on for a few months before UEFA opted for mercy-killing both them and the national team.

My 'downpage filler' appeared on September 18 – the day before I rang Sammy for succour. The end of the Brodie era couldn't come soon enough.

'The end' was Sinatra-esque. Malky attended countless 'farewell' dinners and was rightly lauded by various sports bodies; the Shiny Suit got many outings. Even the masonic press lodge, whose membership boasted quite a few Tele staff, and the Northern Bank – custodian of the Brodie riches – marked the occasion.

The one that really mattered, however, was held at the Culloden a few days before Sammy's inauguration.

This was the 'official sports desk do', during which Malky would deliver an intimate speech.

Typically, it was dripping in MB nostalgia. The soon-to-be pensioner recalled one of his first major stories; an interview with 20-year-old Jimmy Jones in hospital, December 1948 – the day after the Belfast Celtic striker had his leg broken by so-called Linfield fans at Windsor.

Malky regularly referred to that shameful incident as the darkest hour in local football, one which reverberated around the world and hastened (and not slowly either) the end of a legendary club.

Another notorious Windsor event – the 'Battle of Belfast' in December 1957, when the Northern Ireland v Italy game was marred by disgraceful behaviour both on and off the pitch – got an airing.

Malky couldn't understand the bemused looks when he mentioned Arthur Ellis, who'd been put on standby to referee in place of a Hungarian official who'd been fog-bound in London.

Those of us who'd gamboled through fewer summers knew Ellis better from popular BBC game show It's A Knockout, which Malky had never heard of.

But as he explained, Ellis couldn't make it either, and – only 15 minutes before kick-off and with 50,000 in the stadium – what should have been a crucial World Cup qualifier was dramatically reclassified as a friendly, with Lurgan ref Tommy Mitchell in charge.

"Some friendly that was," said Malky.

"We'd players kickin' the crap out o' each other, supporters attackin' Italians an' getting baton-charged. International diplomacy was ruined; all good copy for me, of course."

Malky said it was the first time the Tele had allowed comment in what was ostensibly news copy; an American technique pioneered on this side of the pond by Malky's flamboyant pal (and Munich Air Disaster victim) Henry Rose.

"The display of hooliganism by a section of the crowd cannot be condoned.
It left a bad taste with the Italians and did irreparable damage to Ireland's international soccer reputation. This was one of our blackest hours. Any sporting-minded person must have thoroughly ashamed. The jeering of the Italian anthem made me blush when I thought of the stillness in Rome when 'God Save The Queen was played'."

He found time to recall colleagues from the good old days, such as the tall, elegantly dressed, 'Ralph the Rover' (Billy McClatchey), junior football correspondent Leslie McCullough, Brian Munn and Derek Murray, the 'baby of the team' who joined straight from school.

The sports desk's unofficial colleague or 'fifth Beatle' – Sam Casey, owner of the Brown Horse – also got an honourable mention.

And as former sports desk secretaries (Mary McCarrison, Emily Reif, Margaret Lynn, Maureen Dickson and Bernie McCool) were all present as special guests, it was only right that they got name checks too, along with Angela (Angie) Klein.

But not one journalistic colleague sitting in that dining room heard Malky utter their name; not even Jack or Walker, who were retiring around the same time.

Even Malky's successor didn't merit a "good luck for the future, Sammy".

Colly was more pragmatic about what I regarded as an indefensible, thoughtless snub.

"Why the fuck would Malky get all misty-eyed over guys he'll be back speaking to next week?" said Colly.

"He'll be ringing every day, and you two lovers have all those exotic trips to look forward to."

Sammy was the Tele's second sports editor, and first *proper* one. Unlike his predecessor, he was office-bound most of the time, concentrating on content and presentation. He'd little interest in stories about sports administrators; on his watch, competitors would always have centre stage.

It can't have been easy for Sammy at the start, what with having to cope with the loss of the desk's three biggest stars and a new company directive which prevented him from hiring a deputy, although that eventually changed.

He was good at talent-spotting and Lyle Jackson, David Kelly, John Taylor (aka 'The Captain'; sadly, John passed away in July 2020 after a long illness) and Peter Hutcheon were excellent recruits.

As Ronnie Harper said: "It was Best-Law-Charlton under Malky, but Shirley {Sammy's wife's name; don't ask} has turned us into Giggs-Ince-Keane-Kanchelskis-Cantona."

I concentrated on ridding the Tele of its 'groin strain paper' epithet. No longer would we lead the back with a crocked footballer, unless it was a big name with a career-threatening set-back. Managers habitually lied anyway, their players rising Lazarus-like on Saturdays after being maimed for life the previous day. No, the News Letter are welcome to Lee Doherty's groin strains from now on.

Malky sent pieces on my day off – Thursday, normally – and, after two weeks, I covered my first Northern Ireland match as the 'main man'; a Euro '92 qualifier against Austria. The first time ever that the 'doyen' had *not* reported on one for the paper.

For me, however, this wasn't a Tony Blair-style 'hand of history on my shoulder' moment, probably because I'd been doing preview pieces for three years, as well as covering Republic matches. And let's not forget the Belgrade 'fun and game' a few months earlier.

"Pleasure not known beforehand is half wasted," wrote Thomas Hardy. "To anticipate it is to double it."

Well, we anticipated a pleasing performance from Northern Ireland at

Windsor Park last night and we got one.
Not a classic, it must be said, but certainly novel.

I tried too hard with that one. Contrived and forced. But Colly loved it, and he was my go-to barometer.

I sat beside Malky during the game (which finished 2-1, Iain Dowie and Kingsley Black scoring their first international goals to yield 'successive victories' for the first time in seven years), although, metaphorically, I was now occupying his seat.

If he was smarting about this dramatic change in status, he showed no sign of it.

Then, the day after the match report:

GLENTORAN PLAN £1M INJECTION
Oval club ready to propose radical new share issue

By Malcolm Brodie

Glentoran directors have called an extraordinary general meeting at the Oval on November 7, when a proposal will be placed before shareholders to increase the share capital of the company from its current £3,000 to £1m.

I wasn't sure what this meant, but it sounded a lot better than my bog-standard preview of Portadown v Ballymena – not that I'd been given the courtesy of a Malky-style 'what have ye got' from Sammy, who laid out the back page with the Glens share issue as the splash.

"What's up with you?" he asked. "You're standing there with a face like a Lurgan spade. Are you huffing because Malky's brought in a big story?"

I searched for a witty retort, but nothing came.

"I'm not huffing, Sammy, and it sounds like a good story, but I can't help wondering about the timing."

"What do you mean by that?"

"Well, did you know Malky's on the Kelly Show tonight; is there a chance this story is connected to that?"

"*Now* you're getting paranoid. Look, it's just a good bloody story and it's the back-page lead. Get over it."

Gerry Kelly's opening screed that night: "Well Malcolm, you're supposed to have retired, but what's this in my hand – tonight's Tele, with Malcolm Brodie as the back-page lead. It's just business as usual!" {*Studio audience applauds}.*

Sammy's craggy face the next morning told me that he'd seen the Kelly Show, and that "shut the fuck up" could well be the response if I said anything.

Glentoran's sensational '£1m share issue', incidentally, never came to pass.

Welcome to the new era. But hasten slowly.

CHAPTER 22

I appreciate this whole seduction thing you've got going on here, but let me give you a tip: I'm a sure thing.
(Julia Roberts' character Vivian Ward, Pretty Woman, 1990)

Malky's abdication in 1991 coincided with the end of Terry Nicholson's reign as Glenavon manager.

But there were no farewell dinners or backslapping for 'Nicky', whose abrupt sacking was as big a shock to everyone else in local football as it was to him.

The former Crues, Coleraine and Distillery goalkeeper had moulded the Lurgan Blues into a formidable outfit, with a delicious strike force of McCoy, McBride, Ferguson and Ferris the envy of every other club in Ireland.

Under Nicky's guidance they'd followed up the sensational 6-1 Budweiser Cup rout of Linfield with the League, Gold and Mid-Ulster Cups.

They'd also been Irish Cup finalists a few months before the sacking, losing 2-1 at Windsor Park to a Stevie Cowan-inspired, Double-clinching Portadown, who had pipped their neighbours to the league title by a solitary point the previous year.

According to the Lurgan Mafia, however, Nicky's face no longer fitted the Mourneview board's profile of a Glenavon manager for the 90s.

And, following the death of the club's ebullient, Nicky-supporting chairman Wilfie Geddis earlier in the year, it was only a matter of time before the axe fell.

Nicky was therefore a classic dead man walking after Glenavon's away goals exit to Finnish side Ilves in a Cup Winners Cup tie – not because of how they played, rather the behaviour of some of the travelling party before and after the game.

A few got wasted on the outward journey, having taken cognisance of one notable aspect of Nicky's earlier, exhausting 'fact-finding mission' which revealed that beer and wine on Finnair flights was free (but you had to pay for spirits).

Finnish TV crews were subsequently treated to footage of some of the visitors' star players being 'poured off the bus' on arrival in the southern town of Tampere.

Club directors were also shocked at finding an empty bottle of Buckfast, bearing a Northern Ireland off-licence label, lying in the hotel corridor.

I wasn't on that trip but there were reports, too, of an inebriated player falling out of a broom cupboard, still entwined in the arms of a young Finnish lady after a bout of *in flagrante delicto* he obviously felt would help take his mind off the heartbreaking Euro exit (2-1 on the night, 4-4 on aggregate).

And, on checkout, the club was saddled with a bill for damage to the hotel.

Nicky admitted to me after his dismissal that there had been "some horseplay" which gave his detractors the ammunition they needed, but added: "It was nothing out of the ordinary for an away match in Europe." He's not wrong. Those football trips were as synonymous with "birds and booze" as they were with disappointing performances – although, to be fair, the former generally followed the latter.

As Oscar Wilde once said: "I can resist anything except temptation", and on these exotic excursions, temptresses could be hard to resist, even for those who were happily married – well, from the waist up, anyway.

An Icelandic journalist once told my colleague Jim Gracey, who went to a European match in Reykjavik (with Glenavon, who else?): "There are only two things to do in Iceland, my friend – fishing and fucking. And in the winter there is no fishing..."

The golden rule about 'what happens on tour stays on tour' was often exploited to the 'nth' degree by players, supporters and suits liberated by unspoken, communal assurances of anonymity and discretion.

I've seen a few eye-popping fleshpots on my travels; the 'Four Floors of Whores' in Singapore (ladyboys on level 4), the Memo Club in Addis Ababa (where women literally fight over male patrons), the spotlessly clinical Rappongi district of Tokyo, the hotel in Kiev where ladies of the night were allowed to wander the corridors, offering the type of 'room service' certain to melt the chocolate on your pillow.

Weirdest of all, however, was 'Miari Texas' in Seoul, which myself and Jim Gracey 'researched' prior to a 2002 World Cup game.

You encounter the dubious delights of Mairi Texas by entering through a set of blink-and-miss-them curtains (no, really) which lead into an area of cobbled streets the size of Glengormley.

No short skirts, plunging tops, fishnet tights or wagging 'come and get it' fingers here; instead, each brightly-lit shop front had on display a dozen young South Korean girls kneeling down, dressed in elegant pearl-coloured wedding dresses and with butter-wouldn't-melt expressions on geisha-style painted faces.

During our time in this surreal environment, we spotted some well-known celebrities 'window shopping'. Let's just say you'd be surprised. I'm not being pious or judgmental here; I regularly accompanied players on post-match rampages – and joined other members of the entourage on pre-match ones.

One morning in Vaduz, Liechtenstein, I was tucking into breakfast with Malky when Irish FA vice-president Ivan Marshall remarked that I must have "turned over a new leaf" by making it down in time for croissants and coffee.

"New leaf ma arse," said Malky.

"This wee ballix stepped out o' a taxi ten minutes ago. The only reason he's here is because he hasnae been tae bed yet..."

The late, avuncular Ivan, who'd been filling in for the IFA's ambassadorial president Jim Boyce on that 1995 alpine excursion, had tried his hand at high-level diplomacy during the traditional international committee bash the previous night.

Stepping forward to meet his opposite number, the mid-Ulster pensioner reached out his hand and said: "Sooo very pleezed to meet you, Meester President. Tell me... do you speaka da Engleesh?"

The Liechtenstein FA president replied: "I certainly do, Mister Marshall – and a lot better than you, by the sound of things."

Normally, the players were a model of discipline until after the game, when they were allowed to 'let their hair down'.

Unlike the fans, the media and the suits, they'd been confined to their rooms most of the time, and these were the days before mobile phones and tablets helped relieve the boredom.

Post-match shenanigans would often start off in dimly lit 'hostess bars', where scantily clad women extort large amounts of money off punters for 'champagne' and promises of carnal pleasure.

Visitors often found themselves fleeced, as was the case in June 2001 when members of the Northern Ireland squad were arrested in the Czech Republic after a row over an outrageous drinks bill.

The 'Prague Five' – Michael Hughes, David Healy, Glenn Ferguson, Peter Kennedy and goalkeeping coach Tommy Wright – were detained for 10 hours before being released without charge. And if you were wondering why *enfant terrible* Keith Gillespie missed the fun, he'd been forced to sit this one out through suspension. (The Irish FA's 'duty of care' to their beleaguered players? Boarding the first Belfast-bound plane and leaving them languishing in jail.)

Malky didn't mind frequenting those bars. He wasn't interested in the women, though – and that was precisely the point.

As a bloke approaching his eighth decade, I believe he got a kick out of telling attractive, bemused females trying to proposition him: "Look, love; Ah'm tryin' tae enjoy ma Johnnie Walker Black in peace with ma son here... scram!"

Various acts of seduction were commonplace when word spread that a football team was in town and groupies would breeze in to compete with – and undercut – the in-house hookers.

"Like flies around shite," was Malky's eloquent summation.

One fly was still buzzing around the squad's breakfast table one morning, much to the chagrin of a club chairman who bellowed at his manager to "say something" to the besotted player.

Under pressure and clearly flustered, the manager stood up and hollered the first thing that came into his head: "Oi, Johnny... did you get your hole?"

On another occasion, on the team bus, I overheard a player relating his debauched exploits to a gaggle of team-mates.

The braggart, 'Marty', perhaps clocking my incredulous expression, subsequently produced a camcorder; essential kit for your common or garden miscreant before smartphones and online 'sextortion'.

"Have a gander at this," he said.

I peered through the viewfinder at the acrobatic amateur porn for a short while – until the picture started rhythmically undulating.

"Holy shit, Marty... was there someone else in that bedroom?"

"Oh aye," says he, pointing towards blushing team-mate 'Bertie'.

"Bertie recorded it for me. You can't do close-ups when the camera's sitting on its own."

"No Marty, I suppose not. And it must have been difficult for Bertie to control equipment like that with just one hand..."

The salacious recording had already been neatly dated and labelled as 'match highlights', and would hide in plain sight back home.

"If the missus thinks it's football, she won't look near it..."

'The missus' even bought him a neat wooden case for his recordings. ("Don't forget to store them in the proper chronological order, dear...").

(You may be wondering why I haven't touched on Northern Ireland's notorious 1995 Canada trip. Fear not; I'll get to that fiasco later.)

You could debate ad nauseam the morals and ethics of men behaving badly; my philosophy on the peccadilloes of consenting adults was always 'who am I to judge?'

That said, I encountered a repulsive, game-changing moment on one trip – and no players were involved.

Frankly, the antics of some paunchy, profligate suits could flush the cheeks of the younger, red-blooded sportsmen they accompanied.

Next time that hoary old chestnut about an 'all-Ireland football team' is discussed, consider this: it would mean just one set of suits carousing around the world on freebie trips – and those turkeys ain't gonna vote to sack Santa.

Another east European city. After etching, I decamped to a nearby hostelry. The only available seat was beside two local girls in their early twenties. They ushered me to sit down and a civilised conversation began.

My new pals, both of whom spoke passable English, told me they were students in third year at university. They were enthusiastic about advising me on the best local restaurants and other places of interest.

"Not that we can afford those places," said one. "We have to get by on fifty dollars a month."

Four of the visiting football club's suits then entered the premises. Their compatriot was immediately spotted; within seconds, four more chairs were dragged across the floor.

To be fair, the craic was initially good; neither girl seemed to mind the sudden invasion by a raucous quartet of middle-aged beer bellies.

Indeed, the convivial couple happily agreed to join the male quintet for a nightcap back at the hotel. Then things took a more sinister turn.

Suit One suggested 'a party' upstairs in his spacious suite; again, the girls felt that this was an acceptable request. They even located a decent music channel on the television as a waiter arrived with a trolley of drinks.

Not long afterwards, Suit One's mask slipped. Why is that, to properly feel 'entitlement' to sex, you have to be either stinking rich or depressingly poor?

"Right girls, time for a bit of fun. How about a striptease for the tourists?"

Our guests looked uncomfortable, even frightened.

"You have misunderstood us," said one, firmly.

"We are students, we are not prostitutes or lap dancers."

The reply: "Look, love, as the great Winston Churchill once said, 'we've already established what you are, we're merely haggling over the price'. So, what's it to be?"

With that, he threw two twenty-dollar bills onto the oversized bed.

The girls remained seated, drinks tightly held, as Suits Two, Three and Four began chanting "get your tits out for the lads."

They stayed motionless, staring across as the nauseating Suit One

146

continued to throw down greenbacks.

But when the pile reached over 200 dollars, the girls' resistance evaporated. They rose slowly and began to 'dance' in the most half-hearted way imaginable, faces frozen in a fearful rictus while disrobing to wild cheers from the neanderthal scumbags in the room – a group which, I'm ashamed to say, briefly included me.

I left before the girls' indignity was complete, disgusted at being party to this deplorable iniquity and racked with guilt at having associated myself with such depraved dickheads.

A chastened Suit Two assured me the next day that "nothing untoward" had happened, that the girls had kept their knickers on and departed intacto, which was scant consolation. What exactly was his yardstick for 'nothing untoward' after what had already occurred?

I've never told anyone that grubby, humiliating episode until now.

Tour talk tended to be laced with more 'acceptable' anecdotes, such as the legendary lore of 'Sandy and Dominic' which most football hacks from that era will be familiar with.

Randy Sandy – a slim, dapper suit well into his sixties when I got to know him, had no interest in football.

People on the game, rather than at it, were his focus of attention abroad and, if there was a willing lady (or ladies) to be attended to, the businessman's patient, virtuous friend Dominic would be dropped like the proverbial stone.

"He blows at least five grand on these women every trip," white haired, round-faced Dominic told me after I'd located him – alone again, naturally – in the hotel lobby while whoremeister Sandy did the hokey-cokey with a buxom fraulein upstairs.

"Why do you bother, Dominic? It's not as if you two have much in common."

"Well," said the softly-spoken, good-natured Dominic – whom we nicknamed 'The Reverend' because he was an indefatigable pillar of his local church and perpetually quoting from the Good Book – "He's not like this back home."

"Yes, Dominic, but that's because they don't have a Pussycats Club or a Playmates Escort Service in Lurgan."

"Well, John, we're all sinners in our own way."

His friend's propensity for sin was indefatigable.

One time, in a former Soviet republic, Sandy ordered four 'escorts' within an hour of arrival and didn't emerge from his hotel room until 48 hours later – when the quartet of ladies, either concerned about their client having a cardiac arrest or feeling guilty about how much he'd lavished on them, took him out for a slap-up meal, with one even treating the old goat to a gratis 'happy ending' afterwards.

(I had to compliment Malky on his rapier wit the day his reservation got mixed up with Sandy's. "It was an administrative mistake, Mr Malcolm", said the contrite receptionist. "We had two rooms wrongly booked under Mr Sandy's name." Malky's reply: "That's nae mistake, love. Sandy needs one o' those for a waitin' room...")

Dominic's take on things was that Sandy believed every woman could be 'talked to' at the right price.

Didn't I know it. Malky and myself would reminisce about the time we befriended a Swedish doctor and her medical student daughter in a Baltic town centre.

The pair told us they'd come over on the ferry from Stockholm and had taken time out of their shopping trip to enjoy a coffee in the afternoon sunshine.

They were pleasant company; witty, intellectual and multilingual. They could even understand Malky's Glaswegian.

Then a sozzled Sandy, accompanied by a saturnine, head-shaking Dominic, clocked us from across the cobbled square.

For a short time, the exchanges between the six of us remained congenial – but eventually Sandy's patience expired and the cunicular libido took over.

"Okay ladies, it's time to cut to the chase here... how much for some girl-on-girl action back at the ranch...?"

On a later occasion, at breakfast, Sandy approached myself and Jim Gracey – who'd joined us on this particular trip because the game fell nicely for Sunday Life – with an unusual proposition.

"I'm going to check out a high class hoor-house the bell-boy told me about; fancy coming along for the ride?"

"Are you taking the piss?" asked Jim; "It's eight o'clock in the morning... a bit early for a ride, if you ask me."

Sandy wasn't easily deterred.

"Where's your sense of adventure, Jimbo? This is the best time. It'll be nice and quiet."

"I think you mean 'closed', you idiot."

"Och, guys, stop giving me grief here. Look, just keep me company until I get there, then you and John Boy can go for a cappuccino somewhere."

Jim: "What you really mean is, you're shit-scared of some Albanian pimp knocking your pan in, and you need us to protect your bony arse."

Twenty minutes later, the taxi pulled up outside the Corpus Club. Jim was wrong; the place was open, much to the delight of the salivating Sandy, who was ushered in by the smiling madame.

"Give me an hour," he barked. We didn't.

Three hours later, Dominic was seen helping his paralytic friend into the hotel lobby, where crumple-suited Sandy promptly soiled himself.

"He'd clearly overdone it in the brothel and lost control of his faculties," a penitent Dominic later told Jim, who replied: "I used to have an oul' dog who did that. Where's Don Juan now?"

"Back in his room. I shovelled him into the bathroom and left him to it; even Christian humanity has its limits."

There was no sign of Sandy for the rest of the day.

But later, at closing time in the lobby bar and after Malky hit the hay, myself and Jim spotted two women looking rather disorientated close by.

"I wonder who ordered them at two in the morning?" said Jim.

"Ladies, you're looking a little lost. Can we offer some assistance?"

Escort One: "We have an appointment in Room 172."

Jim: "An appointment, eh? Do you know your client is nearly 70 years old?"

Escort Two: "Yes, but the fire is still burning."

Jim: "You're not wrong there, love, especially with the amount of methane gas in that room."

Escort One: "I'm sorry, we don't understand."

Jim: "Never mind, private joke. So, what do you ladies charge for 'entertaining' a pensioner?"

Escort Two: "It's 100 dollars each for an hour".

Escort One: "But we only get 15 dollars each. Half goes to our employer, and the rest to the doormen and barmen for letting us come in."

Jim: "Christ, that's a bit lopsided. Your client, by the way, is a wealthy businessman, so tell him Jimbo and John Boy said yous were to get a decent tip. Go up one flight of stairs and turn right through the double doors. Good luck."

Then: "Let's leave it a minute and then gatecrash Sandy's party. We'll say we're choking for a nightcap from his minibar; frustrate the smelly bastard."

I hung back a little as an emboldened Jim strode towards Room 172.

"This'll be a hoot," he said.

Rat-ta-tat-tat. "Room service! Drinks for the ladies. Open up!"

The countdown began.

Five, four, three, two, one… the door opened – and Jim's trademark ruddy face turned white.

"Fuck me... IT'S DOMINIC!"

CHAPTER 23

December 19, 1992...

Dear John,

I am writing to tell you that I have not put on a Rangers scarf since the day Mo Johnston signed for them.
I am now going to do the same with my Linfield shirt because a lot of rubbish has been talked this week in the papers.
As I write this I don't know if Linfield are going to sign that player from the Republic of Ireland but if they go ahead and do it I won't be back at Windsor Park.
I have followed the Blues since the 70s and we never had to resort to signing those sort of people before.
There was no talk of bringing in outsiders when Linfield were going well and winning the league year in, year out.
Just because they have had a couple of bad years does not mean they should break with tradition and bring a mixed team to Windsor Park.
I am not being sectarian here but one of the reasons I, and a lot of others, follow the Blues is because they are the pride of Ulster and usually have eleven Ulstermen in their team.
That gives them an identity and it gives us something to identify with.
I ask you John, what is wrong with going along and supporting 'our boys' every week? It is the way it has always been and I don't know many people who want the thing to change.
Catholics can have their Celtics and their Cliftonvilles and good luck to them, so why can't we have our Linfield and our Rangers as well? That's the way the supporters want it.
It's not a case of a bigot shouting his mouth off, so please don't call me one after you print this.

Yours in sport,
'True Blue'
(Name and address supplied)

Malky hated the Have a Rattle page.
"When are ye gonna bin that Dear Abby crap? Everyone's talkin' aboot it..."

I hadn't a clue what 'Dear Abby' meant. It was left to Colly to assuage my ignorance by expounding on Abigail van Buren's hugely popular syndicated newspaper letters column of the 50s and 60s.

"Ergo, comparing Have a Rattle to something 'hugely popular' could be considered a compliment, but Malky clearly didn't mean it like that," said Colly.

"I think his use of the word 'crap' might be more elucidative."

Crap or otherwise, the ISN Have a Rattle page ran for over a decade (until it was killed off by online forums) and, at one stage, was attracting over 100 letters a week and making minor celebrities out of regular contributors such as Eddie the Seagull.

Yet it started purely by accident at the end of 1991.

We always printed supporters' letters as part of the Brodie Soccer Page; that continued after he left.

Then, for the December 28 edition, a Glens fan (Eddie Sharp), wrote in to complain that his team's 7-0 win over Carrick, which put them top of the Irish League table, had been poorly covered in the Pink. I stuck a reply onto the end of his missive, suggesting that the Glens NOT beating Carrick would have been more of a story.

Things snowballed after that and, within a few weeks, we had to find extra space for what was originally labelled, rather unimaginatively, as 'Soccer Scene Extra'.

Our graphics artist, Gerry Patterson, then came up with an illustration of a grumpy football fan, complete with scarf and rattle (geddit?) and, again more by accident than design, the new page got its name.

The Rattle's biggest postbag arrived not long before its first birthday, after I'd broken one of the biggest stories of my career.

Saturday morning, December 12, 1992: I'd called Big Ronnie for a quote about one of the Pink stories I was working on.

As the call was winding up, he tossed in a hand grenade.

"Oh, by the way, the Blues are signing Dessie Gorman."

"Fuck off, Ronnie. Dessie Gorman? You and me both know he's a..."

"A *striker*? Indeed he is, John, and a good one too."

"You know full well what I'm talking about, Ronnie. A Catholic... and from down south as well. Good God, he's also a former Derry player. This would be another Mo Johnston."

"You better get moving on it then. And I didn't hear 'thanks Ronnie, you're a great pal, Ronnie, I owe you one, Ronnie'. Bye..."

Wow! The old ticker began to pound. Could this really be true? It must be; Big Ronnie knows Gorman, and has tried a couple of times to sign him for Portadown. But if he turned *them* down, why in God's name would he say yes to Linfield? And who'd confirm this; the Blues never tell you anything until after it's actually happened.

More in hope than expectation, I rang Shelbourne owner Ollie Byne, whom I knew from the Derry days. Surprisingly, he answered.

"I can't confirm anything about Linfield and Gorman," he said.

"But you're not denying it either, are you?"

"John, take this down verbatim and don't put extra words in my mouth: 'Shelbourne have always enjoyed a good relationship with Linfield and I don't regard it as unusual that they may be interested in one of our players. If they pursue their interest and the player wants to go, we won't stand in his way'. End of statement."

"And the player; Dessie Gorman?"

"Go away, John."

Bingo! I had enough to run a story which, like Malky with Jackie Milburn 35 years earlier, was published on the front page of the Pink that night – causing a similar sensation.

Some three and a half years on from Mo, Rangers' blues brothers from across the Irish Sea had finally bitten the bullet themselves.

But, like Linfield's recruitment of squad player Chris Cullen earlier in the year ("sprat to catch a whale," as Malky had called it), we initially steered clear of Gorman's religion; "the first southern player at Linfield since Davy Walsh" was how I put it, adding that it could cause "similar controversy" to the Mo Johnston signing.

The message was clear... and so was the response. The letter you saw at the start of this chapter, which didn't deign to mention Gorman's name – merely to *'that player from the Republic of Ireland'* – was one of the milder, printable ones.

Many of the Windsor faithful simply couldn't believe the club had resorted "to signing those sort of people", as 'True Blue' had put it.

But the following week, after an understandable bout of pre-wedding nerves, the 28-year-old 'Dundalk Hawk' put pen to paper and a dubious, age-old bastion was breached at last.

James Morgan from the Herald in Scotland later described my Gorman story as "a sensation, a transfer that made front page news and dominated the Irish sports pages for weeks."

It was a nightmare for Malky, though. His principal 'cor' paymasters, the Sun, Daily Telegraph and News of the World, were constantly demanding an exclusive interview with the man who'd 'broken the mould' at Windsor.

But none was ever forthcoming.

"In the end Ah told those diddies, absolutely straight: get off ma fucking back aboot this or go get someone else to write for ye. MB has tried, and MB is doin' nae more..."

Ironically, although he never agreed to interviews, in private The Hawk never shut up.

Another irony was that the much-travelled striker – who'd also represented French club Bourges and home town Dundalk – was a more consistent player with Linfield than anywhere else.

The man who'd ultimately become a Blues legend once told me: "I knew it was best to say nothing in those days, in case anything was misinterpreted. It was a volatile time, and I was well aware that some Bluemen weren't keen on me being there.

"Windsor was a big stage where you couldn't hide, but that suited me. All I wanted was to prove I wasn't a token signing; that I was there because I could make things better."

Not only did the fleet-footed, crowd-pleasing Hawk make things better, he made the club itself more accessible. Soon, the likes of Pat Fenlon – affectionately nicknamed 'Billy' by the fans – Garry Haylock and Martin Bayly would follow Gorman across the border.

And, the summer after Gorman's arrival, Linfield would also snaffle Glentoran's leading player, Raymond Campbell... yes, another high-profile Catholic. That must have hurt.

"I met Soupy in the corridor just after he'd signed," said Gorman, whose goals helped the Blues to back-to-back league titles and other silverware in his first two seasons.

"I said 'welcome to Linfield, Soupy' and he replied: 'I'm only here because of you, mate.' I took that as a special compliment."

Another five years would pass before it was deemed safe enough for Linfield to return to Cliftonville's Solitude home following an exile of nearly three decades but, hey, Rome wasn't built in a day.

Incidentally, the most controversial Linfield recruit of all time rang me in August 1996, shortly after Sammy Hamill had left the desk.

"I see your paper is advertising for a new sports editor," trilled The Hawk, adding: "That could be the ideal job for yours truly."

Me: "What makes you think that?"

Hawk: "Well, it says you guys are looking for someone with a high profile, someone who knows their sport. That sounds tailor made for a bright boy from Dundalk who's heading towards his mid-thirties and seeking a new challenge."

Me: "It also says you have to be a journalist, so I'd call that a bit of an impediment, wouldn't you?"

Hawk: "It's a bump in the road, I'll give you that. But I tick a lot of the other boxes and I'm going to apply for it. What are my chances, do you think?"

Me: "Honestly, Dessie, I don't think you've much of a chance. Sorry, mate."

Hawk: "Well, they said Linfield would never sign a Catholic, let alone one from the south. Maybe you've forgotten; I'm the man who can make the impossible happen."

Me: "Oh, trust me; I'll never forget you, Dessie, Nobody will. Good luck with the application."

I never heard another cheep after that.

Footnote: When David Jeffrey left Linfield in 2014 after 17 hugely successful years as manager, Pat 'Billy' Fenlon was one of the names tipped as a possible successor.

The Belfast Telegraph reported at the time that, if Fenlon (who was appointed 'general manager' at Windsor four years later) took the job, he would be the first Catholic in modern times to manage the Blues.

The paper's "scurrilous, anachronistic and gratuitous" reference to Fenlon's religion prompted widespread derision on social media from irate Linfield fans. Good.

CHAPTER 24

Things that love night, love not such nights as these.
(Extract from the Tele's Scotland v Northern Ireland match report, pre-publication).

Football fans who enjoy a night out would not have enjoyed this one.
(Extract from the Tele's Scotland v Northern Ireland match report, post-publication).

The success of Have a Rattle, and the Dessie Gorman exclusive, were the unrivalled highlights of 1992; my first full year as the 'main football man'. Malky's antics on the Gerry Kelly Show had me on guard against any future possible subterfuge, but our first away trip together – Northern Ireland's 2-1 Euro qualifier defeat by Denmark in Odense, November 1991 – was, the result apart, enjoyable enough.
I discovered on that trip that no rock star could trash a hotel room like Malky; books and files strewn all over the bed and floor, half eaten meals lying around, soaking towels on the bathroom floor – and underwear drying very slowly on bedside lamps. ("The maid hasnae got here yet...") We spent a lot of quality time together, and I even read out my topical match report intro to Malky for his approval:

"Is this Dane the greatest? Probably, thought Billy Bingham, after Flemming Paulson's two cracking goals put the skids under Northern Ireland last night..."

"Whaaa? Ah dinnae get that."
"You don't? It's a reference to the famous Carlsberg ads. They claimed their lager was 'the best in the world' but they've just been banned from saying that, and now they're making a big deal out of being forced to use the prefix 'probably'.
"Quite frankly, Ah've never heard o' that, and naebody Ah know will understand it. John, if ye ask me, Ah think it's far too convoluted for a match report."
"Well, I don't, Malky. Contrived, maybe, but not convoluted."
There was no disagreement on our next sortie, to Malky's home city for a friendly against Scotland in February 1992.

It was a steaming pile of horse manure on a stormy night, settled by an early Ally McCoist goal.

"One of the worst Northern Ireland performances Ah've seen in years," said Malky as we trudged out of Hampden's gargantuan press box which, sadly, would soon be demolished as part of the old stadium's revamp.

"I'm with you on that, Malky. And, to borrow one of your legendary phrases, I'm not going to miss them and hit the wall tomorrow."

What skill, what drama, what excitement... sadly, these were the questions, not the exultations, after last night's international – a friendly match, but not a supporter-friendly occasion.
Football fans who enjoy a night out would not have enjoyed this one.
A bitterly cold Glasgow evening, a near empty stadium, an instantly forgettable 90 minutes...

The second paragraph should have read "things that love night, love not such nights as these" –pretentiously borrowed from the dramatic storm scene in King Lear, which I'd studied for A Level English Lit.

Back in Belfast, this Shakespearean reference was somehow lost on Stoker, who'd been tasked with subbing my copy. Assuming a copy-taking error, he changed it to the clunkier *football fans who enjoy a night out would not have enjoyed this one.*

A bemused Colly immediately altered Jim Stokes' time-honoured nickname to *Stokespeare*..."the only man in literary history who felt it necessary to rewrite The Bard."

I got the impression there was more frantic rewriting done after Bingy declared post-match that he was "rather pleased with quite a few aspects of our performance."

He added: "Our defence was, in general, sound, and our approach play from midfield was encouraging with Michael Hughes showing up well in the second half after Kingsley Black had done really well in the first."

Oh, yes; the inevitable bigging up of Kingsley which, by that time, had become a running joke.

As telly reporter Mark Robson, who did a wicked Bingy impersonation, would often remark: "Well, gentlemen, I accept that it's challenging to find positives after an 8-0 defeat by Gibraltar but, of all the Northern Ireland plures, I thought Kingsley emerged with most credit..."

Perhaps Bingy felt he had to gush about the Luton-born winger who had surprisingly chosen Northern Ireland (his father hailed from Castlerock) ahead of England, who'd selected him for the under-21 side in the late 80s.

He had his moments – and, in 1991, became Northern Ireland's most expensive player ever when Forest's legendary manager Brian Clough signed him from Luton for £1.5m – but the softly-spoken, introverted Kingsley never really lived up his early promise.

Bingy's successor, Bryan Hamilton, dropped him for good after just one senior appearance, while Forest ultimately offloaded him to Grimsby Town for a mere £25,000.

And, despite what Bingy claimed, the 30-times-capped Black was, like most of his team-mates, woeful against the Scots that wintry night.

But that wasn't what Malky wrote in the following day's Daily Telegraph. Instead, we got a 'Billy's battling boys go down fighting' eulogy, with special praise reserved for – guess who – Black and Hughes.

Similar sentiments appeared in the News Letter – *et tu*, Brian Millar – and, on UTV the following night, Bingy hailed the performance as "a useful exercise", adding that he was surprised by "negative remarks from *one member* of the local press."

My only reaction was disappointment that he hadn't mentioned me by name. I'd called the game as I saw it, and don't recall any diehards uttering the one phrase no football hack ever wants to hear: "that wasn't the match I was at."

I likened the Scotland episode to those Hollywood critics who'd hail every new Coen brothers creation as 'a masterpiece' after listening to the siblings talking bollocks in the run-up to their latest release – then admit years down the line that 'Burn After Reading' was actually a load of grandiloquent garbage.

I didn't feel particularly stitched up by Malky in Glasgow, just dismayed that he'd said one thing and written another, having been swayed by Bingy's smooth, highly subjective post-match patter.

Parochialism is one thing, integrity another – and this was, after all, Malcolm Brodie. How many times in the past had professional footballers bleated that "it meant a lot more when Malcolm praised me."

Perhaps the notorious 'Auf wiedersehen, Pat' episode had been a cathartic moment.

There was no need for anything but superlatives after the next away match (another friendly), this time against mighty Germany in Bremen. And Bingy didn't have to explain afterwards how wonderful Michael Hughes was that evening in early June.

Naturally, we'd been expecting our lads to be routed by Berti Vogts' side, who had clearly regarded little Northern Ireland as cannon fodder in the run up to Euro 92.

But Larne man Hughesey, making just his fourth appearance, stunned the Weserstadion's 24,000 crowd by opening the scoring with a brilliant first international goal on 22 minutes.

Latching onto a defence-splitting ball from Kevin Wilson, the 20-year-old (who, like myself and Michael O'Neill, was an alumnus of St Louis Grammar) cut inside Guido Buchwald before rifling a screamer, left-footed, past Bodo Illgner.

(Brilliant – but, for me, not the best by a Northern Irishman in 1992; that honour goes to Raymie McCoy's stunning solo effort for Glenavon against Ballymena in the Irish Cup semi-final at Windsor a few weeks earlier. I know it's 'only the Irish League', but as Bestie once said of his incredible 1981 individual effort for San Jose Earthquakes against Fort Lauderdale Strikers: "If that had been on a park pitch against 10-year-olds, it would STILL have been a great goal". Glenavon went on to beat Linfield 2-1 in a final once again marred by terrace violence at the Oval; it became known as the 'Piss-pie Final' after a few resourceful Linfield followers urinated onto the soil for missiles to hurl at Glenavon fans...)

Manfred Binz equalised for the Germans just before the break, and after that it was a one-way autobahn with Tommy Wright producing a lifetime-best performance.

Typical Northern Ireland... as Danny famously remarked at the 1958 World Cup: "our tactics have always been to equalise before the other team scores." The late Robert Dennis Blanchflower was of course referring to another epic draw against the Germans in Malmo.

The unexpected Bremen result once again brought the mystical 'aura' upon Malky who, after we'd found a small, welcoming bierkeller just off the north western city's iconic Bottcherstrase, held court with nostalgic tales about his favourite footballer – 'Peter the Great' Doherty, who'd died a couple of years earlier at the age of 76.

"Yes, Malky, I enjoyed – if that's the right word – reading your excellent obituary on Peter," said a relaxed Jeekie as he sucked on a Benson and sipped his first Smirnoff Blue of the evening.

"But, Doyen, I had to smile when you asked – what was it – 'who will ever forget this bus conductor from Magherafelt helping Man City win the title in 1937?' I take it that was a rhetorical question? I mean, even if you had a telly back then, you'd need to be walking around with a zimmer frame now to remember that..."

Malky resorted to feigned indignation.

"What crap is The Singer spoutin' now? Speaking o' rhetorical questions, is this the same Jeekie who shouts 'who else?' every time someone scores?"

Now it was Jeekie's turn for scornful affectation.

"Care to elaborate on that scurrilous remark, Herr Brodie?"

Herr Brodie: "What about last month's Irish Cup final, when McGaughey scored; ye said in yer commentary 'who else but McGaughey?' Well, what about Baxter; is HE not someone *else* who scores loads o' goals for Linfield? Mark ma words, by the way: that was the last goal Buckets will *ever* get for the Blues. MB has that on good authority."

Jeekie: "Ouch! The Doyen is in feisty form tonight."

Malky: "Aye, he is – and let me tell you another thing, Jeekie, absolutely straight, end o' ball game: Ah DO remember those Peter the Great days, and Ah don't see any zimmer frame in this bar, do you?"

In Malky's opinion, silky inside-left Doherty was Northern Ireland's best-ever player; yes even better than Bestie and "in the same bracket as Stanley Matthews, Raich Carter, Tommy Lawton, Wilf Mannion and Tom Finney".

He noted my mild bemusement.

"These may be just oul boys' names tae ye, Victor, but tae folk o' ma age, these men were gods, and Peter the Great was one o' them."

He told us about the time Northern Ireland's first manager (prior to 1951, the team was chosen by selection committee) – showed him one of his most treasured possessions: a dog-eared telegram from Glentoran in the early 30s with just six words on it... *Selected for the first team. Saturday.*

"It's hard tae believe Peter started in junior soccer wi' Coleraine Crusaders, and was rejected by Coleraine themselves before the Glens took him," recalled Malky.

"Ah remember him telling me that his debut for City was a disaster, when even his own fans chanted 'what a waste o' money' {Doherty had cost The Citizens a club record £10,000 in 1936, over five times what Blackpool had paid the Glens three years earlier) after seeing him struggle against Preston.

"But he was being man-marked by a wee Scottish terrier – 23-year-old Bill Shankly – who told him afterwards: 'Sonny, ye need tae up yer game... yer in with the big boys now."

Doherty clearly took Shanks' advice, his 30 goals helping City to their first ever top flight title.

Malky couldn't resist an ironic smile as he told us about City's 'bonus prize' that summer of 1937; a trip to the Olympic Stadium in Berlin. (The invitation came from one A. Hitler).

"The Fuhrer had his minions write a letter saying his countryfolk would love tae see players o' the calibre o' Peter Doherty, Alec Herd, Fred Tilson and Ernie Toseland challenge a German select.

"And they did, although they lost 3-2 after ma old pal Frank Swift {City and England goalkeeper who became a reporter with the News of the World and died in the 1958 Munich air disaster} threw one in."

The Doyen, fortified by Johnnie Walker Black and assured of a rapt audience, was now in his element – and getting louder by the minute.

"Peter told me there were 70,000 at that match, which was still 5,000 less than City had got against Arsenal in the title decider a few weeks earlier. According to him, scoring that day {in a 2-0 win} was his finest moment as a player.

"Mind you, that goodwill Berlin trip didn't stop the Krauts bombin' the shit out o' Manchester in 1940..."

Jeekie: "Malky, with our genial hosts listening, this is perhaps not the best moment to reminisce about that. Here, tell us about how you and Peter the Great got on in 1958..."

(Malky's diplomacy could occasionally be found wanting, not least in Tokyo, 2002 when, exasperated at the Japanese waiter continually failing to grasp what a 'cremated steak' meant, the septuagenarian finally bellowed: "HIROSHIMA!")

Those awkward 'hands across the water' moments apart, you'd rarely tire of listening to the Doyen when he was in full flow about the good old days.

Back at the hotel, an exuberant Bingy joined us for a late nightcap – and to remind us that, with him having already masterminded unprecedented home and away wins against West Germany in the European Championship qualifiers a decade earlier, we shouldn't have been so surprised by what we'd witnessed at the Weserstadion.

Jeekie (with a sly wink in my direction): "Obviously young Hughes and Tommy Wright will get the plaudits, Billy, but I thought Kingsley had a great game too."

Bingy: "Oh, did you think so, Jackie? I agree, and I thought he dovetailed well with Hughes – although a certain gentleman was skeptical about that partnership working in today's Belfast Telegraph..."

SHIT... the BELFAST TELEGRAPH! It was the early hours already, your Jeekies, Malkys and Bingys had long finished their work – and I hadn't even started mine.

"Guys, gotta hit the hay here. Early start. *Gute Nacht*, all."

I woke up at 8am... not particularly late, if you disregard the inconvenient truth that the flight to London was departing in 90 minutes' time, and that the buses had left for Hans Koschnick Airport an hour earlier.

After calling reception to hail a cab, I rubbed my eyes, which resembled two piss holes in the snow (a Ballymena saying), stuffed my clothes into a holdall and sped off, hungover and unwashed, to the airport.

After check-in I grabbed a pay-phone, reversed the charges and started barking, note-free, Walker-style, at the copytaker.

There'd be no time to phone over both the match report and the back-page follow-up, but if the plane reached Heathrow as scheduled I'd manage it – and at least I could work on the second piece in transit.

The first thing a grinning Malky said when I finally reached the departure gate was: "*Guten morgen*! So ye finally made it..."

The red mist came down. "No thanks to you, Malky. Why the fuck did you let the bus leave without me? I'd never have done that to you."

Malky's mirth instantly evaporated.

"Ye wouldnae have had tae do it wi' me – cos Ah woudnae have lay on in ma fucking bed in the first place. Nobody else did. Don't take yer lack of professionalism out on me, boy."

He was right. This was the most unprofessional the 'boy' had ever been. It was Malky himself who'd always drilled it into me: "Get yer work done first, Schemer, and play later."

That said, he'd immediately order a large vodka if I claimed (always disingenuously, following the Bremen debacle; you learn quickly) that I hadn't started etching yet.

My 'play' in Germany had got under way long before the match, after bumping into Winkie and the boys in the sunkissed old town area.

Those half litres of Augustiner felt manageable enough, but not when you top them up later with vodkas and light cola that augmented the post-match craic.

So I couldn't really blame Malky for my highly irresponsible behaviour – although the fact remains that, had the shoe been on the other foot, that bus would not have left without him on board.

What was the memorable line from the Will Smith movie Enemy of the State: "It's not paranoia if they really ARE out to get you."

And the paranoia resurfaced at the FA Cup final a year later, when I opted to forsake the pre-match press refreshments in favour of drinks with old friends I'd bumped into at the Wembley Hilton.

"I've already got the teams," said Joyce after I got through to her. "Malky phoned them in earlier. He thought you hadn't turned up."

"He WHAT?"

"He also asked Sammy if we wanted *him* to do the match report..."

Half time: "Malky, what made you think I wasn't here?"

"Well, when Ah didn't see ye in the press room Ah thought something had happened wi' yer mother."

"Look, Malky, if something *had* happened with my mum {who was very ill at the time} I'd have called Sammy to let him know."

"Fair enough, John. Sure we're both here now and there's nae harm done..."

Actually, there was. Three days later, a FA press liaison officer rang to ask why I hadn't gone to see Arsenal play Sheffield Wednesday in the association's showpiece event.

"You know your non-attendance will affect future accreditation," she said.

"What are you *talking* about? I WAS there. I was sitting beside Brian Woolnough of The Sun, and I was with Malcolm Brodie at half time..."

FA woman: "It was *Malcolm* who told me you hadn't arrived, and you didn't sign in at the press room."

Me: "That's because I didn't *go* to the press room. When did Malcolm tell you this?"

FA woman: "Just before the match started. Said he couldn't find you anywhere, and that he had to phone over your copy... look, John, get Wooly and Malcolm to write confirming that they saw you, and we'll leave it at that, okay?"

Mmm. Maybe there had been some chicanery in Bremen after all.

It was Ian Wooldridge who, a few months before Bremen, had written in the Tele that Malky was "the meanest man in journalism" when it came to usurping his rivals.

And Wooldridge's Fleet Street contemporary, the revered Sunday Times sports journalist, Brodie compatriot and fellow doyen/don Hugh McIlvanney, once told me: "Malky would swamp you with kindness at the bar... then slit your throat in the toilets to be first with the story."

That's probably why people remember the cigar-chomping Hugh for his litotes-infused prose – and the whisky-swilling Malky for his world exclusives. (When Hugh died in January 2019, a local, irony-free radio reporter referred to him as "the Scottish version of Malcolm Brodie...") Whatever. I started thinking that Malky, having honed me in the first place, was now regretting the thing he'd created; maybe Colly was right about 'Shelley' after all.

I never read the ad libbed Bremen match report – too scared/ashamed to – until just before writing this chapter, over a quarter of a century later.

The wall down the road in Berlin was no problem compared to the one built by Billy Bingham last night.

Germany have developed a habit of pulling down barriers in recent years but they hadn't reckoned on a Northern Ireland team with Tommy Wright in goal.

What a magnificent display from the goalkeeper, what a magnificent result for Bingham's men.

Bremen had not witnessed a bombardment like it since the war, but Wright held firm, denying the slick Germans again and again...

...and on it went, for another 1,000 words. In retrospect, passable enough, apart from that ridiculous, Basil Fawlty-esque mention of the war. I'd regularly ad libbed ISN match reports, but never one this length – or this important.

Perhaps during that frantic, stressful morning in Bremen I'd finally risen to the challenge set by Colly: "learn to operate like Walker." This was nothing to be proud of, though.

The week after Bremen, Malky – just like in 1958 – flew off to Sweden to cover a major championship.

Ironically, Euro 92 was the first time the Tele hadn't sent a 'staff man' to such an event; instead, we opted to save money by hiring a freelance – ergo, Malcolm Brodie.

Coming so soon after the self-inflicted wounds of Bremen, this was the irrefutable low point of 1992.

And although I'd known months earlier that (with neither Northern Ireland and the Republic qualifying) I wasn't getting the gig, and was pragmatic about the post-*rivers of gold* era financial restraints, it was still a hard punch in the solar plexus when 'From Malcolm Brodie in Malmo' appeared on the back page.

Pragmatism is one thing, perception another. And the impression given here – although clearly not intended – was that the paper's fledgling hack

164

wasn't good enough to cover this tournament and we were sending the wise old owl instead.

Malky later admitted that his Telegraph fee amounted to less than 10% of what he ended up spending in exorbitant Sweden. "Cost me a bloody fortune, that trip..."

Yeah, but you knew that would be the case long before you left... and you still went.

From Machiavellian Brodie in Malmo.

CHAPTER 25

Never have I read such poppycock in the southern papers, or heard such rubbish spouted on RTE.

FAI secretary Sean Connolly, who appears to have more faces than the Albert Clock, says he's concerned about the Republic's team travelling north, but forgets to mention that we travelled through bandit country to Lansdowne Road in March.

Let's be clear about the matter – the Republic have lost their bottle and are frightened about coming to Belfast.

They're quaking in their boots... don't be surprised if they end up wearing yellow – BECAUSE THAT'S JUST WHAT THEY ARE!
(Brian Millar, News Letter, November 5, 1993)

"What's up wi' you?" asked Malky, "yer lookin' a bit pally-wally on it."

That's because I felt a little 'pally-wally' ('off-colour' in Brodiespeak).

"Ach, Malky, it's this RTE news programme I've agreed to go on; I suppose I'm a bit anxious about it."

"But why? Sure ye've done live telly loads o' times..."

"Yeah, but this is different. It's just the whole atmosphere, you know; the way things are at the moment, it wouldn't take much to say the wrong thing."

Malky – who normally thrummed his fingers, annoyingly and incessantly, in coffee shops – was, on this occasion, the mollifier.

Ostensibly we'd met up – Wednesday morning, November 3, 1993 – to plan a forthcoming eight-page ISN special on 'the big match', so my anxiety was hardly a left-field deviation on the subject matter.

"Look, John, take ma advice, keep it simple and just stick tae the facts. What are they gonna be askin'?"

"It's Pat Kenny, and of course it'll be about the Dublin rags saying the match is going to Old Trafford."

Malky couldn't have looked more contemptuous.

"Right, mark ma words right here and now. You go on that programme and tell them this, absolutely straight: 'yous 18-carat-gold diddies are wrong; that fucking match is at Windsor'... full point, end par."

"Maybe I'll not put it exactly like that, Malky. But how can you be so sure about this? Both the Times and the Indo – and RTE, Sky too – are adamant the game's being switched to Manchester."

Malky jabbed his finger on the table-top; a sure sign he'd reached optimum emboldenment.

"Because, John, Ah know what Ah'm talkin' aboot, and Ah know the folk that matter. Trust me on this; ye'll be right and them diddies will be wrong."

Mmm. Trust in my former boss had waned somewhat following the Kelly Show, Bremen and Wembley incidents.

We had, however, spent a considerable amount of time together in 1993 – impoverished Tirana (described by Malky, who'd been there before, as "the land that time forgot", although it was more 'the hotel that basic sanitation forgot'; Northern Ireland beat Albania 2-1), Dublin (a 3-0 thrashing at Lansdowne), Seville (3-1 to Spain, after Kevin Wilson had the temerity to give us the lead), Vilnius (Iain Dowie bagged the winner against Lithuania), Riga (beat Latvia 2-1) and Copenhagen (lost 1-0, terrific performance, heartbreaking late goal from Brian Laudrup).

I felt like 'ma son Victor' again; surely the man sitting across the table wasn't setting his illegitimate boy up for a humiliating fall?

Pat Kenny: "So tell us, John, how is Belfast reacting to this morning's big news about Old Trafford?"

Me: "Well, Pat, I have to say that folk here are bemused by those headlines, because the match is going ahead as planned at Windsor Park on November 17. The days of our international football team leading a nomadic existence because of the Troubles ended 20 years ago" {I'd rehearsed that strident opening gambit en route from the coffee shop}.

Pat: "Really? That's not what we're hearing here. Do you think many fans from the north will travel over to Manchester?"

Me: "I'm not sure you heard me earlier, Pat. I've already said that Northern Ireland versus the Republic will be in *Belfast*. Sorry to mess up your scripted questions..."

Pat: "You have to admit, however, John, that – if you're correct, and it's a big *if* – persisting with a volatile World Cup qualifier in Belfast would be highly irresponsible in the light of what's been happening in the north over the past month."

Me: "The only irresponsible thing I see is the Football Association of Ireland's blatant attempt to use recent atrocities as an excuse to get this match switched to a neutral venue. If the Republic hadn't lost at home to Spain a fortnight ago, we wouldn't be having this discussion."

Pat: "Maybe not, but we are where we are. And I suspect that where we'll be in a fortnight is Old Trafford..."

Those '18-carat-gold diddies from Dublin' still seemed cocksure of themselves but I put my trust in Malky's sources and, thankfully, it turned out to be justified.

The following day, the Irish FA and their southern counterparts confirmed that, despite the almost unbearable tension in the aftermath of the Shankill bombing, Greysteel massacre and on-going, tit-for-tat sectarian murders (26 people killed in just 18 days), the final Group 3 qualifier between our boys, who couldn't qualify for USA '94, and their lot, who could, would indeed take place in Belfast.

The FAI's reluctance to come north, however (and their scurrilous lobbying of Fifa to get the venue switched), had ramped up an already highly charged atmosphere.

Even the News Letter's sports editor Brian Millar – a man not renowned for his overtly strident views – appeared to get swept up in the emotion of it all.

His astonishing back page comment piece on Friday, November 5, was described – by the Daily Mail, no less – as a "frenzied attack" on the FAI. I suspect that the short, stockily-built 'Skipper' (also known as 'Hollow Legs' because of his legendary tolerance for alcohol) had indulged in one sherbet too many at the Windsor social club the previous afternoon.

Even so, he'd caught the mood leading up to the notorious 'Night in November'.

So did Bingy who, like Skipper, ditched traditional diplomacy in favour of anomalous, goading invective – for instance, labelling the Republic's non-Irish-born players as "mercenaries" and "carpetbaggers".

I could hardly believe my ears as the new, bombastic Bingy ranted: "They couldn't find a way of making it with England or Scotland. I take a totally cynical view of the whole business, and I'm happy to state it is our intention to stuff the Republic."

Holy God! Was this the same Bingy who'd gone through 117 previous internationals in charge of Northern Ireland in two spells over 17 years without uttering a contentious word?

It was as if he'd thought "fuck it, this is my last match and I'll say whatever the fuck I want."

It probably influenced Bingy's thinking that he'd nothing to play for but pride. The Dublin hacks were suitably aghast.

"It's as if he's regressed to being that wee Billy Boy from east Belfast once more," said Charlie Stuart (the chain-smoking, northern-born Irish Press veteran and Big Jack's go-to man when it came to cadging fags).

168

He added: "In the interests of preserving a precarious peace, I'll not remind Mr Bingham of where Kevin Wilson, Danny Wilson and his beloved Kingsley Black were born..."

A few days before the match, the Belfast Telegraph and other newspapers published one of the most chilling pictures of the Troubles – Greysteel killer Torrens Knight snarling back at a jeering crowd as he was led, handcuffed, into Limavady courthouse to face eight murder charges. Politicians from all sides called for calm, and for Northern Ireland supporters to behave responsibly at Windsor, where the attendance had been restricted to 10,500; home fans only.

Wise words... so why was Bingy, of all people, inciting the crowd with animated gestures during the warm-up – something he'd repeat at half time?

This was a side of Bingy I hadn't seen before – and didn't particularly care for.

I'm all for sports tribalism, but this seething cauldron of naked sectarian hatred was by far the most depressing I – but not Malky, who was sitting between myself and Jim Gracey – had ever witnessed.

"That Linfield-Celtic business in '48 was worse, as was the Battle of Belfast {nine years later}," he insisted.

"And let's not forget the Donegal Celtic debacle here; that wasnae so long ago."

(No, it wasn't; 1990, a sixth round Irish Cup tie, a controversial switch of venue from west Belfast to Windsor, a delayed kick-off, an inadequate security presence, running battles in the stands, baton rounds fired on the Spion Kop, DC's hard-as-nails Brendan Tully collapsing on the pitch as if he'd just been shot after an invading Blues yob kicked him, riots on the streets afterwards.)

With the ground having such a shameful rap sheet, the prelude to this tinderbox encounter required a calming influence, not the gross irresponsibility being displayed by someone like Bingy who should have known better.

As Malky remarked: "Ah've known Bingy, man an' boy, for over 40 year, and Ah've NEVER seen him act like that. Frankly, Ah find that kind o' thing completely unedifying."

Malky thought Bingy's uncharacteristic behaviour was a legacy of the Lansdowne Road tanking eight months earlier (the day our boys wore that ghastly blue 'butcher's apron' strip) when jubilant Republic fans chanted "there's only one team in Ireland".

"And don't forget, Malky, what Charlton said to us in Albania: 'I'm not in a flap about playing Northern Ireland'. Remember Bingy's face when we told him that?"

Malky: "Aye, and it was Bingy who told Charlton he was welcome tae bunk in wi' us in Tirana... let's see what sort of a flap we get him intae tonight."

In fact, the long-necked Big Jack was flapping like a demented ostrich by the time he arrived in Belfast. His 'mercenaries'– shorn of injured Steve Staunton, Ronnie Whelan, John Sheridan, Kevin Sheedy and Kevin Moran – needed a win to ensure qualification; a draw would only be enough if their other Group 3 rivals, Spain and Denmark, failed to share the spoils in Seville.

Charlton had wanted the match to be played at noon, but Fifa insisted that both qualifiers had to kick off simultaneously at 8pm.

Not only that, but it was decreed the Republic squad would have to fly to Belfast – even though their training camp was the Nuremore Hotel, just across the border in Carrickmacross, Co Monaghan.

That meant going south; would such symbolism extend to their World Cup ambitions?

As the huge media presence indicated, this ethnological showdown was plainly of global interest.

That said, with the country's paramilitary murder gangs having gone mercifully quiet over the previous fortnight, national tabloids had switched their attention to other, more pressing, matters; the furore over photographs of a spread-legged, leotard-clad Princess Diana taken surreptitiously in a gym, Michael Jackson confessing that he was hooked on prescription drugs, 'Turnip Taylor' facing the sack from England – and the prospect of Mr Blobby succeeding Meat Loaf at the top of the singles charts.

The Republic's team bus – with its interior lights switched off and apprehensive players cowering on aisle seats rather than up against the windows – arrived at Windsor from the Dunadry Hotel in Co Antrim to jeering natives who trained imaginary rifles at them and made throat slash gestures; welcome to Belfast.

Charlton strode onto the Windsor pitch for only the second time since October 1966 – when he and his England team-mates, the newly-crowned world champions, played their first match on 'home soil' since defeating West Germany at Wembley.

There were nearly 48,000 in the stands that day; Jack once told me he'll never forget the warmth of the welcome afforded to his lot "by the Irish".

And of course there was that lavish reception in the Belfast Telegraph boardroom, hosted by You Know Who.

Predictably Jack got dogs abuse as he walked down the Windsor touchline this time.

On arrival at the dugout, cigarette already in mouth, he searched in vain for a lighter.

In desperation, he turned to the fans behind the fence and, seconds after baying for his blood, they were falling over themselves to be the first man to light a grateful Big Jack's Benson & Hedges.

Save for the two unforgettable goals, it was a tension-riddled stinker of a game, the soundtrack of which was a cacophony of hatred and bile cascading down from the stands.

The almost incessant wall of vitriolic noise reminded me of an Old Firm derby, only this time the hostility was unilateral.

The musical accompaniment began with a more raucous than usual God Save The Queen; the playing of Amhran na bhFiann (Soldier's Song) had been deemed as ill-advised.

"Why aren't you blow-in fenian fuckers joining in?" was a rhetorical roar from one wild-eyed local diehard at, presumably, the seven starters in the 'Plastic Paddy' team who'd been born and raised on Her Majesty's mainland manor.

Amid the inevitable party songs was a topical new entry to the ignominious playlist: chants of "trick or treat" – a chilling, revolting reference to what one of the murderous UFF gunmen is reported to have shouted prior to spraying Greysteel's Rising Sun bar with bullets.

(One wonders what the modern-day Green And White Army – rightly regarded as one of the most hospitable and impeccably behaved supporters in world football – would have said to their abhorrent predecessors that night, and seven years later after the death threats when Neil Lennon, who had just signed for Celtic, voiced his support for an all-Ireland football team.)

Republic defender Alan Kernaghan – the Yorkshire-born, Bangor-raised Protestant, former Northern Ireland schoolboy international (and future Glens manager) – heard his mother being described as "the Pope's cock-sucking whore." His father and brother, sitting ashen-faced and incognito in the stands, heard it too.

Kernaghan, whose paternal grandparents hailed from these shores, wasn't eligible for 'the north' at senior level because, unlike their counterparts in Dublin, the IFA hadn't yet resorted to the controversial 'granny rule'.

171

"Ah, the irony," I remarked to Malky as the "Pope's whore" and "turncoat" chants gained traction in the old wooden South Stand. Malky corrected me.

"It's nae irony," he said. "Even those clowns are aware of Kernaghan's background. But he's wearin' an Ireland shirt now, and that's all that matters tae them."

All the same, irony and nuance weren't hard to find on that toxic night. The same stadium that had been such a welcoming citadel for Tony Coly and Sam Khammal five years earlier was now an amphitheatre for vile monkey chants directed at Paul McGrath (best friend of Windsor terrace hero Norman Whiteside) and Terry Phelan.

The stunning volley that put Northern Ireland 1-0 up on 71 minutes was scored by a Newtownabbey Catholic whose family fled Rathcoole in the early 70s... one of the first to congratulate Jimmy Quinn on his wonder goal was his close pal, Northern Ireland skipper Alan McDonald, who was raised a few hundred yards away.

And assistant manager Jimmy Nicholl (Canadian-born but another alumnus of the sprawling loyalist estate), completed a Rathcoole 'hat-trick' by brandishing two fingers and screaming {what was reported as} "up yours" at his Republic counterpart Maurice Setters – although, knowing 'Jimmy Nick', I suspect it might have been more in the "fuck you" envelope.

That goal, at the Railway Stand end, sparked the most ear-splitting crescendo of ecstasy at Windsor since... well, since another Catholic number nine, Gerry Armstrong, scored against Israel to send our boys to the 1982 World Cup finals.

Never, in my experience, had the 'Billy Boys' been delivered with such gusto than in the moments following Quinn's marvellous 72nd minute effort, two and a half hours short of his 34th birthday.

 A decade before Fergie coined that immortal phrase, it was 'squeaky bum time' for Big Jack and Co.

Another good pal of the "horse-hoofed" Quinny – Big Mac's term of endearment, not mine – was Alan McLoughlin (ex-Swindon team-mate of the Northern Ireland and Reading striker), who hadn't featured in any of the previous qualifiers, hadn't scored at international level – and had failed to rate a single mention in the copious column inches that precursed this nauseating hate-fest.

The southern hacks in the heaving press-box looked baffled when little known Portsmouth midfielder McLoughlin – a Mancunian whose previous claim to fame was that he'd gone to school with Oasis star Noel

172

Gallagher – came on in place of Houghton just before his old Swindon team-mate Quinny, latching on to Kevin Wilson's clever knock-back, managed to lift the ball over Packie Bonner from 20 yards out, even though he'd both hoofs off the ground at the time.

(It was his 23rd goal of the season, a Paolo De Canio-like effort and sensational succour for the terrific strike controversially disallowed in Copenhagen a month earlier.)

I remember screaming – like thousands of other Norn Iron fans – "that's NEVER a free kick" after Nigel Worthington was adjudged to have shoulder-charged Eddie McGoldrick near the apex of the Spion Kop and North Stand three minutes after Quinny's goal.

Denis Irwin floated the hotly disputed free kick over, McLoughlin latched onto Gerry Taggart's weak clearance header and the rest is history (although Charlton missed it; he was too busy bollocking substitute Tony Cascarino – whom he referred to in happier times as "the ice-cream man" and who, it later emerged, had no Irish ancestry whatsoever – for leaving his match shirt in the changing room).

Lurgan man 'Tags' would later quip that they should have granted him the Freedom of Dublin after that historic 'assist' for McLoughlin, whose 77th minute guided missile whizzed past Tommy Wright and briefly plunged the stadium into an eerie silence.

The press box was largely muted too, save for a muffled yelp from the Irish News man in the 'Northern Ireland' section – which prompted ironic guffaws from Jim: "He's the one celebrating, but that goal means *you and me* will be on the plane to America next summer."

Distracted by the frenzied atmosphere, I hadn't considered that, but Jim was right; with all four home nations failing to qualify for USA '94, the UK media – including ourselves – would clearly be adopting English World Cup winner Jack's boys as their own. If the scores stayed the same, that is.

Those were the medieval days; before every sentence started with 'so' and contained the adjective 'amazing', before someone's worth was measured in 'likes' rather than deeds – and before smartphones. Only those who'd brought transistor radios knew if ten-man Spain had held onto Fernando Hierro's 64th minute goal.

The Republic players' post-match ejaculations were premature.

While they indulged in gawky jigs and reels on the pitch, there was still time for Denmark to equalise in the Estadio Ramon Sanchez Pizjuan.

That would have meant *adios muchachos* for a suddenly ashen-faced Charlton, who'd been (wrongly) informed by McLoughlin that Spain had already won – and responded by angrily buttonholing Bingy and vengefully 'reciprocating' the earlier Jimmy Nick/Setters encounter. Charlton's instant karma meant he was forced to watch the final throes of the Seville game on a monitor near the players' tunnel, surrounded by hacks, photographers, his FAI 'boss' Sean Connolly and other equally anxious players.

Talk about skin-of-the-teeth... Jack's boys finished level with Denmark on 18 points, and with an identical goal difference (+13), but squeezed through courtesy of 'goals scored' (19 to the Danes' 15) during the 12-match campaign.

McLoughlin – who afterwards told me in the chaotic tunnel that he was dedicating his goal to all the people "back in Ireland" – clearly made an indelible mark on the Republic's sporting history.

But there'd also be a toast to absent friend John Sheridan, whose 73rd minute goal against Spain in Dublin a month earlier was regarded at the time as a mere consolation following the morale-sapping 3-1 defeat, but ultimately became just as crucial as McLoughlin's.

Despite security men urging him to board the airport-bound bus soon after the poisonous encounter had ended, a chastened, emotional Charlton opted instead to gatecrash Bingy's press conference in the bowels of the South Stand, just as the retiring legend was telling us, one last time, how well Kingsley had played.

There was an audible gasp as he walked up to the podium, holding a parcel.

Jack: "Can I say something, please?"

Bingy: "Who IS this man?"

Jack: "I said something to Billy after the match which I shouldn't have said, and I regret it. I'll regret it for the rest o' me life. We've been friends for a long time, and I apologise."

Bingy: "Forget it, let's have a drink. By the way, is that a retirement present you have for me?"

I was glad Bingy hadn't lost his final game and, from a professional point of view, delighted that the Republic were going to their second *Mundial*. There was a sense of an ending that night, and not just with regard to Bingy's illustrious career.

No, as the Windsor floodlights dimmed, you couldn't help feeling that a violent, horrific storm engulfing our troubled wee country had finally passed.

The following morning, tens of thousands gathered at 16 separate rallies, demanding "peace and a better future" for Northern Ireland.

174

And just as there had been no further atrocities in the two weeks preceding this game, that would also be the case for the rest of November 1993.

Sadly, it wasn't the end of the Troubles, merely the conclusion to one particularly horrific chapter.

CHAPTER 26

NICHOLL IS THE CHOICE
(Belfast Telegraph first edition, February 15, 1994)

HAMILTON IS THE CHOICE
(Belfast Telegraph final edition, February 15, 1994)

"How can ye be so sure about this?"
I had to laugh when Malky asked that.
"That's the same thing I asked *you* last year when that Old Trafford thing was raging – and what was your reply?"
"Ah think it was 'trust me, John' or words like that."
"Exactly. So now I'm saying 'trust *me*, Malky'. I spoke to Jimmy Nick last night, and again first thing this morning. He's been offered the job, he wants it – and a four-year contract is being rubber-stamped by the committee's nodding dogs as we speak.
"Jimmy's waiting by the phone to hear from Bowen, then jumping on a plane for a press conference at Windsor Avenue this afternoon. Read my lips, Malky: Jimmy Nicholl is the new Northern Ireland manager."
Two hours later, at the Irish FA's ornate headquarters, general secretary David Bowen unveiled Bryan Hamilton as the new Northern Ireland manager.
You could have heard an unequivocal intro drop. There were audible gasps of astonishment from the assembled press corps, one of which felt the blood drain from his head and his legs buckle.
Over 100,000 copies of that day's Tele were already on the streets proclaiming, in huge banner headlines, that "Nicholl is the choice."
I dashed, gasping, into Bowen's plush office and grabbed the phone. Another desperate, Walker-style ad lib to a copytaker followed. We got the splash changed for the Sixth Late (final edition) but the damage was already done.
I returned to the press conference in time to hear a beaming Hammy outlining his "vision" for the next four years – and Bowen ridiculing "certain sections of the media" for focusing solely on "one particular candidate".
Oh ye of forked tongue.

The incredulity had nothing to do with Bingy's successor per se; Hammy, a 50-cap former international and experienced football manager, was a more than credible candidate.

It's just that 37-year-old Jimmy Nick was such an overwhelming favourite it was untrue – which, of course, it turned out to be.

Former Man United and Rangers full-back Nicholl had been 'groomed' (it was a more innocent word back then) for the main post having been Bingy's assistant for two years.

He'd also been a successful boss in his own right with 'Jimmy Nicholl's Raith Rovers' (copyright Radio Ulster) in Scotland.

And it was Bowen – not "certain sections of the media" – who had him on standby to board a Belfast-bound plane that cold Wednesday morning.

So what happened?

A shell-shocked Jimmy Nick – who never made it onto the flight from Glasgow – announced later that day: "I was offered the job on Tuesday night. There was a difference in what they'd offered and what I wanted, but it wasn't outrageous... we're talking tuppence here.

"There were other candidates for the job, however, who were out of work... and possibly prepared to accept anything..."

The "nodding dogs" of the 12-strong IFA international committee were chaired by an ancient bloodhound who still had lacerating teeth: Sammy Walker, who'd just replaced the retiring Harry Cavan as association president.

His no-nonsense approach to the first item on that day's agenda, Nicholl's wage demands, was: "He wants too much, he's not getting it... next candidate."

Just like that, as comic genius Tommy Cooper used to say. But no laughing matter for me, who feared this unforgettable 'exclusive' would become a Gordon Smith-style, career-defining moment.

(A few years ago, I spoke briefly to the popular ex-Scottish international, who bagged 117 career goals but will always be remembered for missing a last-gasp, would-be winner for underdogs Brighton against mighty Man U in the 1983 FA Cup final. I asked him if, three decades on, he still gets reminded about that. His reply: "only about 20 times a day".)

Today, my erroneous story would have gone out first online, the gaffe instantly corrected, the embarrassment fleeting and swiftly forgotten. But back in 1994, you couldn't explain to print edition readers that you were "right at the time of going to press", but wrong by the time the paper hit the streets.

177

(Something similar happened after I 'revealed' that Distillery's Seamus Heath had 'retired' from football. Whites boss Billy Hamilton read the story, rang Seamus, coaxed him out of quitting immediately, played him in a cup match that night – and made me look like a right idiot.)

Vulnerable and racked with self-pity, I reached out to Malky for sympathy. And didn't get any.

"John, Ah told ye only this mornin', ye have tae be 100% certain o' these things. At the end o' the day, we're a paper o' record and, as far as the punters are concerned, that story was wrong, no matter how ye coat it." There was no answer to that; well, not then.

It would be two more years before I could reply: "What are YOU on about? You're the fool who sat up all night in Nuremberg writing a 2,000-word obituary on Frank Sinatra. And what was it Flan {Jim Flanagan, Tele deputy editor} said after you'd phoned it over? 'Brilliant piece, Malky. You were clearly a huge fan. Only one small problem: Ol' Blue Eyes is still very much alive and kicking'. And what did you say? 'Whaaa? The German waiter told me he was deed'. The waiter? Don't preach to me about being '100% certain' before you etch..."

A more immediate retort was heading in Brian Millar's direction. He'd bragged in the following day's News Letter about correctly predicting Hamilton's appointment, with a 'rag-out' to prove it. That irked, because the disingenuous 'Skipper' had also, on previous occasions, 'predicted' Howard Kendall, Terry Neill – and Jimmy Nick – as possible Bingy replacements. Where were *those* rag-outs?

The Saturday afternoon following the Hammy debacle, and shortly after I'd arrived in the Windsor press box with Malky and Jim, Brian shouted over: "Hey, John, everyone's talking about your story".

To which I replied: "Yes, Brian... but NOBODY ever talks about one of *yours*..."

Hardly *per aspera ad astra*, and I wasn't proud of that riposte; Skipper was a mate, and a welcome colleague on international trips. I apologised immediately.

In any case, I was wrong about Skipper; his 'frenzied attack' on the FAI from three months earlier was one of the most talked about back pages in years.

But Malky insisted of my retort: "It's one o' the best put-downs Ah've ever heard". Really? His other favourites were Groucho Marx: "I never forget a face, but in your case I'll make an exception" and the Queen's feisty sister Margaret replying to a fawning female interviewer who asked "what's it like being a glamour princess?" with: "Oh, I don't know... what's it like NOT being one?"

Skipper bore no ill will, but I knew I was in for months of barbs from players, managers and punters: "And what makes you such a football expert, John... sure you couldn't even get the fucking Northern Ireland manager right..."

These days it would have been *#FuckwitLaverty* on Twitter, and troll nirvana.

To be fair, Hammy didn't elicit similar sentiments when I rang him to formally introduce myself.

He did, however, unnerve me with an assurance that there'd be "no hard feelings" about wanting Jimmy Nick in the job and that "the slate was wiped clean".

What slate? I'd never spoken to Hammy in my life, and just because I'd written – correctly at the time of going to press, remember – that Jimmy was the chosen one, didn't mean I favoured him over his former international team-mate. (Although I actually *did*; after two years of 'working' with Jimmy, I'd grown very fond of him. Rated him too.)

Bygones all round. Hammy, who named Gerry Armstrong as his assistant, had big shoes to fill and deserved our full support; he was also a long-time friend of my boss Sammy Hamill, and proved the 'slate' had been 'wiped clean' by giving us exclusive access to his "four-year mission plan for Northern Ireland football".

His infectious enthusiasm wasn't shared by a Leicester City fan who wrote into Have a Rattle a few days later.

Describing the ex-Foxes manager's appointment as "a terrible decision", the 'Filbert Street Faithful Supporter' (name and address supplied), added: "Hamilton will keep himself in the job at least 18 months longer than he deserves to, due to the one thing he IS good at: talking bollocks". Not exactly a *billet doux* to our new boy.

We removed the word "bollocks"; Colly suggested replacing it with 'prolixity'.

I nodded knowingly but had to look it up: *verbosity, long-windedness, wandering, boring verbiage.*

(Modern-day exponents of prolixity include Roberto Martinez and the even duller Tony Pulis, who feels it necessary to remind us which sport we're covering: "I'm just trying to win *football* matches for Middlesbrough *Football* Club...")

A bit harsh, that. Subjective too; true, former Linfield, Ipswich and Everton midfielder Hammy had made a telling contribution to Leicester's top-flight relegation – reports of 'dressing room unrest' at Filbert Street didn't help – but he'd done well in two spells with Wigan, so give the man a chance.

And, from a media point of view, the articulate 47-year-old certainly had the jump on Jimmy Nick.

'Filbert Street Faithful Supporter' was right, though; four and half years later – and having been in borrowed time for at least a year – Bryan Hamilton became the first Northern Ireland manager in history to be sacked.

The Euro 96 campaign, while far from disastrous by our standards (let's not forget Bingy's dismal final years), was irrefutably shambolic and infuriatingly unpredictable.

We lost at home, 2-1 to a slick Portugal and 4-0 to a rampant and vengeful Republic of Ireland – yet carved out terrific 1-1 draws away to those same opponents. We beat Latvia away, 1-0, then succumbed to a calamitous 2-1 defeat to the Baltic no-hopers at Windsor.

Hammy inexplicably dropped Gerry Taggart for the first Portugal match (preferring Steve Morrow alongside Big Mac) and crowd-pleaser Keith Gillespie for the Latvian debacle – although the decision may not have been football related. More about that later.

"Hamilton just wiped 2,000 off the gate," said one exasperated international committee member at the squad's Chimney Corner hotel base after it emerged that 'Gilly' wouldn't be starting.

On the other hand, Hammy appeared to have unshakeable belief in utility players such as Crystal Palace's Darren Patterson – or Darren *Hamilton*, as Big Mac rechristened him.

The Euro qualifiers also included home and away victories against Liectenstein and, more impressively, Austria.

Speaking to the Tele in 2010, Hammy recalled: "In the first campaign we were joint second in the group and only missed out on qualifying for Euro 96 in England through our head-to-head record with the Republic. Another point would have got us there."

Mmm, not *entirely* correct. The 'head-to-head' he spoke of never kicked in because the Republic, on the same number of points following a poor second half of their campaign, finished ahead of Northern Ireland having scored one more goal. And 'another point' would actually have got us into a play-off at Anfield against the Netherlands, who comfortably defeated Charlton's dog-eared veterans 2-0.

180

The less said about the subsequent World Cup series the better; a solitary victory against near-useless Albania – who would administer catastrophic revenge in the return fixture – home and away defeats by Ukraine, the failure to beat Armenia in both ties and the descent to hitherto unplumbed depths of 75 in Fifa's world rankings. We also got a 'now I've seen it all' moment in April 1996 when goalkeeper Aidan Davison was booked for time-wasting in a friendly against Sweden at Windsor; we were losing 2-1 at the time...

It wasn't all desolation and despondency: the 2-1 victory in Vienna (October 1994) was superb, the cherry on that sweetest of cakes being *wunderkind* Gilly's stunning volley ("A goal that made you glad video recorders were invented," I wrote) which earmarked Fergie's *Class of '92* fledgling as the latest 'new Bestie'.

The 1-1 draw against Germany in Nuremberg (November 1996) was even better; Hammy's men, unlike Bingy's back-to-the-wall battlers two years earlier, gave as good as they got against the newly-crowned European champions, raining on their homecoming parade with Tags emulating pal Hughesey courtesy of a shock opener.

It was that epic performance that prompted jubilant defender Barry Hunter to interrupt Hamilton's post-match interview (with the BBC's Winker 'Stephen' Watson) by coining the immortal phrase: "What about our wee country?"

We'd also drawn 1-1 with the Germans in a Windsor friendly earlier that year, and there would be a morale-boosting 3-0 win over a useful Belgian outfit in another non-competitive game in early 1997.

But, after four years, the stats were incriminating; under Hammy, Northern Ireland won only eight matches out of 31, losing 15.

The manager's overall win ratio? 34.4% (Bingy's was 43.5%), which, at face value, was respectable – and considerably better than his ill-fated successors, Lawrie McMenemy and Sammy McIlroy.

But it was the nosedive from an impressive 57.7% in the first campaign to a dismal 23.3 in the second, allied to a series of unacceptable home performances and that pitiful away display against Albania from what was, on paper at least, a relatively talented squad, which brought this production of 'Hamilton' to an ignominious end.

That, and the spectre that had haunted the Belfast man in a previous life: dressing-room unrest.

There was friction, too, with 'Certain Elements Of The Press'.

"That's yer new nickname," quipped Malky.

CHAPTER 27

Everything ends badly, otherwise it wouldn't end.
(Tom Cruise's character Brian Flanagan, Cocktail, 1988)

Hammy run-in 1: Providence, Rhode Island, June 1994. For a laugh, I'd got dressed up as an American dude; extra-long shorts, sneakers, basketball shirt – even a bandana. I looked ridiculous.

Later that day, there was a knock on the door of the hotel room I shared with Jim. It was Hammy. All 'hail fellow well met' at the beginning, but then he started on me: "Out here, it's important to remember that we're representing our country, our families – even our employers – but especially ourselves. The onus is on us: not to do anything that may in any way reflect badly on people out here, or folks back home. Players, officials, media; we're all one team, pushing in the same direction. You see where I'm coming from?"

Me: "Erm. Not really, Bryan."

He repeated the mantra, then: "Jim, *you* know what I'm trying to say, don't you?"

Jim: "I do surely, Bryan, and you're absolutely right. A good point well made."

A few more pleasantries, then Hammy left.

Me: "What the fuck was all *that* about?"

Jim: "I haven't a fucking clue. Maybe he doesn't like your new Beavis and Butt-head wardrobe."

Me: "So why didn't he just say that, instead of spouting cryptic messages? Let's hope his team talks aren't like that."

Hammy's philosophical sermon would have been more apt a year later – when he clocked me smuggling ciggies and dubious reading material into certain players' rooms at the Killiney Castle hotel in upmarket Dalkey.

Our would-be porn-addled nicotine addicts in the squad still battled their way to a creditable 1-1 draw at Lansdowne, but my behaviour that day was disrespectful and unprofessional; I *had* let down my country, family, employers, etc.

To be fair, Hammy didn't make a big deal of it, and for that I was profoundly grateful after my pathetic, shameful attempt at currying favour with some of 'the lads'.

182

Run-in 2: Vienna, October 1994. Needing a line for the paper, I asked Hammy about fit-again midfielder Michael O'Neill, who'd been ill/injured and hadn't got a look-in since Bingy retired.

"To be perfectly honest with you, I regard Michael as the form player in the squad," said Hammy, adding: "I've been very impressed with him over the last few weeks; his recall is richly deserved."

The following day's headline read: 'O'Neill in from the cold', with *John Laverty in Vienna* confidently predicting that the Hibs man would have a key role in the Euro 96 qualifier.

The 'key role' consisted of Michael's bony arse warming the subs bench for most of the game – another bollocks headline in the country's biggest selling paper.

Not in the same ball park as 'Nicholl is the choice', but I was still feeling bruised and hypersensitive about that.

With our boys winning 2-1 in the freezing Ernst Happel Stadium, however, the wisest counsel was to keep schtum.

The front-page headline when we got home was 'Peace at last', with Gusty Spence announcing that he, his son-in-law Winkie and other loyalist godfathers were going to emulate the Provos by declaring that war was over.

A personal conflict was, however, just starting.

I didn't confront Hammy at the time about the O'Neill bum steer, but it was decreed that he would have to pay for making me look like an idiot. I mean, what already fading credibility would I have left if the Tele's 'man on the spot' couldn't even deliver basic team news?

The squad's long-serving kit man Derek McKinley remarked – after spotting a reconnoitring Jack Charlton with a Tele that had been handed to him in the Vienna hotel – "Well, at least your story will confuse *him*".

My *fatwa* would take the form of playing down/omitting Hammy's pre-match quotes. Derek, a good friend (whose son, Stuart, later joined the Tele sports staff), would give me a steer on the starting XI.

(In those days – before oversized earphones, social media addiction, obscene salaries and irreversible detachment from reality, when the lads played cards, not Fortnite – you could wander in and out of footballers' rooms and it was no bother getting a line about the forthcoming game.)

Also, nothing about the manager if Northern Ireland actually won or got a creditable draw. Best if Hammy's words were only associated with a disappointing result.

(I engaged in a similar vendetta with Jacko after high-spirited Glens players locked me – a claustrophobic – in the bus's toilet en route to a

1992 European Cup tie with star-studded Olympique Marseille in France. One minute trapped in that stinking hell-hole felt like an hour – and I blamed Jacko. From then on, in Have a Rattle, I persisted with the illogical, juvenile theory that, to be a successful boss, you had to have a moustache like Big Ronnie, Trevor Anderson, Roy Walker, Billy Hamilton and Nigel Best, not clean-shaven like Jacko.)

It wasn't long before Hammy cottoned on.

"I know what you're doing, but *why* are you doing it?" he asked.

"Because, Bryan, in Vienna, you started a sentence with 'to be perfectly honest with you' and then lied to me about Michael O'Neill."

Hammy remained even-tempered.

"I didn't *lie*, John. I merely said I was really impressed with O'Neill's current form. I can't help the way you interpreted what I said."

Wrong answer.

Run-in 3: October, 1997. The day after Hammy, the juggler who'd run out of arms, was sacked, I wrote a less than flattering piece headlined 'NO MORE, MR NICE GUY'. ("It's the comma that changes it from so-so to brilliant," remarked Colly).

Later, BBC Radio 5 Live's Nick Higham called to say he loved my article – and would I mind him reading it out on air, then we'd talk about it? Oh yes, Nick, I'd love that.

An hour later I sat, smug and proud, phone glued to my ear, as Nick delivered my *chef-d'oeuvre* to the nation...

Bryan Hamilton is a decent, honest bloke.
A tireless, enthusiastic servant of Northern Ireland football. A diplomat, a worthy ambassador for this country.
Courteous, considerate, knowledgeable; Bryan would turn up to open a crisp packet, then talk for 40 minutes about its contents.
He was a media man's dream, too; he'd let his favourite dinner go cold, or miss a TV show he'd been dying to watch, before he'd hang up on you.
A polite, proud, patriotic gentleman; a genuinely nice guy.
Unfortunately, he wasn't a very good manager...

(A few pars later, I'd added: *'there's only so many times you can warn people that they're playing for their country, family, pride, themselves, etc and make it stick'*)

I awaited Nick congratulating me on my wonderful prose.

Instead: "Some strident views from John there... and we've got Bryan Hamilton on the line to talk about them..."

Bastards stitched me up! Christ, this is awkward.

To be perfectly honest with you, as Hammy would say, I can't remember a lot about the subsequent exchange.

I do recall "disappointing" and "stabbed in the back". What, you or me Bryan... or both?

Despite the run-ins, I liked Bryan; a favourite framed photo features him, myself and UTV's Mark Robson larking around in Miami. I really wish he'd been a success.

Instead the pay-off line – which wasn't read out on 5 Live – summed up that era.

The manager continued to travel all over, assessing players, attending functions, vigorously defending the image and reputation of Northern Ireland football.

He was a master at public relations – something the IFA themselves failed to emulate by delivering the bullet via phone call rather than in person.

But the PR thing was a double-edged sword, which Bryan eventually got in the back.

I recall him at a function a couple of years ago; smiling, signing autographs for kids, talking endlessly to disabled fans, spending quality time with anyone who sought his company, being an altogether good egg.

"You wouldn't have seen Billy Bingham running about like that", I whispered to a senior IFA official.

"Bingy never HAD to," was the droll reply.

Ed Curran had that faraway look in his eyes.

"I can see it now," he said; "Laverty at the Masters, Laverty reports from the Monaco Grand Prix, Laverty at the Australian Open..."

The editor had just announced that he was promoting me to 'Chief Sports Writer'.

"Sammy and myself are agreed on this; no more chasing after Irish League beer bellies; this is the big time," said the man who'd taken over from Roy Lilley two years earlier – and whom I'd turned down for a job on Sunday Life in 1988.

"So what do you think, John?"

"I don't know what to say, Ed. But there's nothing to think about; I'd love to do this, and thank you so much for the opportunity."

185

A month later, April 1995…

"You're going to think I'm a complete heel, John."

Heel?

"We've been ordered to make stringent financial cuts to the editorial budget.

"We'll have to put your promotion on hold, indefinitely. I hope you understand."

"Don't worry about it, Ed. These things happen. It's not your fault."

Then: "There's something else, John."

What *else* could there be?

"We've had to look at other areas of sport as well, notably foreign trips. Sorry about this, but we're not sending you on the Canadian tour. Bit of a double whammy, I fear."

Now I know what *heel* meant.

"But Ed, the Tele has *never* missed a Northern Ireland game, home or away. If you don't mind me saying, this is a terrible precedent to set."

The heel nearly cracked.

"You think I don't know that, John? You think I want to be the editor responsible for this unfortunate milestone? But I have to make tough decisions, and this one's been made."

He added: "Malcolm will cover the Canada thing. Let's be honest, John, it's only a glorified training session. Who's going to care about *that*?"

BOOZY SOCCER STARS DRINK CANADA DRY
NI player urinated against my desk says horrified receptionist

SHAME AS FOOTBALL ACES GO ON DRUNKEN RAMPAGE
NI coach's fury at players' all-night benders

FIGHTING IRISH! SOCCER ACES BRAWL IN PUB
Golf buggy ends up in lake after NI footballers' jamboree

(Various media outlets, June 1995)

David Neely had raced across to the sports desk even before I'd got my coat off.

"Have you seen this morning's headlines?" the news desk veteran asked, not waiting for a reply.

"You'll have to get onto this, find out exactly what went on in Canada."

"Okay, Davy – but it was *Malky* who was out there, not me. We paid *him*

186

to cover it; maybe you should call him first."

Malky rang a few minutes later.

"Yer man Neely just called, wanting chapter an' verse about Edmonton," he said.

"I told him, absolutely straight: 'MB was there to cover football matches, full point, end par. MB does not do sleazy tabloid tittle-tattle'. He got short shrift, let me tell ye."

Aware that the news desk would ultimately return, I kept Malky on the phone, then called Big Mac, who helped Jeekie and me smoke our brains out on continental flights. Big Mac would keep me right.

Malky: "A few of them were gettin' pissed at Heathrow, and nearly missed the flight oot."

Big Mac: "Hammy wanted a dry plane. A transatlantic flight with free booze? You must be joking."

Malky: "Bryan gave up on tryin' tae stop them swillin' but then horsed the shit out o' them with a training session in Edmonton."

Big Mac: "Nobody wanted to do anything after we got through immigration. We were hammered – well, some were – and all of us were jet-lagged. It would have been better just letting us hit the hay, but I think Hammy saw the training as revenge for us defying him."

Malky: "They wised up a bit before the Canada match, but the shit hit the fan after."

Big Mac: "It was a shite game and a keek performance. We left the pitch {after the 2-0 defeat} pissed off and dehydrated. All we could think about was downing a few."

Malky: "Most of them hit the nearest bar as soon as they got back from the Commonwealth Stadium; didn't even go tae their rooms tae get changed."

Big Mac: "It wasn't long before Gilly was off his trolly; that's when he and Jim had a right go at each other, but Gerry managed to separate them."

Malky: "Gillespie was out o' control. Magilton and Taggart had been playin' pool with Canadian internationals Paul Peschisolido {the future 'Mr Karren Brady'} and Frank Yallop; Keith kept sneakin' up, moving the ball and Jim eventually whacked him on the knuckles with his cue. Then it all kicked off."

Big Mac: "Gilly didn't actually piss up against the reception desk, he pissed onto Tippy's tracksuit bottoms. Hey, that could be the headline: the piss de resistance."

Malky: "Hamilton tried tae have a word wi' Gillespie but he bounded off towards the North Saskatchewan river... with Gerry flailin' behind him."

187

Big Mac: "We were laughing on the golf course the next day about fat 40-year-old Gerry trying to catch the wonderkid. Like something from the Benny Hill Show. But Hammy didn't see the funny side and ordered Gilly to stay teetotal for then on. Yeah, right! This was an end-of-season jolly; surely Hammy, who'd been one of the lads himself, should get that. And as for turning the golf cart into a boat; I'm not mentioning any names."

Malky: "The bigwigs at Goose Hummock Resort were furious about the golf cart. Ah wasnae there – and Ah was in bed when the fire alarm was set off that night.

"Ah do remember Hammy goin' over tae the bar and tryin' tae negotiate a curfew with McDonald – and bein' told where tae go. Quite frankly, the insubordination was the worst Ah've ever seen."

So why didn't he write about it?

"If Hammy had sent one or two hame {and there was talk that he'd actually do that with Magilton and Gillespie} for misconduct, of course I'd have reported it. But all he did was drop Gillespie for the next match {which Chile won 2-1}.

Gillespie was also dropped (along with Phil 'Tippy' Gray; PG Tips, geddit?) for the match they'd ostensibly been 'preparing' for – the crucial home qualifier with Latvia on June 7.

Those lurid headlines from the Alberta capital only appeared *after* that shambolic game, which finished 2-1 to the visitors and put the final mockers on the campaign.

Unaware of exactly what had gone on across the pond – although one player provided an off-the-record summary – I delivered the most condemnatory match report of my career.

Go home, lads. Sit down in the drawing rooms of your plush suburban homes.
Reflect on the dross you served up in the name of football at Windsor Park last night. Bury your heads in your hands and beg to be left alone. And, if you don't feel like doing that, today of all days, then don't bother coming back.
Thousands paid good money to watch this. They were entitled to get some value from it, some semblance of entertainment.
Instead, they witnessed highly-paid players pushing back the parameters of ineptitude...

I expected a backlash as we mustered for the next challenge, a Sunday night encounter against Portugal in Porto's Estadio das Antas that

September. There was nothing.

Perhaps they feared another drubbing – and subsequent media laceration – in front of 50,000 on the Iberian Peninsula. At least that's what I thought.

It was a different story after the morale-boosting 1-1 draw, goalkeeper Alan Fettis' heroics helping to earn a worthy (though ultimately futile) point courtesy of Hughesey's brilliantly taken second-half free kick.

It was the first time Figo and Co – who racked up 32 goalscoring opportunities – had dropped home points in Group 6. A 'typical' Norn Iron display, one worth celebrating.

Steve Morrow was the first to pounce after I entered the changing room to congratulate the team.

In the aftermath of an epic defensive performance against world class opponents, the Arsenal man felt he'd the right to say his piece. I'd no issue with that; I'd had my tuppence-worth, and now it was his turn.

Next morning at Francisco Sa Carneiro Airport, midfielder Steve Lomas, a short-fused young man, took things a little further by persistently kicking my holdall at check-in.

I just let the Hanover-born (his dad was a soldier), Coleraine-raised Lomy, whom I liked and rated highly, get on with it; what the hell, they needed to let off steam.

(When the hot-blooded Lomy, who'd start an argument in an empty room but enjoyed a promising stint as St Johnstone boss, took over basket-case Millwall – and him an ex-Hammer – in June 2013, I predicted he'd be out by Christmas. He was sacked on Boxing Day.)

Of all the Northern Ireland players I worked with, Big Mac was by far my favourite, followed by Hughesy and Tags. I was devastated when Big Mac, who was only 48 years old, dropped dead on a golf course – a few hundred yards from where I lived – in June 2012. I love you, man. God rest you.

I fought with, and made up with, Big Tommy a lot, depending on whether I praised or criticised him after a match.

I never really clicked with Nigel Worthington (ironic, considering we'd played together in the Ballymena youth team), and Mal Donaghy (ironic, considering most people I know say he's one of the nicest guys they've ever met).

I retain huge admiration for Mal as an all-time great player for our wee country, but he was recalcitrant and unhelpful in virtually all my dealings with him. Christ, he wouldn't even confirm that he was leaving United for Chelsea in 1994, even though every UK paper was reporting the deal as imminent/done.

Sorry Mal, but "sure you wouldn't know" wasn't the sort of quote I needed that day.

I tactfully (well, perhaps not) reminded Mal about that when he rang looking for a favour a few years later.

On September 17, 1997, Gilly had the match of his life, for Newcastle against Barcelona in an unforgettable Champions League tie at St James Park.

Faustino Asprilla dominated the headlines with a hat-trick in the 3-2 victory over Louis van Gaal's visitors, but the 22-year old from Islandmagee was man of the match.

Repeatedly torturing Barca's world-class left back Sergi – "on this form he could have nutmegged a mermaid," said one commentator – Gilly showed why Magpies boss Kevin Keegan insisted on him being a key constituent of the controversial £7m transfer that took Gallowgate goal machine Andy Cole to Man United in January 1995.

"That jammy wee fucker Gilly got a £175k signing-on fee and two grand a week before bonuses – at 19 years old," Big Mac told me after Gilly became Northern Ireland's first £1m (his declared value in the swap deal) 'home-grown' player; Luton-born Kingsley doesn't count.

Gilly's brilliant display against Barca led to their irate Dutch manager firing the club's scout, whose pre-match dossier hadn't even mentioned the threat posed by Newcastle's young wing wizard.

The hapless spy was replaced by a lad called Jose Mourinho, who'd been hanging around the Camp Nou like an office cat after his stint as Bobby Robson's translator ended.

Unfortunately for Hammy, Gilly produced one of the *worst* displays of his career just seven days *before* that masterclass against Barcelona. The dismal 1-0 World Cup qualifier defeat against Albania (played in Zurich due to civil unrest in Tirana) came days after Princess Diana was laid to rest (Mother Teresa, a hero in the 'home' team's homeland, had also just died) and the aftermath felt just as funereal. Time to sharpen the pencil once more.

A minute's silence before the game. Several hours of it afterwards. This was a performance so reeking in ineptitude, it rendered you speechless. Pathetic? It didn't even reach THAT description. Rolled over in Switzerland by the worst team in the group, although the Albanians might now give you an argument about that. We were no match for the nomads, and

190

that's probably the most damning indictment of all; a disgusting, embarrassing shambles from start to finish.

It was Keith Gillespie who set the tone for this calamity by blasting a shot ten yards wide – from ten yards out – early in the game. That was as good as it got. Honestly.

Inconsistency prevented Gilly, who proved to be both a gift and a curse for Hammy, being remembered as genuinely top drawer; although more a creator than a scorer, his record of just two goals in 86 internationals (the cracker in Vienna, and more straightforward effort against Wales at Windsor in October 2005, came almost 11 years – 4014 days, to be precise – and 64 caps apart) is particularly underwhelming for someone of such unquestionable ability and early promise.

That, and forsaking the rod-of-iron environs of Fergie's Old Trafford in his teenage years for the "birds and booze" temptations of Geordieland, which one Toon-based hack described to me as a "shagger's paradise" in the mid-90s. He added: "No wonder they blew a 12-point lead against United. If they'd scored as often in the Prem as they did at the Bigg Market and Julie's Nightclub, they'd have walked that title race. I swear their bony arses were still wobbling when they stepped onto the pitch." Gilly's off-the-field antics have been, wrongly, likened to Bestie's; not within a beagle's gowl of it. He clearly enjoyed female company and a boozy night out, but there was no suggestion of the debilitating alcoholism that pulverised Bestie's liver and ultimately killed him at 59. What *did* bring Bestie to mind was the Co Down native's good looks, inherent shyness and unflappable belief in God-given talent.

Gilly's main *bete noire* was, as we know, gambling. I remember quietly marking his card in 1995 that The Sun had been made aware of his eye-watering flutters and that he should watch his step. (A News International pal had – rather unprofessionally – spilled the beans about their upcoming investigation.)

I doubt if Gilly heeded the warning; the Currant Bun exposed his gambling addiction in a front page exclusive a few months later.

Hammy, meanwhile, was the proverbial beaten docket after that 1997 defeat by Albania.

He'd long lost the dressing room – something I witnessed with my own eyes after visiting Slieve Donard Hotel on April 30 that year – the day after a scoreless Saturday afternoon draw with Portugal at Windsor. The atmosphere was poisonous that evening, Hammy was uncharacteristically tight-lipped – but, in a quiet moment, Derek

191

McKinley explained that a number of players had reneged on an organised golf outing, having (legitimately, as it turned out) booked themselves into Belfast hotels for a post-match Saturday night on the tiles.

As the squad prepared to depart on the Monday morning for another important World Cup qualifier in Kiev, one senior player told Malky at the airport: "We didn't need another 'team-building exercise'. We'd been together a week and were sick of the sight of each other".

Incidentally, Jim Magilton – man of the match against Portugal – was dropped, with no explanation given, for the Ukraine match. And Iain Dowie was relieved of his stand-in skipper's duties (final score, 2-1 to Ukraine).

The dreary campaign hobbled to its end with defeat by Portugal (1-0) in Lisbon's Estadio da Luz on October 11, 1997; a much-improved performance than a month earlier in Zurich, but the die had already been cast.

The axe fell 12 days later, a unanimous decision – although virtually every member of the 12-strong international committee would later insist (via phone calls and conversations with Gerry) that they were the outlier who *hadn't* voted for dismissals.

It should have happened earlier, though. To be perfectly honest with you.

CHAPTER 28

I finally made it to the 'big paper' in 1974. Julie Welch of the Guardian had just made headlines as the first woman to write about sport and Malcolm said "We need a lassie too. When can you start?"
(Wendy Austin, BBC)

David Trimble stole a glance at the mirror and liked what he saw.
Lookin' good, Davy-boy. Look. Ing. Good!
He wouldn't normally don the glad rags on a Saturday, but this particular date demanded it; a huge number of constituents congregating in one place, an irresistible photo op – and no hecklers.
How often to you get *that* in Northern Ireland politics?
But, as Dylan sang, the times they are a-changin'.
It's late April, 1994: they're saying an IRA ceasefire is imminent before the end of summer, with loyalist paramilitaries expected to follow suit.
If that comes to pass, someone with fortitude and courage within the Ulster Unionist Party should probably go public with his idea of a Stormont 'assembly' that would undoubtedly play a significant role in eradicating violence for good.
After all, the Shinners need a mandate if they're to prove their commitment to democracy and exclusively peaceful means. Surely that would be a major leap forward in the peace process?
Not only that, but there's speculation that this will be Molyneux's last full year as UUP leader; time for a new, resourceful, dynamic man at the helm, obviously. Young(ish) too – maybe someone still under 50 – and not a recalcitrant dinosaur like John Taylor.
Yep, such a man could solve the Drumcree issue, lead Northern Ireland into the promised land as an inspiring First Minister, maybe even pick up a Nobel Prize for his statesmanlike elan, striding the corridors of power like a colossus before it was time to take his rightful place in the Lords.
The more immediate challenge, however, was finding Mourneview Park, home of Glenavon FC.
They're playing local rivals today in A Really Big Match. A genuine 'winner takes all' encounter.
Naturally, the MP for Upper Bann would have to be completely neutral, impartial and non-partisan. *Mais oui!*
Such an effortless marking; congratulate the triumphant captain,

commiserate with the losing one, soak up the atmosphere in a stadium heaving with potential voters... sorry, fanatical supporters. A win-win situation, if e'er there was one.

So why did that April 30 afternoon end with David Trimble ruining his favourite shoes in the middle of a muddy pitch, with all four stands having been emptied at breakneck speed by gutted fans – and, if you excuse the pun, being press-ganged into an emergency live post-match analysis alongside some bloke from the Belfast Telegraph... because both managers were too upset to face the cameras?

"Ha-ha-ha-HA... ye went tae the wrong game!"

Malky was in The Inkspot, and in his element. He wasn't long back from seeing Linfield retain their Irish League title with a 2-0 win over Glentoran at Windsor – and I'd just returned from my double-act with Trimble.

"Ye know, John, Ah had a funny feeling they'd fuck it all up at Mourneview today."

"Did you now? Funnily enough, I didn't get that impression from your preview pieces. What was that killer line: 'you pays your money and takes your choice'? Not exactly Mystic Malky..."

"Oi, bartender... get ma son a drink here. He's gettin' rattled cos he went tae the wrong game."

The 1993-94 Irish League climax was the most thrilling one ever.

On that final day, any one of three – Portadown, Glenavon and Linfield – could win the Gibson Cup.

With the Blues blowing their crucial game in hand by drawing 1-1 at Newry on the Thursday night, all three contenders entered the climactic day with 67 points from 29 games.

Ports, however, had the best goal difference (+55 to Glenavon's +40 and Linfield's +39). It boiled down to this: Big Ronnie's men WOULD win the title if they beat Alan Fraser's Glenavon, the Lurgan men MIGHT finish top (for the first time in 34 years) if they got all three points in this epic Mid-Ulster showdown – and Linfield COULD be champions again if the Mourneview match was drawn, or if they saw off the Glens by two more goals than Glenavon beat Portadown. Simple!

Trevor Anderson's Blues – technically at least – had won the previous year's race on goal difference, but the final league table of 1992-93 is deceptive; they actually pipped Roy Walker's up-and-coming Crues with a match to spare.

This one was going to the wire, though – or, as the wry Anderson remarked afterwards, "*beyond* the wire."

194

And, despite Malky's Saturday night *schadenfreude*, Mourneview *was* the place to be. It promised to be an unforgettable occasion and it was – but not in the way either team intended.

Portadown, who'd lost to Linfield the previous Saturday and were then handed a fortuitous life-line by the Blues' Newry slip-up, didn't play like a team determined to make the most of their unexpected opportunity.

A slick, fired-up Glenavon deservedly went ahead early on through Raymie McCoy, and should have been out of sight before Stevie 'Macker' McBride made it 2-0 after the break.

With no goals at Windsor, this was the cue for a wild-eyed Billy Ireland to grab me by the lapels and pin me against the press box wall.

"The team you never write about... the team you're always making sarcastic jibes about... where's that team now? I'll tell you, John – top of the Irish League and about to be crowned champions! Get the blue and white ribbons on that trophy, right now..."

Gasping for air and trying desperately to extract myself from the Lurgan Mafioso's bear hug, I squeaked: "It's not over yet, Billy..."

The reply: "Oh, go boil your head, son! It's over all right. The Gibson Cup is coming back to where it belongs."

He then burst into song: *"All the lads and lassies, smiles upon their faces. Walking down the Tandragee Road, to see the Mourneview aces..."*

Just after Billy released me, Macker missed a glorious chance to make it 3-0 – and word came through from Belfast that Billy Fenlon had put Linfield ahead.

Then Radio Ulster reported a second Blues goal, this time from the Hawk. Then Portadown pulled one back through Sandy Fraser – who promptly bagged another: 2-2.

Billy's face turned as white as his hair. The blue half of Mourneview fell silent. And Portadown, a poor second best in this game, suddenly began playing like the only ones capable of winning it.

Back at Windsor, their match had ended but the collective anxiety was just beginning.

There was still enough time for a fired-up Ports to complete a sensational comeback against by-now demoralised opponents still ruing that Macker miss, and two earlier ones from skipper Paul Byrne.

Then: Martin Russell lobbed the ball over a static Glenavon defence into the path of Robert Casey, who beat the offside trap and bore down on Robbie Beck's goal.

Some 25 miles away at Windsor, thousands hung on to Radio Ulster commentator Michael 'Foghorn' Hammond's every word. Then...

"... and Russell has sent Casey through, he's onside... IT'S CASEY FOR PORTADOWN..."

This could have been one of those great moments in football commentary, up there with Wolstenholme's "they think it's all over" from '66 or Moore's "it's up for grabs now" when Michael Thomas raced through at Anfield in '89.
Instead, as Casey flicked the ball past the onrushing Beck, Foghorn shrieked...

"AAAARGH!"

Malky recalled: "We hadnae a clue what 'aaaargh!' actually meant. If was probably only a second or two before he started talkin' again, but we'd no idea if Casey had scored or messed it up."
In the end, what would have been the most dramatic Irish League title-winning goal of all time drifted centimetres wide of the far post.
And, a full six minutes after the Windsor torment began, the massed ranks of Bluemen could finally celebrate.
It was a less taxing wait for Irish League president Morton McKnight and secretary Harry Wallace to charge up the M2, armed with the Gibson Cup, from their half-way house at Nutt's Corner.
Conversely, there was bugger-all to cheer at a deserted, funereal Mourneview. Myself and David Trimble did our best as understudies to the absent Big Ronnie and 'Fraz'.
"It's something you don't see every day," said the MP. Indeed.
Trevor Anderson was in philosophical form when I rang to congratulate him.
"Who'd have thought, after being cheated out of an historic win in Copenhagen last September, that we'd be put through *another* six minutes of injury time waiting for something special to happen?" he said.
"It must have been written in the stars. I've never known an atmosphere like it; the long, agonising wait, followed by the unbridled joy."
He added: "Of course you missed all that, having been at the wrong game..."

December 19, 1994...

"Sports desk."

"John, Kenny Shiels here."

"Kenny! Are you calling to wish me happy Christmas?

"That's one reason. Must say, I never thought I'd see the headline 'Sinn Fein at Stormont' on page one of the Tele. McGuinness and Kelly grinning for the cameras; who the fuck saw *that* coming?"

"We're certainly in uncharted waters, Kenny. But I suspect you're not calling to discuss our tortuous peace process. What's up?"

"What I'm calling about is the Belfast Telegraph linking me with the vacant Coleraine job."

"*What*? You're barking up the wrong tree, Kenny. I can assure you, mate, we've never put anything in the paper linking you with the Coleraine job."

"That's true, John, and that's the reason I'm calling. *Why* haven't you?"

December 20, 1994…

Bannsiders get ready to tempt Shiels

By John Laverty

Kenny Shiels is top of Coleraine's wanted list of candidates to replace Felix Healy.

The Bannsiders' board is expected to convene in the next few days to consider a replacement for Healy, who quit the club for Derry City last month.

And there is little doubt that Carrick Rangers boss Shiels will emerge as a strong favourite.

Shiels, who works without a contract at Taylor's Avenue, was today remaining tight-lipped about the speculation.

"I haven't had any official approach so I cannot comment," he said.

"All I can say to you is that I am currently the manager of Carrick Rangers and nothing has happened so far to change that situation."

December 22, 1994…

Delighted Shiels gets his dream job

By John Laverty

Kenny Shiels was today installed as the new manager at Coleraine.

Shiels answered a call from the Bannsiders yesterday and will meet the

197

players at the Showgrounds tonight.
"I couldn't have lived with myself if I'd have let this opportunity pass,"
said the lifelong Coleraine fan.

March 9, 1995...

"Sports desk."

"John, Kenny Shiels here."

"Kenny! What about you? How are things with those unmentionables from down the A26?"

"Going well at the moment, John. Completely different from Carrick. Bigger club, more demanding. And you get paid to hate Braidmen."

"Never thought of it like that. Anyway, what can we do for you, Kenny? I see the Gunners have just sacked George Graham. Want us to link you with the vacant Arsenal job?"

"Very funny. No. This is serious. John, I've just discovered that a scenario exists in which a team might have to lose on the last day to avoid relegation."

"What are you talking about, *lose*? How can *that* be?

"John, listen carefully. This is the legacy of those clowns voting for aggregate placings over two seasons to sort out promotion and relegation, rather than points accumulated.

"Say, for instance, we get to the last day with Bangor, who are struggling, playing Ards, who aren't. It might be more beneficial for Bangor to lose – and then Ards would leapfrog over one of Bangor's relegation rivals, thus condemning *them* to the drop. You get what I'm saying?"

"Er, no. But I'll look into it, Kenny. I promise."

"You do that, John. There's definitely a story there."

Three hours later: "What's that crap ye've put in today's paper, John? Ah can't get ma head round it."

Irish League club may have to LOSE to stay up, says Shiels

"Malky, at the start I thought it was just Crazy Kenny being... well, you know his schtick. But he's right. Such a scenario *does* exist, at least potentially."

"Maybe so John, but *really*? The odds against that actually happenin' are so astronomical, it's nae worth talkin' aboot."

Sunday Life, April 30, 1995...

WHAT A JOKE! WHAT A FARCE!

By Jim Gracey and Lyle Jackson
Irish League football was the laughing stock of Europe last night as Bangor deliberately lost to Ards – in order to secure their place in next season's new Premier Division.
But Coleraine didn't see the funny side. They didn't lose yesterday – but are still relegated despite finishing four places above Bangor in the 1994-95 table and accumulating more points over the last two decisive seasons.
On a day of high drama and tension, there was the farcical sight of Bangor supporters cheering Ards' second goal in a 2-0 win. That goal helped lift Ards above Coleraine in the table – and doomed the Bannsiders, who would only manage a scoreless draw at home to Ballymena.
So, despite finishing a comfortable seventh in this year's final league table, Kenny Shiels' men are one of the eight teams that will form the new second tier of Irish League football next season...

"Ah owe ye an apology, Schemer. Ah honestly thought ye'd lost yer marbles printin' a story like that. Ah dismissed it as hyperbole ye shouldnae have risked publishin', especially after last year."
Cheers.
"Naebody followed up on it, includin' me, and Ah always copy yer stories for ma cor pieces. But Crazy Kenny was right behind the 8 ball after all."
"He was, Malky – although he didn't imagine his own team being the fall guys. Are Coleraine still going to sue?"
"They're talkin' aboot it, but they havenae a leg tae stand on. At the end o' the day, it was a monumental fuck-up, although naebody raised any objections two year ago, so tough titty. And who'd have thought, wi' Crues winnin' the league at a canter, that there'd be another final-day drama this year?"
Crazy Kenny's tip-off that Thursday morning produced one of the most bizarre scoops of my career.
And Malky was right; no other media outlet followed up on it, presumably because they, like me initially, thought it was too ridiculous to be true. Then the Irish League became 'the laughing stock of Europe'. This was the last time any football body in the world would use 'aggregate placings' rather than accumulated points to split a unitary

league into two tiers.

Never again would we see a player-manager such as Bangor's Roddy Collins careering like Stevie Wonder towards the corner flag after being put clean through on goal.

It still feels surreal typing this:

It was between Bangor and Coleraine for the final relegation place.

To have any hope of staying up, the Seasiders (whose optimum aggregate placing was 8th) had to lose by two goals to their north Down rivals, ensuring that Ards finished fourth in the 1994-95 table (and 5th on aggregate placings).

Beating Coyler's Ards would not have improved Bangor's position, but losing would save them if Coleraine failed to get the better of an already relegated Ballymena and finish with an 8.5 instead of a redeeming 6.5. (Even then, Coleraine would still have survived had either Linfield or Crusaders scored one more goal in their respective games – but let's not expand the 'mindfuck', as Shiels called it, any further than necessary).

The Bannsiders' fate was in their own hands – and they blew it by not beating opponents who'd nothing but pride to play for. After Shiels got over the devastation, the mindfuck and the immediate sense of injustice, he appreciated the bitter irony.

Malky quoted a defiant Seasiders chairman Gifford McConkey thus after the shameful north Down derby: "If you want to blame anyone for this farce, blame Cliftonville. It was them who proposed aggregate placings, and the League accepted that."

He added: "Don't forget that, last season, we had fifth place wrapped up long before the campaign ended, and rested key players with the Irish Cup final coming up. If it was points, not places, at stake, we'd have acted differently. When all is said and done, however, we did what was necessary and Coleraine didn't – end of story."

Crazy Kenny, meanwhile, would be involved in another pantomime a few months later: oh yes, he was sacked by Coleraine... oh no, he wasn't.

What happened was this: on Wednesday, October 18, a group of board members opted to fire the manager following a disappointing start to the new First Division championship; a squad boasting the likes of Tony Gorman, Tommy Huston, Stephen Young and John Devine should not be losing to Ballyclare Comrades, they said.

The volatile Magherafelt man wouldn't accept that, however, arguing that four senior directors – including club chairman Hugh Wade – had stormed out of the acrimonious meeting, leaving it bereft of the quorum required for such a seismic decision to stand.

As Crazy Kenny scathingly remarked – to panic-stricken presenter Adam Coates live on Radio Ulster the following morning – "How could anyone take this seriously? "The sacking was proposed by an old woman and seconded by someone who can't string two words together..."
Coatesy (whom Malky referred to as 'The Chooghter'): "I'm pretty sure Coleraine Football Club wouldn't challenge those descriptions..."
(The 'old woman'? Legendary ex-chairman Jack Doherty.)
Kenny then rang me: "I watched the OJ Simpson verdict a fortnight ago and thought nothing else could shock me. But to be sacked after only ten months, and with the season hardly started, is ludicrous.
"I gave up my day job to manage a club I've supported since I was a child, and I'm not going to take this lying down. I was kicked in the teeth by people who tried to take advantage of seven board members being absent from the meeting. How's that fair?"
October 20, 1995...

Shiels back as Coleraine boss!

By John Laverty

Kenny Shiels will be back in charge of Coleraine tomorrow!
The manager, sacked on Wednesday night, was sensationally reinstated today and will assume control of team matters against Larne at the Showgrounds.
Shiels said: "I have been asked to take charge of the team tomorrow and have agreed to do so. There will be a meeting next week to decide on the future, and I expect that meeting to have a full complement of board members.
"If it's decided I should step down, I'll accept this as a democratic decision. If they want me to carry on, I'm happy to do so."

Kenny (off the record): "Well, John, as Sinky {Billy Sinclair} would say in his book, 'don't let the bastards grind you down'.
"At least this story has given you media guys a break from the 'Marc Kenny saga' {ex-Bangor player fielded by Glenavon while technically suspended} and 'Fulton-gate' {Portadown expelled from Ulster Cup final for using 'unregistered' youngster Gareth Fulton}, so you owe me one."
"You're not wrong about those yawn-a-ramas, Kenny. As my editor would say, 'important, but not interesting'. And I think *you* owed *me* one as well, after that 'come and get me' plea last year..."

Despite their inauspicious start, Crazy Kenny's gang – bolstered by club record signing Packie McAllister, Dubliner Greg O'Dowd and the boss's free-scoring brother Sammy (who'd nearly died in late 1994 when complications set in after he broke his leg playing for Carrick) – steamrollered the inaugural First Division title, finishing a whopping 18 points clear of Ballymena.

And the club relegated from the new Premier Division to make way for rejuvenated Coleraine? Bangor.

CHAPTER 29

I feel what you feel when you're far away
It's been a hundred days
(Jessie Reyez, Far Away)

Roy Keane looked dog-tired. He was wearing his FAI tracksuit – three oversized white stripes on one side, an oversized OPEL sign on the other – and sweating profusely. He was surrounded by half a dozen Republic supporters. They were attempting to hail a taxi for the brilliant young Man United star.

"He can come with us," Jim told them.

"We're staying in the hotel across the road from the Hilton; we'll get him home safely."

This idea initially found favour with Cork-born Keano's self-appointed henchmen. Then one of them – I'm sure he had a northern accent – spotted our Press accreditation lanyards.

Instantly, he adopted a confrontational stance. "If you put one word about this in the paper," he told Jim, "I'll knock your fucking pan in."

Jim doesn't do fear. Uncontrollable rage is more his thing.

"And what will *I* be doing, arsehole, when you're *knocking my fucking pan in..?*"

Jim and the green-and-white bedecked diehard began squaring up to each other like rutting stags.

Then: WHOOP, WHOOP!

The police car drew to a halt, and two heavily armed officers stepped out. "What's going on here?"

"Nothing," chorused Jim and fellow stag.

"Right. Let's all take it nice and easy here, okay? You soccer fans move away to the next street, right now. You guys with the press badges? Step into the back of the car, please."

"Are you arresting us, officer?"

"No, I'm giving you bozos a ride home..."

God bless America!

CHAPTER 30

The American Dream got off to a nightmarish start.
You know those embarkation cards you had to fill in? That ridiculous question:

Are you applying for permanent residency in the United States for the purpose of committing espionage?

Jim Magilton couldn't resist penning an equally ridiculous reply: *I sure am, yes siree!*
Immigration officers at Boston's Logan International aren't fabled for their sense of humour.
Two hours would pass after we'd 'deplaned', and before it was accepted that the repentant Magilton was indeed a professional footballer, not a spy. I suspect the bastards knew all along.
Having spent eight boozy hours on the jumbo from Heathrow, we could have done without this.
No mind; only another hour's 'transportation' from Boston, Massachusetts to Providence, Rhode Island.
May 31, 1994: The cheery hotel staff had planned to make the travelling party feel right at home; an Irish tricolour flew from the building, with smaller ones presented to bemused guests on arrival.
"We'd planned to play the Soldier's Song, but couldn't find a recording," said the apologetic receptionist, adding: "You guys are on floor 14. There isn't a 13; *RI* folk are a superstitious lot..."
An opportunistic lot too; it wasn't long before we realised, courtesy of the bedroom TV's 'check your bill' facility, that we were being hit with a whopping $10.22 'connection charge' each time we made a phone call.
Jim Gracey, our self-appointed unofficial shop steward, demanded to see selected printouts of the party's running totals.
He discovered that everyone was being hit with the same outlandish charges – including breakfast they hadn't ordered – and that one or two had also developed a penchant for late night pay-per-view entertainment such as Dirty Debutantes, Naughty Co-Eds and Horny House Mates.
("I've no idea how *they* got onto my bill, Jim; these gangsters are obviously charging us for all kinds of stuff we haven't used...")
Tenacious Jim got the connection charges removed, but this capped a fraught opening to Northern Ireland's two-match transatlantic tour, which had been set up by US-based ex-pat, multi-millionaire businessman

(and Malky's long-term friend) Noel Lemon, brother of former Linfield star Jim.

It should have been a three-match sortie, but Saudi Arabia reneged on a friendly in Atlantic City, New Jersey.

There were still two other World Cup-bound opponents – Colombia at the Foxboro Stadium just outside Boston, and Mexico, in Miami's Orange Bowl – for the 18-man squad to look forward to.

The post-arrival angst wasn't helped by Hammy's bizarre lecture in my bedroom ("It's very important to remember that we're representing our country, our families – even our employers – but especially ourselves...") or the failure of the new Tandy laptops presented to myself and Jim prior to departure.

These were the days of dial-up modems, irritating chirrups, peeps and squelching noises, and repeated connection failures – although that's not what our rapidly expanding hotel bill was recording.

Must get these things fixed; can't be phoning masses of copy over at 2.30am (7.30am UK time); it would take aeons.

Luckily the tech department of Providence's world-famous Brown University was just a few blocks away, and 'Dan' was delighted to get his soldering iron out and help the Irish guys get connected. Cheers, Dan from Brown.

By Thursday, June 2 – our second full day in the Rhode Island capital, and the day before the Colombia game – we could finally relax and enjoy the surroundings.

Me, to a Westminster Street coffee vendor: "Is it true that Providence has some of the finest churches in New England?"

Vendor: "Yeah, and some of the finest titty bars too..."

Malky suggested lunch and a few Sammy Adams in a little place he'd spotted in Elbow Street, a short distance from the hotel.

It came across as a typical American bar; dark interior, neon beer signs, lots of wood, two pool tables.

We were among the first customers of the day; the place was so quiet, we could actually hear the TV news report on the horrendous Chinook helicopter crash back home, in which a large number of high-ranking intelligence officers died on the Mull of Kintyre.

"Today's Tele puts the death toll at 29", said Jim.

Malky: "How do ye know that?"

Jim: "I've arranged to have the front and back pages faxed over every day. No doubt those extortionists back at the hotel will charge a fortune for it... 'facsimile reception fee' or something like that. You get a good show on today's back page, John; 'Boston to boycott Hammy's boys', or something like that."

(I'd written a piece about Boston's Irish-American politicians calling for football fans to shun the Northern Ireland team after the 'Night in November' fiasco.)

Within an hour, the bar had morphed into a Frankie Goes to Hollywood video – with the Village People as guest stars.

Me: "Malky – did you know this is a *gay* bar?"

"Whaaa? It looked okay when Ah walked past this mornin'. Hold on, Ah'll get the tab..."

Me: "No, no, it's *still* okay. It was just a bit of a shock when those blokes started kissing a minute ago."

Jim: "Tell you what, Malky; we'll order the check and then have ourselves a wee dance when YMCA comes on..."

I rattled out my preview stuff on the temperamental Tandy that afternoon; young midfielders Neil Lennon of Crewe Alexandra, and Crystal Palace's Darren Patterson, were hoping to win their first caps on this trip, as was George O'Boyle, who'd been in good form for Dunfermline.

I'd check later that the copy made it across the Atlantic – before that, it was off to a highly recommended hostelry on the banks of the Seekonk River with Jim, Jeekie and BBC NI's slim, fair-haired, meticulously groomed, Pringle jersey-wearing, head of sport Terry Smyth.

Jeekie: "Are you joining us, Malky?"

Terry: "Apparently this place does the best USDA cremated steak in New England. You don't wanna miss that."

Malky: "Nah, Ah've got a bit o' work tae do upstairs. Ah'll just order room service."

Jim: "Maybe Malky's planning a sneaky return to The Tasty Truncheon."

Malky: "Very funny. But Ah notice you couldnae stop jivin' wi' that bloke in the leather troosers and the handlebar moustache. See yous anon."

The craic was ninety, but Providence (founded in 1636 by Reformed Baptist theologian Roger Williams) is not New York, and late-night taxis aren't easy to come by.

For the first – but evidently not the last – time on this two-month odyssey, the local cops gave us a ride home. In two City of Providence PD squad cars, no less.

At one point – and egged on by a sozzled Smyth – the friendly officers briefly raced each other, 'blues and twos' in full emergency mode,

206

through picket-fence neighbourhoods, onto the I-95 and into downtown Providence (or 'The Twilight Zone', as Jim had rechristened it). Happy days!

Quick call to the office at 2.30am: yep, we've got your stuff, great. Night night.

CHAPTER 31

I don't mind what you did. I mind the way you did it.
(Woodward to Bernstein, All The President's Men, 1976)

Jim came into the bedroom the next morning, brandishing a fax of the Tele back page.

CASSIDY IS NEW GLENS BOSS
Former NI international takes charge at the Oval

From Malcolm Brodie in Rhode Island

Glentoran have appointed 43-year-old former Northern Ireland midfielder Tommy Cassidy as their new manager.
In a shock move, Cassidy has been appointed to take over from Robert Strain, who has resigned but will continue in an assistant capacity at the Oval.
"We have now formed a management team which will be of tremendous benefit to the club," said Glentoran chairman David Chick, one of the Irish FA official delegates on Northern Ireland's current US tour.
"I know there is a tremendous amount of work to do at Glentoran and I'm keen to get started right away," said Cassidy.

I felt light headed, nauseous, disrespected, embarrassed, denuded of dignity – and incandescent.
"That treacherous wee snake has stitched me up yet again. He must have known about this all along. That's why he didn't come with us last night."
Jim: "He's made a tit out of me too; so much for my big Sunday Life back page exclusive about Strainer getting a 'vote of confidence' and a 'big war chest' for the new season. It looks like Malky was just waiting for the right moment."
 "Yeah – the right moment for optimum humiliation; the start of my first big marking as the Tele's main man; the first without him, the great globetrotter. pulling all the strings. Oh, they'll be fairly gloating about this back home; 'trust Malky to get the big yarns, while wee John's rattling on about Neil Lemon, or Noel Lennon, or whatever the fuck he's called'.
Well, I'm fucking finished with him, Jim."
"But John, it IS a good story."

208

"It's a *great* story, and he's got chapter and verse. It's not what he did, Jim, it's the *way* he did it. If he had mentioned this yesterday, I'd have applauded him. Instead, he's gone and shafted me. Fuck... FUCK!"

Some 20 miles south west of the Twilight Zone, there's a quaint little colonial town called Coventry. As far as I was concerned, Malky had just been sent there.

I wasn't alone; Jim, Jeekie, Terry and others were, to various degrees, taken aback by what I called the 'treachery'. It wasn't what he did, it's what he didn't do. The unspoken truth and the spoken lie are merely two sides of the same betrayal coin.

What was it McIlvanney said: "Malky would swamp you with kindness at the bar... then slit your throat in the toilets to be first with the story." Rhode Island may be an idyllic location in the summer but Mephistophelian Malky was about to encounter a sudden cold front. He may have been well read, but must have missed that bit in the Tao where it says 'to hold on, you have to let go'.

We still spoke, of course – Christ, we're not 10 years old – but any exchanges were, on my part, terse, frank and frosty. I desisted as much as possible from engaging with the prince of darkness; monosyllabism from now on, pal.

Malky, not normally behind the door when it came to gasconading about an exclusive, remained uncharacteristically mute about this one. That June 3 evening, we executed the half hour journey to the 60,000-capacity Foxboro, home of the New England Patriots, in virtual silence.

Outside the massive gridiron stadium, desperate hawkers attempted to sell Republic of Ireland shirts and scarves to anyone in the 21,000-strong crowd wearing green instead of yellow.

Our lot were comfortably beaten 2-0 – Hammy's first defeat – by a slick Colombian side missing outrageous scorpion-kicking keeper Rene Higuita – who'd been banged up for his involvement in a kidnapping – but featuring crazy-haired superstar Carlos Valderrama, future Newcastle favourite Faustino Asprilla, Real Madrid-bound Freddy Rincon and classy defender Andres Escobar.

Fit-again skipper Escobar, (nickname 'El Caballero', The Gentleman) didn't feature in highly-fancied Colombia's qualifying campaign but certainly looked the part against us.

As Malky dictated to the Daily Telegraph: "Michael Hughes got little change out of the impressive Escobar, who played as if he had all the time in the world."

(As we know now, the 27-year-old's time on this earth was violently truncated; shot dead in Medellin, his home city, 10 days after scoring the own goal against USA in Pasadena which effectively ended Colombia's World Cup aspirations.)

Malky looked agitated as he wrapped up his dictation.

"Did somethin' happen at the very end there?" he shouted over.

Me: "Nah, it was handbags, Malky. Nothing to get excited about."

PITCH BRAWL ROCKS TOMMY
Attacks on NI goalkeeper mar Boston 'friendly'

By Jim Gracey in Boston

Northern Ireland keeper Tommy Wright told last night how he was punched and kicked by Colombia stars in an amazing pitch battle.
Wright also described how he was the victim of a sneak attack by Colombia's top player Carlos Valderrama during a last-minute brawl that marred a 2-0 Northern Ireland defeat at the Foxboro Stadium.
Fists and boots flew after debut boy Darren Patterson sent Colombian substitute Antony De Avila crashing into Wright's penalty area. A furious De Avila lashed out at Wright with his boot and then threw a punch.
An amazing free-for-all then developed, involving almost the entire Colombian team, with coaches and subs rushing from the bench to join in the fracas.

Okay, so I lied.

CHAPTER 32

To borrow the mandatory ending of all school trip reports ever written, it was a tired but happy group who boarded the bus.

The destination – Manhattan – might have had something to do with it. Much to their manager's discomfort, the players repeatedly sang "we're all going on a Hammy holiday", to the tune of Summer Holiday, throughout the four-hour, 200-mile journey down Interstate 95.

Earlier in the week I'd quoted Hammy, whom I described as a strict disciplinarian, thus: "This isn't a holiday. It's a serious tour, we're carrying the flag for our country..."

That theory was severely tested on the Liberty Island pleasure boat the next day, when Northern Ireland's merry men organised an impromptu dancing/safety-rail-sliding competition to the delight of some but obvious disdain of many others.

The budding hoofers later showed up at Kennedy's on West 57th – a hostelry owned by one of Malky's old friends, Gerry Toner, who treated them to further refreshments while regular patrons wished them luck for their forthcoming World Cup opener against Italy across the Hudson in Noo Joisey.

A few wondered why 'Coach Charlton' hadn't come along; after all, there was a huge poster of the big man alongside a framed monochrome photo of JFK supping Guinness in Kennedy's.

Ardoyne native Gerry introduced myself and Jim to revered actor Roscoe Lee Browne – a fascinating character whom I'd spend quality time with on my 'solo' return to Manhattan in July.

The multiple Emmy and Tony-winning thespian (and Kennedy's frequenter) appeared impressed by my ability to recall lines his distinctly rich, burr voice had uttered in 1972's The Cowboys – spoiler alert: John Wayne's character is killed off *long* before the end.

Many's an enjoyable hour this amateur film buff would pass in 72-year-old Roscoe's company; indeed, that first night in the Big Apple, I stayed on with him in Kennedy's while Jim and Jeekie opted to check out one of the city's legendary night clubs.

For a man with over 100 appearances on the silver and small screens (and probably best remembered on this side of the pond as acerbic butler Saunders in popular US comedy Soap), Roscoe wasn't fond of Hollywood, although he kept a property in LA.

"Broadway's the real litmus test in acting," he told me.

"From my unremarkable time in the studio system, Wayne was one of the biggest stars, but a dreadful actor, Eastwood and McQueen weren't too hot either... and Charlie Bronson? Heaven help us.

"But they had 'charisma' and 'screen presence', and that's what mattered. Bobby {De Niro} and Alfredo {Pacino} got the kudos, those other guys got the big bucks. It's the same story today with Arnie-fucking-Schwarz-whatever and Wee Tom."

Roscoe, son of a Baptist minister, told me he only drifted into serious acting in the 50s, when he was 35.

"Before that, my only conspicuous role was as a failed athlete, a deluded Jesse Owens wannabe..."

(Not true: I later found out that Roscoe, who died in 2007, aged 84, won an 880yd/800m race in 1:49.3 – the second fastest time in the world in 1951 and, back then, one of only 25 sub-1.50s recorded.)

He bristled at the word 'blaxploitation' – "40 years in this business, and I still don't know what the fuck that means; was the late Jimmy Cagney, a good pal of mine, a victim of 'Irish-ploitation' in the 40s? It's just bullshit media words.

"I was a New Jersey boy, and happiest when treading the boards across the river. I didn't *need* Tinseltown, so I could afford to turn down the 'token negro' roles. I wouldn't accept a part a decent white dude couldn't do equally well."

I retain fond memories of Roscoe, still enjoy seeing him pop up on screen from time to time. I'll quickly gloss over the night he invited me back to his apartment at closing time; the impulsive 'don't go there' look on the barman's face intimated that, unless I was on the same wavelength as the openly-gay *RLB*, this might not be such a good idea.

CHAPTER 33

Less than two hours after we'd booked into the majestic Eden Roc hotel on Collins Avenue, there was a major commotion in the pool area.

"Help, HELP! I can't swim, for God's sake help... I'm going to lose... I can't live without..." cried veteran Irish FA suit Joe McGorman.

It was George O'Boyle who bolted from his sun lounger and dashed to the rescue.

"Don't panic, Joe," the ripped ex-Linfield star bellowed, before plunging head-first into the deep end.

The rest of us held our collective breath as intrepid George, displaying scant regard for his own safety, did likewise. After what seemed an eternity, he resurfaced, to enthusiastic applause from staff and bathers alike, clutching Joe's false teeth.

"Man, I've seen it all now," said the pink-suited bell boy as a deeply indebted, fully clothed Joe shook George's hand and reunited the dentures with his bereft gums.

Later, in one of the Roc's myriad of restaurants, the hastily rechristened 'Jaws McGummin' would send his clam chowder back, complaining that it tasted of chlorine.

Miami was fun; considerably more relaxed than New York, where the service industry's argot mainly consisted of "shut the fuck up", "all right already" and "do you need change?" (i.e. "don't even *think* about dodging the tip, buster").

In Florida, the customer is king (or queen), hence: "Good morning sir, my name is Jennifer. It's my pleasure to be serving you today, sir. How may I help you, sir?"

All extremely ersatz, as epitomised by the foul-mouthed Cuban-born *Miamense* bartender who'd jar with us in Harpoon Mickey's after his shift at the palatial 600-room Roc (built in affluent mid-50s America) had finished.

"Fucking hate it, man," said Mateo.

"This nicey-nicey alter-ego shit, it eats your insides out, y'all know what I'm sayin'? Fuckers fired my buddy last week, know why? Cos one of his customer's glasses was empty.

"That's a no-no in South Beach, man. Didn't matter nuttin' to 'em that the poor bastard had been waitin' on 50 other dudes at the time. An' here's another thing; 'acknowledge' a customer within 30 seconds or you're out in the fucking street, man. Two more years of this shit'll do me, if it don't kill me first."

Jim: "Why don't you try New York? With your sparkling personality, it might be a better fit..."

Mateo was 20 years old and single. His former 'chica', a student at the University of Miami in nearly Coral Gables, claimed he was "suffocating" her and, from what he told us, the suffocation continued long after the split.

"Couldn't stop liftin' the fucking phone, know what I'm sayin? Like, I missed her an' stuff.

"Thought she might have a change of heart. In the end, bitch sent a polaroid of her blowing the new guy, with a note on the back sayin' 'NOW do you believe you're toast?'"

Terry: "Man, that really sucks. Sorry, wrong choice of words. So, did you stop calling after that?"

Mateo: "Yeah, but I mailed that fucking polaroid to her mom first..."

Harpoon Mickey's, located in the city's stunning Art Deco District (an architectural masterpiece of hotels, apartments and hostelries erected between the World Wars) became our shelter of choice from the unremitting, sweltering heat (37 degrees Celsius was the norm) during an all-too-brief stay in Florida's biggest city.

"It sure beats standing under a palm tree," said Jeekie.

The decking area outside Mickey's was a terrific vantage point for people-watching; the adjacent South Beach boardwalk, like its west coast cousin, Venice Beach, was a Mecca for some of the most beautiful/narcissistic people on earth; every hour thousands of them strutted, posed, thonged, budgie smuggled, jogged and roller-bladed their way towards, presumably, the nearest mirror. Look up their self-obsessed, pouting descendants on Facebook and Instagram.

How simple the world must be when there's only one person in it. You can't 'ghost' yourself.

Fashion impresario Gianni Versace strolled past one day, wearing a monogrammed bathrobe and slippers. He was with another man dressed in tennis gear.

"That's his 'boyfriend', Antonio", explained Mateo while doing the annoying 'finger quotes' thing.

Me: "His *boyfriend*? I thought he was seeing Naomi Campbell. That's what the papers back home are telling us."

Mateo: "Nah, unless Naomi has suddenly grown a dick; now wouldn't *that* be a story for your dumb Limey tabloids, know what I'm sayin?
"Check this out: Versace and Antonio live two blocks away in Casa Casuarina; eight bedrooms, 10 bathrooms, a bar and indoor pool – just the place for a faggot orgy after a hard night in Twist."
Jeekie: "What's *Twist?*"
Jim: "Miami's 'hottest gay club', apparently."
Mateo: "The porn stars love chilling out there after a hard day banging pneumatic chicks."
Me: "What, are you saying it's gay guys in those videos?"
Mateo: "God, you Irish guys are so fucking naïve. Yes, John, those big bad boys are faggots. You think a straight dude would last that long with two babes going down on him at once, know what I'm sayin?
"And what 'videos' {he did the finger quotes thing again} are you talking about? 'Naughty Nurses' on pay-per-view back at the hotel, perchance?"

Myself, Jim, Jeekie and Terry also 'acclimatised' by necking Tinima Cerveza Claras in nearby Larios, owned by Gloria Estefan. (We never got to meet the sultry Latino songstress, unfortunately, but hubby Emilio was a gregarious host.)
With Malky remaining *persona non grata* to me, and doing most of his socialising with Lemon in the east Belfast-born tycoon's Eden Roc penthouse suite, Gordon Hanna would occasionally join us.
The Lurgan Mafioso loved the supersized lager tins you get in Miami – "oil cans", he called them; we'd take bets on how long he could go without mentioning Glenavon.
(I often wondered if Gordon's sports editor at the Sunday People ever inquired why the Lurgan Blues monopolised the column inches while Linfield, Glentoran and next door neighbours Portadown won all the big trophies.)
We'd also 'adopted' young Chris Morgan, the lucky winner of a 'trip of a lifetime' with the Northern Ireland squad though a scratch card competition.
Chris was himself a promising young footballer, whom Hammy allowed to train with the boys – although with the searing heat, sapping humidity, perilous dehydration and frequent thunderstorms for company, it's debatable how much of a *treat* it was.

215

'The Lad Chris' turned 18 in Miami; it was decreed he should celebrate such a landmark date in the Playmates lap-dancing club.

Our handsome Irish birthday boy got plenty of attention from the scantily-clad ladies; my, how we laughed at his wee childish face as the sequined brassieres were whipped off and the gyrating began.

The joke, though, was on Gordon, who'd suggested this birthday present in the first place; poor, naive Chris actually thought the girls were 'dancing' for him because they liked him. The veteran hack's face turned slate grey when his 18-year-old *ingenu* presented him with a 200-dollar bill (with compliments from Candy and Babs).

Chris would go on to star with Crusaders, Linfield and Glentoran but this was a 'Morgan Day' the rest of us (with the possible exception of Gordon) could recall with affection.

Oh, and lest we forget, there was a match to look forward to on Saturday, June 11, at the Orange Bowl a few miles away in Little Havana.

The horseshoe-shaped college arena (Jeekie hated its vertigo-inducing, high-banked stands and unashamedly held an out-of-shot Terry's hand when reporting live from those eyries) was once home to the Miami Dolphins who, seven years earlier, moved to a fabulous new base, the Joe Robbie Stadium (narrowly beaten by the Rose Bowl in the race to host the World Cup final). Sadly, I never got to meet Dan Marino, my all-time favourite quarter-back.

Jack Charlton flew down from the Republic's base in Orlando, 250 miles away, for Northern Ireland's first meeting with Mexico since another pre-World Cup friendly at Windsor in 1966 (when Bertie Peacock's men beat them 4-1 with goals from Jimmy Nicholson, Alex Elder, Billy Ferguson and Billy Johnston).

The Miami Herald breathlessly revealed that this was the "first time in history" the "two Irelands" had occupied the same American state at the same time, to which Big Jack remarked: "So fucking what? It's not as if we're playing each other."

We *would* be meeting in a Euro 96 qualifier in November, but Jack was only interested in the Mexicans, the Republic's second Group E opponents.

"I thought the final score was cruel on you lads," Charlton told us after the 3-0 defeat in front of 8,500 roasted fans.

"Their first goal was a dubious pen that would have fucked me right off if

it had gone against us, and the second was an unlucky deflection."
Charlton was most exercised, however, at seeing the ref refuse water
bottles being thrown onto the pitch.

"It's a fucking crazy situation," he said.

"I saw some Irish lads feign injury just to get a drink. How do they expect
human beings to run for 90 minutes in 50 bloody acres of a concrete
oven? This game kicked off at 4pm – three and a half hours later than
ours – and the pitchside temperature was 102 degrees fahrenheit.

"Don't they know dehydration can kill? Tell you this: it won't happen to
us, no fucking way."

(Ironically, the Mexican dismissively credited with those two rather
fortuitous strikes against Hammy's men – Atletico Madrid striker Luis
Garcia – would rifle two screamers past Packie Bonner in Orlando's Citrus
Bowl 13 days later.)

There was a tinge of sadness after the Miami game, but not because of
the result; our boys, who sweated like onions in a pan that day, played a
lot better in the Orange Bowl furnace than they did in the significantly
milder Foxboro, and keeper Alan Fettis – who'd rearranged his
honeymoon to make the trip – proved himself an able deputy to Big
Tommy.

No, the thought of boarding a transatlantic plane the next morning was
distinctly unappealing – not that it bothered me, who'd be staying on in
the US with Malky, Jim, Jeekie, Terry and several others, including
Hammy (signed up by UTV).

And with the last friendly falling on a Saturday, I wouldn't have to write
anything for another 24 hours. Time to get wasted, methinks.

CHAPTER 34

No one is perfect, that's why pencils have erasers.
(Wolfgang Riebe)

It's close to 1am in the lobby bar. Malky hadn't had enough Johnnie Walker but he'd unquestionably had enough of me blanking him.

He'd spent most of the evening sitting with David Chick – his presumed partner-in-crime with the Cas story. One or two players were there too; Hammy guessed that most would have decamped for daiquiris at Wet Willie's – having rumbled Magilton and Co on an unauthorised recce earlier in the week.

At the bar, the bulbous, pontifical Lemon was holding court, and reminiscing about the previous night's 'Mrs Florida' competition (you had to be married and over 30) in the hotel ballroom.

Lemon: "You know, I had to fight off a couple of contestants after you guys left."

Jim: "Fuck me, if the Honey Monster can charm women here, there's hope for us all."

Jeekie: "Come on Jim, that's a bit harsh. If it's any consolation, Noel, I don't think you look like the Honey Monster."

Lemon: "It's okay, Jackie, honey monsters have a thick skin."

Jeekie: "Jim, tell Noel why you think America is a third world country."

Lemon: "Really, Jim? Now *this* I gotta hear."

Jim: "I've already written about it in my World Cup diary: 'America would be fine if it wasn't for Americans'. They're the thickest people on the planet."

Lemon: "Now I *know* you're talking bullshit."

Jim: "Am I? What about that idiot in Providence, after we told him Bestie was our greatest player: 'Gee, I can't wait to see HIM playing in the World Cup...'"?

Terry: "That's not a good example, Jim. I mean, someone back home might say the same thing about Joe DiMaggio."

Jim: "Okay then, what about your 'federal laws'? They'll turf you in jail here for smoking in 'the elevator' and you can't even bet on sports..."

Jeekie: "Did he just say *sports*?"

Me: "I believe he did."

Jim: "No I didn't. I said *sport*."

Terry: "I'm pretty sure you said *sports*."

Lemon: "So am I. Maybe Jim's a bigger fan of 'third world' America than he lets on."

Jim: "Not while your big arse points downwards. Christ, if they let 'Mr H. Monster' through immigration, what hope is there?"

Jeekie: "Children, please."

Jim: "As I was saying, you can't smoke in an elevator or bet on *sport* here, but you can waltz around with an Uzi machine gun if you've got a permit – and any dickhead can get one."

Lemon: "That's a wild exaggeration, Jim."

Jim: "You think? What about that mogadon robot at reception, after I'd got locked out of my room and asked for a replacement key? 'Sorry, Sir, can't do that'. And why not? 'Because you don't have ID to prove it's your room, sir'. And I'm going: 'that's because the fucking ID is *in* my room'. And he goes: 'So there's no way you can prove you're a guest here?' And I say: "Well actually, I can: it was YOU who checked me in, you fucking twat.' And then you get: "There's no need for that language, sir'. Under federal law number 2,5 fucking 8..."

Malky joined us.

"Right, who's for a dram here? Schemer, wee vod and coke?"

Me: "No, I'm all right."

It was one embittered snub too many.

Malky: "Look John, Ah dinnae know why ye're actin' like this, but it has tae stop, right now, pronto."

Me: "Does it? And *why* would I be acting like this?"

Malky: "Ah dunno. Maybe it's somethin' tae do wi' that Cassidy story."

Me: "Mmm, so you DO know. How come you haven't been shooting the breeze to everyone about your latest great exclusive? I'll tell you why; because you know it was a fucking stitch-up. You knew rightly, when we were in the gay bar that day, that you'd be going back to write it up. At first I couldn't understand why you were so loathe to come out that night, but now I know."

Malky: "Och, come on, John. At the end o' the day ye're just huffin' cos ye got hit with a corker of an exclusive. It happens us all. Get over it."

Me: "Don't you fucking patronise me, you treacherous wee shit. You've fucked me over for the last time with your slippy-tit ways."

Jeekie: "Come on, John, let it go. You've made your point."

Me: "No, I fucking haven't. This man's hitting seventy, and still that mammoth ego needs its own zip code."

Terry: "Did he just say *zip code?*"

219

Me: "Not now, Terry. First the Kelly Show, then Bremen and Wembley, now this.

"You have to be the great fucking beJesus every time, don't you, Malky? What's this, your *11*th World Cup? You've had your day; can I not get to cover *one* fucking tournament in my life without getting shat upon?

"I'll tell you this for nothing: as soon as the Republic go out, we're finished. You go wherever the fuck you want, I don't want to be anywhere near you."

Bartender: "Guys, you really need to watch your language."

Jim: "And YOU really need to shut the fuck up."

Even the bartender laughed at that. It helped emolliate the noxious atmosphere, and I finally *did* shut the fuck up.

I was way out of line and, boy, did I know it. This bilious, spiteful rant didn't feel anywhere near as cathartic as I'd imagined. Jeekie was right in attempting to curtail it; enough already, as the Americans say.

I glanced across; Malky's eyes had gone all misty. It could have been the copious whisky he'd consumed but my former boss, for once, looked genuinely lachrymose, like he was about to burst into tears.

Next: "John, John, Ah canna cope wi' any more o' this rancour. If it means anythin' tae ye, I'm really sorry ye took this thing so badly. This isnae what we're aboot and it wasnae ma intention. Ah should have said somethin', Ah know that now. The cut an' thrust o' journalism's one thing, but true friendship's another – an' Ah dinnae wanna lose that. Let me tell ye this, John, absolutely straight: and the end o' the day, ye've been like a father tae me..."

Me: "*Father*? Don't you mean *son*?"

Malky: "Aye, that's right. Sorry, sorry; what Ah meant was: Ah've been like a son tae ye..."

Jeekie – pre-roll-around-the-floor – "I, um... I think John now knows what you mean, Malky."

I made a forlorn attempt not to join in with the concerted guffaws but the *tristesse* that had engulfed us since Providence was finally over, and we all knew it.

"Fuck it. Come here, *Daddy*..."

Malky and myself embraced, for the first and only time in our lives. Although we didn't know it then, it would be the last time we'd ever exchange harsh words. Spontaneous applause erupted from the audience.

Bartender: "Why all the clapping; is this, like, a father-son reunion kinda

thing?"
Terry: "Yeah, something like that."

CHAPTER 35

Seventy-five pellets of mescaline
Five sheets of high powered blotter acid
A salt shaker half full of cocaine
A whole galaxy of multi-coloured uppers, downers
Screamers, laughers
Also a quart of tequila, quart of rum
Case of beer, pint of raw ether and two dozen amyls
... not that we need it at all for the trip...
(Hunter S Thompson, Fear and Loathing in Las Vegas)

Malky looked horrified as the Lincoln Town Car veered off the Florida
Turnpike into a large parking lot.
"What in the name of God is *this*?"
"*This*," said Jim, "is what you call McDonald's."
"Ah know *what* it is, Ah'm just wonderin' what we're doin' here."
"We're here because it's lunchtime and I, for one, am starving."
Three months shy of his 68th birthday, Malcolm entered a McDonald's for
the first time in his life.
"Do they do steak here?"
"Burgers, Malky. You look like a Big Mac kinda guy to me."
After 120 miles at a steady 55mph on the world's most boring road –
nothing but white concrete and unbroken lines of cypress trees – we
desperately needed a halfway house comfort break.
There's only so far you can go on coffee, mineral water, Lay's potato
chips and M&Ms; not exactly the necessities of a Hunter S Thompson-
style road trip, but it was far too early for mood-altering substances –
which, in our case, would be Johnnie Walker Black, Woodchuck Cider and
Coors Light.
Press Association photographer Martin McCullough had kindly offered to
ferry us between Miami and Orlando – some 250 miles – in his hired car.
The least we could do was buy him lunch; Mickey D's was his choice.
This was June 12, 1994 – Turncoat Day – when we shamefully switched
allegiance from Northern Ireland in southern Florida to the Republic
further north; geographically ironic, I know.
Jeekie, Terry, Mark Robson and Hammy would fly up the following day
but the Royal Avenue trio, as well as saving on travel costs, were anxious
to get up to speed with how Big Jack and Co were preparing for a second

222

successive 'Group of Death'.

Our chauffeur – he of short, dark curly hair and mad staring eyes – was unintentionally hilarious during the long journey; he told us his then girlfriend was the "fifth best looking woman in Northern Ireland" – and wondered why she wasn't flattered. "I thought she'd be delighted..."

(A year later, Martin was nearly shot dead by Secret Service agents while abseiling down the Europa in a botched attempt to photograph President and Hillary Clinton's bedroom.)

"Why are the Republic based here and not in New York?" he asked Malky, who'd been restored as my bezzie after the regrettable Miami outburst and seemed delighted at Martin directing the question at him.

"Because, Martin, it's a wee bit cooler in New York and they wouldnae get properly acclimatised for the Mexico game; it would be too much of a shock comin' doon tae this kinda heat for a one-off game."

Martin: "And tell me, Jim: how come the New York Giants' stadium is in New Jersey and not New York?"

Jim: "Oh, I don't know. Why is Old Trafford not in Manchester?"

Martin: "What are you talking about? It was in Manchester the last time I looked."

Jim: "Will you guys tell him, or shall I?"

The first person we met after checking into the Holiday Inn at Altamonte Springs, about 10 miles north of Orlando city centre (and a couple of hundred yards from the Hilton, where the Republic were based) was my old friend from Ballymena, Tony McCall, whom I was meeting for the first time since his (1992) wedding in the breathtaking resort of Point Clear, Alabama.

A more than useful contact; Tony, then head soccer coach at Stetson University in DeLand, some 40 miles away, had been appointed FIFA liaison officer for the Republic in Florida, responsible for the squad's travel and training arrangements.

"Big Jack's been in stinking form since we arrived," confided Tony as we settled down for a cold one in the hotel's Why Not Lounge.

"First of all, a lot of the players didn't like being in single rooms and we had to switch things around so they could share. It took ages.

"Some of the lads were already giving Jack grief about why him, Setters and the other FAI bigwigs were in first class on the flight over, while the rest of them were in steerage. Keano, in particular, didn't look too happy about that.

"Then it bucketed down for the first three days {at the superb Seminole County Training Centre, 12 miles away} and Jack, who'd been told it would be too hot even for sunbathing, was doing his nut in about that. All the lads had factor 40 sun cream on, when what they really needed was umbrellas.

"Jack let rip at me when I ordered everyone off the pitch on the third day because a thunderstorm was coming; 'what sort of fucking place is this?' he said – like I was the poor schmuck responsible for the weather. {More rain fell in the Orlando area that day than was forecast for the whole of June.}

"I'd called right, though; we were drenched before we made it to the bus and Jack later apologised. Said he'd make sure I got tickets for the Mexico match. Anyway, he's turned on the press guys now. The Sun printed that there was a serial killer stalking the Irish camp."

Malky: "Robert Reid will have got the blame for that. But Ah'll bet that wasnae the way he wrote it. Tabloid subs will ruin yer life."

Tony: "Jack eventually made a joke about it; something like 'I hope that fucking serial killer gets you first.' But there was another headline on Wednesday: 'Booze on lads, says Jack'. I honestly thought he was going to deck your man Reid for that one."

(At the Tuesday press conference, Charlton had said: "We're not here to prepare like monks. We'll go out and have a pint or two. I did that when I was a player, and it didn't do me any harm...")

Jim: "Wow. We've missed all the fun."

Tony: "I haven't *finished* yet! Jack was raging again today, after he heard the tabloids were going to report that a bust-up between Keano and Setters had taken place while he was away with you guys in Miami.

"He had the pair of them swearing it was all bollocks – but I was there at Seminole yesterday, and it nearly *did* come to fisticuffs.

"Keano got mouthy and told Setters he was pushing everyone too hard, Setters told him where to get off; it got nasty. And everyone knows that, so I don't understand why Jack's threatening to pull the plug on press conferences. He's already banned Sky Sports."

Malky: "Why's that?"

Tony: "Because they wouldn't pay him. Everyone else is: BBC, RTE, ITV. But even *they* got it in the neck for filming him ranting when he thought the cameras had been switched off."

Jim: "Christ, has *nothing* made him happy here?"

Tony: "Oh aye. The Hilton people put a keg of Guinness in his suite; he said it's the best he's ever tasted. And he likes the food too; apparently him, Setters and the other coaches are hitting the Kobe tonight."

Me: "So are we! And the photographers are going too; this should be interesting."

Malky, a culinary traditionalist, was dubious about dining in a Japanese restaurant but Martin assured him it would be better than McDonald's. And he'd take us there in the Lincoln.

He drove down South Westmonte Drive until he reached Wymore Road ("it's important to avoid Interstate 4"), then took a left at the intersection and travelled on for about a mile down East Altamonte Drive. "And this is us," he said, pointing up at the big Kobe neon sign. The journey took around 14 minutes.

(There's a reason I'm being so specific; the following day, while looking for an ATM, I passed the Kobe restaurant – two blocks, or a mere 200 yards, from our hotel. Two minutes' walk if you turn left, Martin; 14 minutes' drive if you turn right. "That fella couldnae find his own arse wi' both hands," said Malky.)

Martin and his pals had a table reserved. We hadn't told him Jack and Co would be there (with the chef cooking meals in front of them while flames lit up their happy faces).

We thought it would be a pleasant surprise, a priceless photo op.

Thing is, the photographers in their wisdom had decreed that, just for once, this would be a camera-free excursion. Oops.

Malky stared over at the grinning Charlton with ill-disguised contempt. "What dae ye think o' yer man Jack over there?" he asked.

Then, not waiting for a reply: "Ah think he's a hobo. Bobby has a bit o' class, but he hasnae any."

(He wasn't saying that four years later in Paris when Sir Bobby, after bumping into Malky, responded to "Bout ye, Bobby?" with "I'm fine, *Jimmy;* how are you?").

Two hours later, Charlton and Setters strode over to our table.

"It's good to see you, Malcolm... and Jim, John; I'm never sure which one's which," said Jack, adding: "Can I get you lads one for the road?"

As he started moving towards the door shortly afterwards, Malky grabbed Jack's hand, got down on one knee, gazed up lovingly at the World Cup winner and gushed: "Jack, Ah'll tell ye this, right now, absolutely straight; what ye've done for Irish football can never, EVER, be reciprocated. Ye are a first-class gentleman and one of the game's everlasting heroes."

Jim, a minute later: "Well Malky, you certainly didn't miss *him* and hit the wall… nightcap back at the Why Not, anyone?"

Next day, I ventured into the neighbourhood with a London TV news crew, fronted by a mouthy female reporter called Debi – at 2am in the Why Not, this excursion seemed like a brilliant idea. Why not, indeed. Their mission was to gauge Americans' interest in the Greatest Show on Earth. The plan: a vox-pop whereby Orlandoans would be asked if they knew who Maradona was.

Later in the Why Not, Debi showed me the finished edit on her video camera: supposedly thick Yanks answering with variations of "She's a pop star from New York".

Hilarious – except, in most cases, the contributors were actually asked: "Do you know who *Madonna* is?" The leading – or, rather *mis*leading – question was then edited out; ta-da! Orlando, 1994… the genesis of fake news.

Also that night: socialising with injured Republic striker/Indo guest columnist and RTE analyst Niall Quinn (who trained with the squad, although not officially involved) and Brendan O'Carroll, the self-appointed court jester of the Republic's travelling party and future 'Mrs Brown'. You can guess who was the funnier of the two; Quinny, you're in the wrong job.

CHAPTER 36

Myself, Jim and Malky – who'd be filing a daily 'World Cup Diary' for the Tele – got a taxi to the Citrus Bowl media centre in West Lakes, the collection point for our official FIFA accreditation.

Although it was only 10 miles from the hotel, Charlton and his colleagues showed no interest in visiting the massive college football arena; the Giants Stadium, 1,000 miles further north, was clearly the only venue on their radar.

East Rutherford, New Jersey, wouldn't be as hot as Orlando – mere sunstroke as opposed to certain death – but the mid-summer heat would still be oppressive – and Jack was still banging on about getting water to the players.

That's not true: he'd stopped banging on about it – until Jeekie and Terry, who'd just arrived in central Florida and who'd missed the earlier, 'waterlogged' press conferences, brought it up again to collective groans.

Later that day, Fifa president Sepp Blatter cooled Charlton's jets somewhat by conceding that the ref in Miami had made a mistake by denying the players rehydration. And if you can't trust a man of integrity like him, who *can* you trust?

"Ah'm surprised nae one's been callin' this Water-Gate," quipped Malky.

"You should keep that for your 'State of the Union address," said Jim.

(Every year at the NI Football Writers dinner, President Malky delivered a showstopping speech.)

Though empty and locked up (except for the media centre), there were fans milling around the Citrus Bowl when we arrived. The revolutionary new 'crowd misting tents', where beer-bellied diehards got sprayed with a fine film of ice-cold water, were proving very popular.

We had to laugh as a partially sighted young lady (one of the 1,100 volunteers helping the city's organising committee) showed us to our 'work stations' – obviously *she* wasn't the object of the mirth, rather her guide dog, who had his own accreditation badge, complete with picture and paw mark.

"Just in case some other guide dog tries to sneak in," said Jim.

Malky didn't fancy walking – or, rather, scampering from one air-conditioned oasis to another – and instead got a taxi back to the hotel, while we 'soaked up the atmosphere' downtown.

Unlike Miami, Orlando was buzzing with pre-World Cup fever and festooned with USA 94 – and corporate – bunting and logos. Even the

City Hall roof sported a 40-foot-high 'soccer' ball – Adidas-branded, of course.

The sweltering home of Disney World and Universal Studios was like a huge melting pot – almost literally – as thousands of early-arrival Belgian, Irish, Dutch, Moroccan and Mexican fans mingled.

It was clear they'd opted to base themselves in the Sunshine State's 'capital of entertainment' and commute north when necessary.

Orlando had beaten Floridian rivals Miami and Tampa in the race to become one of the nine USA 94 host cities. Five matches would be held there: Belgium v Morocco on Sunday, June 19, Mexico v the Republic five days later, Belgium v Netherlands the day after the Mexico-Republic game and Morocco v Netherlands on June 29 – all with 12.30pm kick-offs, to accommodate European television schedules and avoid central Florida's notorious and highly dangerous, mid-afternoon, 20-minute thunderstorms.

Sub-tropical Orlando – or 'Irelando', as it would eventually become – would also host a Round of 16 game (even earlier, 12 noon) between a Group E (Republic's group), and Group F (Netherlands, etc) qualifier on Independence Day.

The tricolour-draped watering holes on International Drive and Orange Blossom Trail were heaving, but most of the organised entertainment was to be found in the city's iconic Church Street Station area (featuring the gargantuan Mulvaney's Irish Pub), which Jim and myself were planning to investigate until we realised there was a cover charge just to get into the street.

"I'm not paying ten bucks to walk down a street," said the indignant Jim, adding: "What if you just want to get to the other end?"

The money collector suggested we take a hike down the parallel Jackson Street, which didn't command 'a toll charge'.

That was where we bumped into Mr Keane and his pugilistic, lobster-legged pal.

Had the £3.75m British record signing overdone it, just days before the biggest match of his life?

I honestly don't know. In those days the volatile 22-year-old, who was nursing a worrying hamstring strain, had quite a reputation for tying one on – and remember, Charlton allowed his players to have a few beers and mix with fans, as long as they didn't take the piss.

Speaking of which... maybe he was just dehydrated; it was, after all, a scorcher. But why did that guy get so aggressive after we'd offered to escort Keano back to the hotel?

228

(Ultimately, none of it mattered; Keano and McGrath, another man with inner demons and alcohol issues, were the best players on the pitch during the Italy game.)

Our friendly smokeys, meanwhile, chatted away as the squad car sped up the I-4 towards Altamonte.

"The Orange County Sheriff's Department and Orlando PD got an extra 700 large to cope with soccer fans over the next three weeks," said one.

Jim: "What did you spend it on?"

Cop 1: "Riot gear and bomb disposal equipment. It was recommended after we heard the Irish and Dutch were coming."

Cop 2: "We've been told to adopt a softly, softly approach – as you've already seen – but to be wary of potential hooliganism and terrorism."

Jim: "I think your barmy bosses have just wasted '700 large'. This is one place where orange and green DO get along."

Cop 2: "*Orange and green*? Sorry, I don't understand what that means."

The Orlando PD squad car let off another whoop, whoop as our law enforcement friends pulled away from the front of the Holiday Inn.

As we approached reception to retrieve our keys, we noticed that our luggage – indeed, all our belongings – had been dumped in the foyer.

CHAPTER 37

Jim: "What the fuck?"

Me: "What the fuck?"

Receptionist: "Sorry, gentlemen, but your rooms have been reassigned to other customers."

Jim: "*Reassigned*? Why?"

Receptionist: "You'll need to speak to the manager. I'll call him."

Manager: "I'm afraid you two gentlemen, and Mr Brodie, are no longer welcome at this time. You have been evicted from the hotel. Please take your bags and leave."

Jim: "This is a joke, right? {To me: "I'll bet Jeekie and Smyth are behind this"}. Okay, the fun's over, now I need to take a shower."

Manager: "There's no joke, sir. According to our security staff, on two consecutive nights, you gentlemen refused to hand over your intoxicating liquor at the specified time."

Me: "What exactly does that mean, in plain English?"

Manager: "It means, sir, that you kept consuming intoxicating liquor in the bar after 2am, even when requested to give up your glasses."

Jim: "Now, you listen to me. Your bartender served us drinks – large beers – two minutes before 2am. Surely you don't expect us to down them in two minutes? Where we come from, customers are given a reasonable amount of time to drink up."

Manager: "And where I come from, it's the law that you hand over your intoxicating liquor at 2am, no matter when you paid for it or how much is left. We let it go with a warning on the first occasion, but then you repeated the offence last night. Therefore, you are no longer guests of this hotel. Good day, gentlemen."

Me: "Fuck me, we're homeless! And where's Malky?"

Receptionist: "If you're referring to Mr Brodie, sir, he has already gone."

Me: "*Gone*? Gone where?"

Receptionist (lowering her voice): "To the Hilton. My friend Cindy works there; rooms are available if you want them."

Me: "I thought the Hilton was out of bounds to everyone but the Irish team."

Receptionist: "No, just the top floor. They've been told not to accept new bookings while the team's there, but Cindy will look after you. Look, I'm sorry about what's happened; my boss is a bit of poker-ass about these things."

Me: "Don't worry about it, and thanks for looking after us."

230

A minute later: "Jim, can you believe this? We're thrown out of one hotel – and get rooms in the team's HQ. Result!"

Jim: "I know, I'm actually too shocked to be pissed off anymore. Christ, they'll not believe it back home when we tell them Malcolm Brodie – *FIFA press liaison officer* – was chucked out of his hotel. Maybe we should call our new Orlando PD pals and get them to help with the luggage..."

CHAPTER 38

The Hilton, on Northlake Boulevard – "conveniently located midway between Disney World and Daytona Beach", it said on the brochure – was a tangible upgrade on the place we'd just been turfed out of.

We'd already been to it a couple of times, to blag a quick word with Jack. And, to the delight of those who needed to watch the pennies, nickels, dimes and quarters, we soon discovered that the Hilton put on a free complementary buffet every lunchtime.

Despite its size – over 300 guest rooms – it had only one bar, which suited the Republic's manager ("it's easier to keep tabs on folk") but its corporate blandness didn't impress Malky.

"Ah'm gonna miss the Why Not Lounge; Ah was startin' tae feel right at hame there," he said.

I replied: "You'll not miss it, Malky; we're going back there tonight."

Malky: "Whaaa?"

Jim: "Did you not see the big sign – 'Non-residents welcome' – outside? Well, we're now non-residents, so it's 'welcome y'all' from here on in..."

Malky: "Ha-ha-ha-HA! Brilliant."

Our short move across the multi-laned I-4 coincided with the arrival of the 'British' press – and that didn't improve taciturn Charlton's mood.

As an Englishman with his World Cup pedigree, in charge of the only 'British Isles' team in the tournament, he knew this day would come.

At least, on this trip, we were spared the supposed 'impartial' UK broadcasters referring to England as "we" and "us", and the faux tabloid outrage at those arrogant Germans pre-booking a hotel for the final. Newsflash: they all to it, including England. What did you expect a football association to do; scramble for vacancies in Bates Motel after winning the semi?

(Incidentally, Jack wasn't the only Anglo boss at USA '94; some bloke called Roy Hodgson – who, as a player, reached the dizzying heights of non-league Gravesend & Northfleet – was manager of Switzerland.)

Jack was also pissed (they don't augment it with 'off' in the US, prompting awkward ambiguity) that the flight to Newark on Thursday, June 16, had been arranged for early morning – even though it was a charter that could have left Orlando virtually any time.

And he was raging with Keano after hearing the irreplaceable midfielder had been nursing "a bit of a groin strain" for two days but hadn't bothered telling anyone.

"No more training for him here," said Charlton who, by this time, had forsaken his trademark duncher for an oversized, all white baseball cap – not a good look.

Us: "But he'll play against Italy?"

Charlton: "Dunno; sure I'm only finding out about this meself."

The night we settled in to our plush rooms – Tuesday, June 14 – the Charlie Stuart of the Irish Press, a self-proclaimed Charlton confidant (and occasional contributor to the Tele and Sunday Life) asked myself and Jim to meet him for breakfast the next day.

"As a thank-you to you guys, who are forever greasing my palm with silver, I've got an exclusive for you," says he.

Jim: "Can you tell us now? We don't usually bother with breakfast."

Charlie: "Yes, indeed; the lure of the Why Not Lounge. Nah, I'll get it confirmed later and yous can do what you want with it tomorrow."

Next day, 7.15am... Bleary-eyed, we sat down with a shifty, furtive looking Charlie. What could the big exclusive be; Keano out of the tournament? Charlton resigning after the World Cup? Had Lord Lucan – or, even better, Charles Lindbergh Jnr – been found alive and well and working in a pub on Church Street?

Charlie's eyes darted left and right, one more time, and then he came out with it: "The referee for Saturday's match is a Dutchman."

Jim looked fit to be tied.

"Are you taking the piss?"

Charlie (clearly taken aback): "No, Jim, it's true. I've even got his name – Mario van der Ende."

Me: "Sorry, Charlie, but I'm not getting what the actual story is."

Charlie: "He's Dutch, and we could end up playing the Dutch in the Round of 16, here in Orlando."

Me: "So what you're suggesting – not that we could print it anyway – is that he might want to favour the Irish over the Italians, thus giving the Dutch an easier path to the quarter-finals. Is that it?"

Jim: "I tell you what, Charlie – next time you come up with a ball-breaker of an exclusive like that, do us all a favour and keep it to yourself. I'd go back to bed now, but I'd never get to sleep after all this excitement."

The British posse's arrival meant a welcome reunion for Malky and Jim with Brian Madley, whom they'd spent quality time with at the last World Cup.

It was clear that the Sunday People veteran, who died in 2009 aged 72, was a man who instantly endeared himself to others.

Like your man Norm from the sitcom Cheers, gregarious Brian sat on the same bar stool every day – and, seemingly, *all* day – chatting to all and sundry.

"It was the same in Italy," said Malky.

"Ah never saw him leave the bar, yet he still managed tae get a world exclusive interview wi' Schillaci's mum in the hills above Palermo..."

With Welsh native Brian clamped to that stool, he'd alert us when 'guest stars' wandered in.

Former world 5,000m champion (and future Fine Gael senator) Eamonn Coghlan rocked up one day, as did Olympic gold medal boxer Michael Carruth, 'singer' Daniel McDonnell, England striker Teddy Sheringham (former Millwall team-mate and pal of Tony Cascarino), who was holidaying with girlfriend Nicola Smith (older sister of 'wild child' Mandy who, in 1989, famously married 52-year-old Rolling Stone Bill Wyman when she was just 18), also paid us a visit.

Even the deposed, disgraced Bishop of Galway Eamonn Casey – he of the Thornbirds-style 'love child scandal' which broke two years earlier – sauntered in to collect his match ticket.

We grabbed a few quotes with the three sports personalities, but what could you ask a defrocked bishop: "So, Your Excellency, are you here for the 'soccer' or to visit {your American ex-lover} Annie Murphy and illegitimate son Peter?"

The Hilton, we'd learn, was very relaxed about visitors – compared with the Secret Service-wannabe security staff at the Seminole training pitch, who prevented us from talking to players we'd shared a breakfast room with an hour earlier.

Ray 'Rayzor' Houghton, despite being under pressure to keep his starting place ahead of young pretender Jason McAteer, was courteous, articulate and friendly; it was no surprise he became a media pundit.

Cascarino taking the same path was a shock, though; the Kent-born English-mangling Cockney came across as barely able to string a sentence together: "We was good against the Germans last mumph, wasn't we?"

To be fair, though, 'Cas' has improved his diction beyond measure and developed into one of the shrewdest pundits in the game.

The night before we left for New Jersey, Houghton, Steve Staunton (Jim Magilton's one-time brother-in-law; they married two sisters) and Ronnie Whelan grabbed a taxi to the nearest cinema to see the latest blockbuster, Four Weddings and a Funeral.

Due to the large crowd – and because no one had a clue who they were – they didn't get in, and had to watch the dire Police Academy 7 instead.

"At least it was all about taking down dodgy Italians," said Houghton afterwards.

CHAPTER 39

So after school, I take a dip in the pool, which is really on the wall
I got a colour TV, so I can see, the Knicks play basketball
(The Sugarhill Gang, Rapper's Delight)

We were halfway through the evening meal when *it* happened.
There'd already been plenty to discuss at our reserved table in Kennedy's.

What a mad day June 17, 1994 was. First up, over a million New Yorkers lining Broadway to see the Rangers ice-hockey team parade the Stanley Cup for the first time in 54 years.

Newly-elected mayor Rudi Giuliani had lifted the 'ticker tape' ban for the city's first 'team parade' since the Mets won the 1986 World Series, leading to the awesome mid-morning spectacle of shredded paper blizzards cascading down from the Manhattan skyscrapers; surely as close to the iconic VE Day scenes someone my age is ever likely to get.

After lunch, we nipped into Rosie O'Grady's on 7th Avenue – a shameless tourist trap, admittedly, but boasting huge TV screens – to see defending champions Germany beat Bolivia in Chicago's Soldier Field stadium, courtesy of Jurgen Klinsmann's goal (a mere tap-in, but President Clinton, sitting alongside Chancellor Kohl, clapped raucously).

We'd arrived hoping to see America's unofficial queen, Oprah Winfrey, emcee the opening ceremony – but the major US networks had opted against showing it live. Even sports behemoth ESPN shunned it, preferring round two of the US Open golf; national treasure Arnold Palmer's swansong.

Only later, in news bulletins, would we see Motown superstar Diana Ross ruin the denouement of 'The Greatest Show on Earth' curtain-raiser by missing a meticulously choreographed penalty; should have seen *that* as an omen.

Oh, and local property tycoon Donald Trump announced that he wanted to buy the Empire State Building.

The Germany-Bolivia game, which kicked off at 3pm Eastern Time (and which Malky showed no interest in), was eminently forgettable; so much for FIFA's new 'three points for a win' rule generating attack-minded football.

This was also the first World Cup to feature the revised back-pass regulation, which had been introduced after the time-wasting, ultra-defensive tactics of Italia '90.

The American 'soccer' commentary was unintentionally hilarious but ultimately excruciating; apart from the ironic plugging of official sponsors ("This game is brought to you, commercial free, by Snickers; Snickers *really* satisfies!"), corner-kick and free-kick takers were 'trigger men', central midfielders 'ideas men', sweepers 'quarterbacks'; Klinsmann's goal made it 'one-zip', a tackle was a 'clean steal', a decent pass an 'excellent downfield feed'; one Bolivian player came close to being 'ejected' while others made timely 'rejections' (clearances).

The 'FIFA World Cup' opener was well down the schedules.

Ahead of it was the breaking news that American football legend-cum-movie star OJ 'The Juice' Simpson – now the chief suspect following the gruesome murders of his wife Nicole and her friend Ron Goldman (their funerals were held the previous day) – had failed to surrender himself to the LAPD at the appointed time – 2pm Eastern, 11am Pacific.

After that, the breathless anchor cued in the Rangers' parade through the 'Canyon of Heroes' – juxtaposed with the Vancouver riots which followed the Canucks' Stanley Cup defeat.

This being NYC, there was a preview of the (World) Gay Games which were about to get under way across the East River in Queens (!), and of course mounting excitement about that night's potentially pivotal Knicks v Houston Rockets showdown (NBA Finals, Game 5; the teams were tied at two wins each) at Madison Square Garden, just half a mile from where we were supping.

Victory would bring the Knicks to within one win of a first title in 21 years. A brief mention too of our *raison d'etre*; the Ireland v Italy game, described by one mouthy Yank commentator as "The Big Apple's Catholic immigrants showdown"– although, with half the city's ten million population being of either Irish or Italian descent, he sort-of had a point. As you'd expect, Midtown traffic was bedlam as we emerged from Rosie's.

To Malky's disdain, Terry suggested we walk to Kennedy's and make the most of the balmy June evening.

"It's less than 20 minutes away; straight up Seventh, then across a couple of blocks. We'll be there in no time," said Terry.

Jim: "*Now* who's starting to talk like an American?"

Terry: "Maybe we'll bump into Big Jack on the way." (Charlton and his wife Pat were guests of honour at a glitzy do for well-heeled Irish-

Americans in Central Park's Tavern on the Green, a few hundred yards from Kennedy's.)

Malky: "Why, is Jack walkin' through Manhattan too?"

We didn't meet Jack, but did come across Irish fans, many of whom were wearing Dublin and Kerry jerseys and gearing up for a June 18 double header, the Leinster Senior Championship quarter-final at Croke Park followed by...

Jeekie (after we'd settled in Kennedy's): "Charlton has looked a lot more relaxed since we got to New Jersey {yesterday morning}."

Jim: "He says he loves the hotel." (The 380-room, castle-themed Sheraton Tara in Parsippany, 31 miles from Manhattan, 22 from the stadium and, to Malky's delight, only half an hour from Hoboken – "where Sinatra was born").

Me: "He *did* love the hotel – until the receptionist started putting punters' calls through to his room."

Malky: "Did ye hear aboot this, Jeekie? She thought 'Mr Charlton' was just a normal guest: every time a fan rang up tae wish Jack all the best for tomorrow, she put 'em straight through, even in the middle o' the night."

Jim: "I thought it was hilarious when Jack led about 50 of us down that big wide corridor like the Pied Piper – when he stopped to talk to someone, everyone else stopped. They were all shit-scared of walking in front of him and getting a mouthful."

Terry: "Were you not surprised, though, when he checked in yesterday, grabbed his room key and just buggered off for the day?"

Malky: "Christ, dae ye no think the man deserves a wee break after what he's gone through already?"

Jim: "Wow, *you've* changed your tune since that love-in at the Kobe. I forgot to ask: how'd you two get on in the hotel jacuzzi?"

Malky: "Hilarious, Jim! Ye know full well Ah didnae get anywhere near it."

Jeekie: "To be fair, Malky, how were you to know that Keano had it booked it exclusively for the whole time?"

Malky: "Ah'll tell ye this, Jeekie; Ah'll be surprised if a jacuzzi clears up a groin strain. We'll soon see if it worked."

Me: "The Dublin lads were saying he'll be fine and, with Babb getting the nod ahead of Kernaghan, this will be the first time the Republic have had three black players in defence; changed times indeed."

Jeekie: "Yes, and all three have African dads and Irish mothers."

Me: "Although McGrath's the only one who's never met his dad."

Jim: "A punter in Rosie's told me that Italians had hawked their tickets to scalpers in Little Italy, and that three quarters of tomorrow's crowd will be Irish."

Terry: "*Hawking*? *Scalpers*? You really *have* been in the States too long, Jim."

Malky set down his Johnnie Walker Black, drummed the table top with his chubby fingers and changed the subject.

"Tell them who we met in the hotel lobby this morning, Schemer."

Me: "Only one John Zachary DeLorean."

Terry: "Wow. Now there's a REAL schemer. I hope he paid for the coffee and doughnuts."

Me: "He must be 70-odd now. I couldn't believe how tall he was. Still looks like James Coburn. Scorching outside, and he's wearing a suit. Lives just a couple of miles down the road with his fourth wife, apparently. The bitchy receptionist told us it's a rather 'modest' dwelling..."

Malky: "Ah met his third wife, Cristina, at the Culloden one night."

Jeekie: "Now *there's* something I want to hear more about..."

Malky: "Nah, it was nothin' like that."

Jeekie: "I'd already guessed *that* bit."

Malky: "She was wi' John Z at a do. Ah made a speech at that one. He told me he remembered it. Fine lookin' lassie, that Cristina."

Terry: "Well, she WAS Cristina Ferrare, the world's hottest supermodel. She dropped your great pal 'John Z' like a stone after that drugs bust in LA... and the thought that she might end up living in a 'rather modest dwelling' in Jersey. I bet she wishes that bloody car really WAS a time machine."

Me: "Guess what... he told us he STILL wants to start up another car company. That guy's self-delusion has no bounds."

Malky: "Ah thought wee Schemer was going tae suggest he funds his new venture from that Cayman Islands account he used to syphon the taxpayers' Dunmurry dough intae..."

Me: "Well I DID ask if he ever thought of revisiting our wee country. Said he'd love to, but he's had to surrender his passport..."

Despite how insanely busy Manhattan was that day, Kennedy's dining room wasn't overly packed, although the main bar was coming down with excited Knicks fans. The management had also erected two screens for any diners interested in the exclusive NBC-broadcast spectacle.

"I'm told that, with this being the first NBA finals in four years not to feature Michael Jordan {who'd retired from the Chicago Bulls to try his hand at baseball}, the TV ratings could well be down," said Jeekie.

Then it happened.

During the second quarter, with the home team leading 45-36.
Suddenly, instead of the Knicks' most crucial game in over two decades, we got a white SUV travelling very slowly down a freeway.
Never have so many bellowed "what the fuck?" in unison.
Amid the wails of derision, Michael Glynn (aka 'Mayor of 57th Street' and Kennedy's Galway-born manager/co-owner) reached for the remote control. To no avail; CBS, ABC, Fox – even ESPN – were showing the same thing.
It was like one of those sci-fi movies where invading aliens, having regarded this earth with envious eyes, simultaneously commandeered all the global broadcast networks to reveal that they'd – slowly but surely – drawn their plans against us (additional reporting by HG Wells).
That once-in-a-lifetime bar scene is brilliantly recreated in multi-award-winning Netflix drama The People v OJ Simpson. It really *did* happen like that; looking back, this may well have been the birth of reality TV.
"If I'm not mistaken, something similar befell NBC once before," said Terry after the initial seismic shock subsided and the drama on Interstate 405, 3,000 miles away, morphed into something indisputably more riveting than basketball.
As a fleet of helicopters bore down on the Bronco, Terry continued: "Have you heard of 'The Heidi Game'? Late 60s; the Jets were smokin' the Raiders with a minute left – and NBC pulled the plug because Heidi was starting.
"Suddenly, 'Broadway Joe' Namath was replaced by a wee Swiss girl in pigtails. It nearly put the network out of business. Not only that, but the Jets conceded two touchdowns in that last minute..."
Jim: "Shut up, Terry, we're trying to watch this."
Me: "I can't get over those people on the flyovers – sorry Jim, *overpasses* – screaming their support for someone who hacked two people to death."
Malky: "The punters in here are rootin' for him too. But it's how slow they're all goin' that takes me to the fair. Does Simpson think he'll get away wi' murder just because he keeps tae the speed limit?"

Jim: "Maybe The Juice is listening to the Knicks on the radio and doesn't want to turn himself in too early. Wouldn't THAT be ironic?"

(Some 22 years later, Al Cowlings – who was driving the Bronco while OJ threatened to kill himself with a loaded Magnum – revealed that his suicidal passenger really HAD tuned into the MSG game and had subsequently ordered his friend to drive as slowly as he could to Brentwood. PS: the Knicks won 91-84 but lost the next two games and the series. And NBC's audience increased by over 900% during OJ's riveting 75-minute cat-and-mouse with a phalanx of California Highway Patrol cars).

An exhausted Michael Glynn, who became a cherished friend until his death in 2013 at the age of 67, walked us to our Jersey-bound minivan at closing time.

"That was one hell of a day," he said, adding: "Thank God there's nothing exciting happening in these parts tomorrow... that right, lads?"

CHAPTER 40

A passenger travelling quietly conceals himself
With a magazine and a sleepless pillow
(Paul Simon, Trailways Bus)

For a moment, it felt as if a dubious moment in history was repeating itself.

A huge stadium nearby. The Republic's team bus which, just minutes before, had been full of players. Empty now – except for a tracksuited Paul McGrath, sitting alone in the darkness, silent, barely stirring.

We'd been here before, him and me. On that ignominious day in October 1990 when a deeply disturbed 30-year-old sat on in the vehicle outside a heaving, expectant Lansdowne Road, repeatedly ignoring pleas to join team-mates as they prepared for an important qualifier.

This, however, couldn't be more different. June 18, 1994, around 9pm Eastern time – and the 'Black Pearl of Inchicore' had just helped pull off a miracle against Arrigo Saachi's star-studded Italy in the Giants Stadium, Meadowlands, East Rutherford.

'Rayzor' Houghton's 12th minute winning goal, in front of 75,338 fans – the vast majority of whom were delirious Irish – would get the big headlines.

But *Ooh Aah Paul McGrath* was the best player on the park – some achievement, when you consider that World Player of the Year Roberto Baggio, Franco Baresi, Paolo Maldini, Billy Costacurta and McGrath's own team-mate (a definitive "fuck me, how good is Keano?" 90 minutes) were on the park at the same time.

That blistering summer's afternoon in New Jersey, McGrath produced the finest performance I've ever seen from a central defender, against the thrice world champions, a team fortified with Milan players who, just one month earlier, had tanked Barcelona 4-0 in Athens to win the Champions League.

It would be another 12 years before anyone (Italy's Fabio Cannavaro v Germany, World Cup semi-final, Dortmund), even got close.

The softly-spoken, introverted Aston Villa man (who'd been secretly nursing an excruciatingly painful left shoulder injury) was so good that day, he made central defensive partner Phil Babb – a decent but unexceptional Coventry player – look world class himself.

Early on, a lacerating pass from Juventus's 'Divine Ponytail' sent Beppe Signori – eight years younger than McGrath and terrifyingly fast – bearing down on Bonner's goal. Somehow, the older man – who'd later repel Baggio three times in ten remarkable seconds – found the speed, strength and sheer will to catch the Lazio striker and steer the ball safely back to a relieved Packie.

"I knew, right then, that we were going to be okay today," said an emotional Charlton after the Republic's first (non-penalty shootout) World Cup finals victory.

That stunning interception – applauded by a raucous crowd which included Jack Nicholson, John McEnroe, Henry Kissinger, Daryl Hall, Rudi Giuliani and Liza Minnelli, past and present *taoisigh* and various Vatican cardinals and bishops – visibly lifted McGrath's team-mates who produced a classic 'what we have, we hold' display following Houghton's opportunistic left-foot lob over the stranded Gianluca Pagliuca.

It had earlier been agreed, win, lose or draw, that the Irish players would spend an hour mingling with fans in the huge Meadowlands hospitality tents afterwards.

And they were true to their word – all except striker Tommy Coyne, who was being treated for severe dehydration, and the inspirational McGrath, who stayed behind, incognito, in the air-conditioned Mercedes coach while his colleagues swilled beer, pressed the flesh, signed autographs and posed for instant Polaroids before departing, later than scheduled, for Newark airport, some 15 miles away.

You'd be forgiven for harbouring suspicions about why someone with McGrath's rap sheet, who'd been so comfortable – no, who'd positively *revelled* – in front of over 75,000 a couple of hours earlier, would shy away from a few inebriated compatriots.

"The only thing that man could be drunk on is Ballygowan," said Malky who, earlier that week, had delivered a meticulously-researched piece about 'hyperhydration' – 'water intoxication' – and subsequently regarded himself as a foremost expert on the subject.

I can vouch that McGrath, raised in Dublin orphanages, regularly beset by self-esteem issues and tortured by the ravages of alcoholism, remained subdued – and sober – on the charter back to Orlando.

I nodded off towards the end of the three-hour flight, only waking after birthday boy Jason McAteer (23) tipped a full ice bucket over me. (Cheers, pal. Must inform readers what 'Trigger' wrote on his US Mastercard application form when 'position within company' was sought: "full-back, but I prefer central midfield").

The fierce heat of that historic afternoon – when Charlton's men earned sweet revenge for their Italia 90 elimination by the hosts in Rome's

Stadio Olimpico – had clearly sapped *my* energy; I can only imagine how debilitating it must have been for the players, especially those in 'centre-field' positions such as McGrath, Babb, Keane, newly-blond captain Andy Townsend and Coyne who rarely got near water bags thrown from the sidelines.

There was another reason for the collective lachrymosity on that plane; word had filtered through about the Loughinisland atrocity when six men – including an 87-year-old who'd been watching the game in the Co Down village's Heights Bar, were murdered by UVF gunmen. There was little enthusiasm for partying after that.

We got back to the Hilton after 2am – too late even for a nightcap.

So, while all around the world, Irish people celebrated the stunning victory with tuneless *ole, ole oles*, the 'New York giants' themselves were tucked up in bed, save for Babb who played video games for a short time in the lobby.

Charlton, meanwhile, was snoring his head off back in Parsippany, having booked an early flight to Washington where Norway would meet – and beat – Mexico in the other Group E opener.

He missed Kjetil Rekdal's 85th minute winner, having left the RFK Memorial Stadium to catch a flight that, unknown to him, had already been cancelled due to inclement weather.

The exasperated 59-year-old eventually boarded a plane to North Carolina, but missed the on-going connection to Orlando and spent the rest of the night on a hard plastic chair at Charlotte's Douglas airport.

"Next time you're doing a piece about the glamour of the World Cup, write that down," said an exhausted Charlton as he staggered into the Hilton lobby mid-morning.

He added: "For all the euphoria about beating Italy, this damned group could well be another one that ends up as tight as a duck's arse."

CHAPTER 41

It's easier to leave than to be left behind
Leaving was never my proud
Leaving New York never easy
I saw the light fading out
(REM, Leaving New York)

"Vaarwel, Johan, as they say in the Netherlands. Good luck and, if the good Lord spares us, we'll all meet again at the final. Netherlands versus Spain; wouldn't that be nice?"
(Lex Muller, reporter, Citrus Bowl media centre, Independence Day, 1994)

"I'm outta here"
(Jim Gracey, Giants Stadium media centre, June 28, 1994)

Michael Stipe was right. Leaving New York's never easy. Leaving Orlando, however, was effortless.
Unlike others in that early-morning departure lounge, whose sunshine holidays were coming to a depressing end, this departee was positively jubilant.
July 5, 1994… the third time I'd jetted off from the former McCoy Air Force Base in as many weeks and, mercifully, the last.
It's no coincidence that I've never gone back to that dump.
Five weeks in, and the thrill of being in America, and indeed the World Cup itself, was long gone. It didn't even feel like the Greatest Show on Earth, more an elaborate extension of the Northern Ireland tour that started it all in late May; different people, same basic colours, similar 'who'll play and who won't?' stories.
Yes, I know: woe is me, get the violins out, you spoilt, pompous, nauseatingly self-pitying, unappreciative bastard.
It's all relative though. I was still cognisant of having The Best Job In The World, a job so many others would, figuratively speaking, die for. But you can still miss home, your family, your partner, your regular buddies.
Privileged people – and I'm not hitching myself to that wagon – don't remain blissfully happy just because others envy them; why do you think so many, who supposedly 'have it all', often suffer depression and suicidal thoughts?

A little obtuse, but four of the Not-So-Famous Five (Jim left on June 24, after meeting Cantona: for him, nothing could top that) were losing the proverbial will to live in 'The Entertainment Capital of the World'.

Well, the glossy travel brochures might say that.

To me, it was a sprawling mass of concrete, neon, cheap hotels, all-day rush hours, churches and 'scrub club' massage parlours (Sodom alongside Salom; a bible-belted Vegas); a former college town, hastily and haphazardly expanded into a heaving metropolis after Mickey Mouse arrived in the early 70s, with a population that literally doubled in the summer, full of 'attractions' but lacking genuine character; hell, even the famed orange groves were disappearing. It brought to mind Billy Sinclair's withering description of Lurgan: "A graveyard with traffic lights."

Enough already; you weren't saying *that* when you arrived here, pal.

True, but there was a tangible change when we returned to the sticky air of central Florida on June 19.

The attitude of the 'Jolly Green Giants' followers, for a start. Hope had turned to rapacious, unquenchable expectation after the Italy game; 'getting out of Group E' was no longer the holy grail, no sir.

I wish I'd a dollar for every time "we're gonna win the cup" paddywhackery spewed out from inebriated punters now frequenting the Hilton.

That place had suddenly become microcosmic of downtown Orlando (whatever *did* happen to their security detail?). And the Why Not Lounge; they'd rumbled that little haven too (although we did feel genuinely sorry for the many who'd been left roomless and ticketless by a rogue, London-based tour operator).

The Oirish logic: Italy boasted nine Milan players – and 'AC' are the best club team in the world – plus they have the best player in the world, so that makes them the best team in the tournament, but 'we' beat them; ergo, Ireland are better than them. And, as Sinatra sang about Noo York/Noo Joisey, if you can make it there, you'll make it anywhere...

A Groundhog Day scenario arose too; breakfast, bus to Seminole, listen to Jack rail against FIFA over waterbags, free buffet lunch (essential; with the obvious exception of Malky, we were running short of cash), retire to room, get work done (sunbathing? Far too hot for that), shower, dinner, hotel bar for as long as you could stand the relentless, hysterical hyperbole, Why Not Lounge to 2am (when we'd politely hand over our drinks), back to Hilton, make reassuring 2.30 phone call to office, zzzzz.

It wasn't just fans shouting/spouting the odds; I picked up a copy of the Indo from July 20 (they arrived a day late), to read hitherto rational colleague and all-round good egg, Philip Quinn, gush: "First Italy, now the rest of the world. Roll on Mexico and Norway..."

(Less than a month later, Italy – and not the Republic – would step out at the Fifa World Cup final, 3,000 miles west of this infernal gabfest).

Two things broke up the tedious monotony. Firstly, a two-day Star Trek convention at the hotel (or 'earth station', as devotees called it).

Malky's horrified expression, after he'd been joined at the urinals by a Klingon on one side and a pointy-eared Mr Spock on the other, was priceless.

And why did Trekkies need taxis from the earth station; couldn't they just beam themselves to wherever they were going?

Secondly, Terry, who had a hire car (a Mazda 929; there's never any budget concerns at the Beeb), suggested we'd all benefit from a day out at Daytona Beach, that bastion of bikers and spring breakers, just one hour up the I-4. Malky opted to sit this one out.

The refreshing sea breeze meant that, for once, we could lie in the sun... bliss. Then lunch in the Boot Hill Saloon – across from a cemetery, naturally.

Now it was Jeekie's turn to look horrified – at the glass jars of condoms on the bar top, discarded bras hanging from the ceiling (no admission to women unless they removed them on entry), open stalls instead of a proper 'bathroom', a tattooed, bearded, pony-tailed barman called Red, an 'Irish Car Bomb' (Baileys and Jameson in a shot glass, dropped into a Guinness) on the menu, sawdust on the floor and a sign saying 'No dogs or children after 7pm'.

Back in Hotel California, we continued to speculate as to how long the punters' unflappable, Ally McLeod-style mass optimism would last.

Well, like Scotland's hilariously deluded manager from Argentina 78, it persisted until they met decent Latino opponents who delivered a savage reality check in the blazing Citrus Bowl (to all except Jack who, to be fair, had been fretting about this game, above all others, from day one).

In the land of thunderstorms, lightning wouldn't strike twice – but *Me-hi-co* striker Luis Garcia did.

Even by fierce Floridian standards, that Friday, June 24 was a brutal, merciless, 120-degree scorcher; I'd left an almost full Americano in Terry's car prior to the game; on my return, four hours later, the coffee was still piping hot. Hundreds of fans were treated for sunstroke and severe burns that day; Ray Houghton said it was so blisteringly hot on the field, his leather boots were starting to scald his feet.

"Come on you boys in green," sang a section of Irish fans until they realised that, having lost the 'traditional strip' toss-up, were wearing all white – and today's 'boys in green' were playing better football.

Apart from Garcia giving McGrath (who was as bad in that game as he was good in New Jersey) the runaround and an appallingly poor rendition of *Amhran na bhFiann*, that ill-fated high noon showdown (watched by 60,790 sweltering fans) is best remembered for John Aldridge sensationally losing it with a bespectacled, hyper-fussy FIFA official in blue blazer, white shirt, striped tie and yellow baseball hat who'd attempted to stop him replacing Tommy Coyne.

As tens of millions watched on television all over the globe, an incandescent Aldo reached boiling point (almost literally), then let fly with both Scouse barrels: "Fuck off, ya twat, ya dickhead, ya fucking, fucking cheat. Fuck off!"

The aforementioned 'twat' then pushed an equally irate Charlton back towards the dugout. Some of the hardest men in football have lived to regret doing something similar.

A priceless interlude which has gone down in the annals of World Cup history – and, to borrow Malky's catchphrase, *Ah was there*. But Ah didnae see any o' it.

Indeed, no one in the air-conditioned press box (positioned in an upper tier which blocked the view of the dugouts) did. So, while everyone back home discussed this unfolding drama, our lot, high up in the aluminium bleachers of the shimmering concrete oven, knew sod all about it. There were some TV monitors, but who's watching the dugouts on telly when the on-pitch action is continuing?

Naturally it was the main topic of discussion in the 'mixed zone' after the demoralising 2-1 defeat.

My first instinct was to alert Malky, who was halfway through dictating a comment piece to the Irish Sun; maybe I was subconsciously attempting to atone for callously misleading him at the Foxboro three weeks earlier. I don't know, it just felt like the right thing to do.

CHAPTER 42

It was nearly 2.30am when my bedside phone started ringing.

"That ye, John?"

"Yes, Malky, is everything all right?"

"Aye. Have ye filed your copy yet?"

"Of course. Hours ago. I'm just waiting to ring the office and check that all's well."

"Ah thought so. Well, when ye ring, tell them tae add a bit in; Charlton's gonna be banned for the Norway match, and hit wi' a heavy fine. It's too late for the morning papers; ye'll have this all tae yerself."

"Banned? What for? Sure it was Aldo doing all the mouthing."

"Tae be honest, John, Ah'm nae quite sure. They've been gunnin' for Jack since he snubbed the draw in Vegas last year. Ah think this is for him slabberin' in general, rather than one specific thing."

"Hey, Malky, thanks a lot for tipping me off. Next question: how sure are you about this?"

I could hear him cackling.

"It's FIFA, John; Ah think ye can assume Ah still have friends in high places. In any case, Ah'm grateful for what ye did for me earlier the day."

The following morning – after Jack and his missus had gone shopping – FIFA announced that the Republic's first non-Irish boss had been given a touchline ban for the forthcoming match on June 28 and fined 20,000 Swiss francs (roughly £7,000; Aldo also got hit for around £2,500).

The statement, however, didn't say what the punishment was for – and Jack looked genuinely baffled when greeted with the news when he arrived back at the Hilton that afternoon.

And he couldn't contact anyone in the FAI to find out – because they'd all buggered off to Disney World for the day; cue the Mickey Mouse references.

"It must be about me row with that Egyptian, but that was nothing," he concluded.

('That Egyptian', incidentally, was Mustapha Fahmy, the Confederation of Africa general secretary, who would later be one of the masterminds behind the 2010 World Cup in South Africa, and ultimately become FIFA's General Coordinator...)

Aldo's late header proved to be, like team-mate John Sheridan's goal against Spain the previous year, more than a mere consolation.

A 2-0 defeat would have left the Irish bottom of Group E and needing to beat Norway; instead, thanks to Aldo, a draw against Egil Olsen's men would suffice.

That leverage did little to improve Jack's mood; indeed, a three-hour delay at Orlando International en route to Newark on Sunday, June 26, further aggravated it.

Subsequently, he manhandled one of the battery of photographers waiting for us in the Tara Sheraton lobby – Charlton's ongoing contretemps with FIFA was now A Big Story – and the following day's press conference was vintage 'Jackattack'.

Asked by an American hack about how he'd get instructions to the players during the game: "If you'd been readin' the papers, you'd know already."

How did he feel about the prospect of meeting Nigeria in the Round of 16?

"Don't know. Stop asking stupid questions about something I know nothing about."

And what will it feel like, sitting up in the stand instead of in the dugout? "It'll be a much better view, and I'll be able to drink a cold beer..."

As we milled around the Giants Stadium press centre before the game, I called out to Jim: "Look who's just walked in."

Jim, whose eyesight isn't the greatest, glanced over – and looked distinctly unimpressed.

"*Mark Lawrenson*? So what? We bump into him every day."

"No, Jim, not *him*... look who's *behind* him."

"Fuck me, it's ERIC CANTONA!"

It was the happiest Jim had looked since we touched down in Boston. Cantona should have been there as one of the star players.

But *Daveed* Ginola's reckless, wayward injury-time attempted cross to that other *Ooh Aah* man (when he should have been playing the game out at the corner flag) against Bulgaria, who promptly scored a breakaway winner, bid *adieu* to all that.

Eric le Rouge posed for a picture (taken by our good pal, UTV cameraman Eric Roberts), said he believed the Republic would get through and added that his club-mate Keano was shaping up as one of the players of the tournament.

Actually, Keane's cultured performance was one of the few things I remember about that dreadful game – one of only three scoreless draws in USA 94 (although the Indo described it as a "thriller") and played, mercifully, in the most benign weather conditions so far.

But not shown live by the American networks, who opted instead for the Italy-Mexico game in Washington, which was deemed as having more "ethnic interest".

Sitting near us was a frustrated and, ultimately gutted, spectator – Norwegian midfielder Alf-Inge Haaland, who'd been yellow-carded against both Mexico and Italy and therefore missed the chance of a first locking-of-horns with Keano, whom he'd replaced at Nottingham Forest. Don't worry, Alfie, your time will come...

Norway's poker-mad manager Olsen had gambled on a winner emerging from the other Group E game in Washington; 1-1, oops. The 'Group of Death' had lived up to its billing, with all four teams finishing with four points and a zero goal difference.

But Mexico finished top, ahead of the Republic because they'd beaten them, the Republic finished second, ahead of Italy, for the same reason; ditto the Italians ahead of the overcautious but luckless Scandis, who departed for Oslo feeling mugged on a muggy day.

An Irish victory in 'Game 29' would have given Jack's boys a chance to stay in New Jersey or relocate to Boston (the 'Dublin of North America'); that would also have meant a showdown with Nigeria or Argentina (now bereft of the wild-eyed, ephedrine-addled, expelled Maradona).

Jack, however, wasn't keen on meeting another team who could handle the stifling conditions a lot better than his ageing milk bottles.

One thing was certain: it was back to Or-bloody-lando – another lunchtime kick-off against an as-yet unidentified foe.

After milking the adulation cascading down from the heaving Meadowlands stands (official attendance 76,322), and an exhausting/ultimately infuriating night of glad-handing and backslapping in the by-now troglodyte-central Tara – which bore no resemblance to the idyllic, peaceful getaway he'd praised 10 days earlier – Charlton jetted off once more to DC to watch Belgium, whom he was convinced would be the Round of 16 opponents, play Saudi Arabia.

Alas, Saeed Al-Owairan slalomed through the Belgian defence for one of the greatest goals in World Cup history, and Jack suffered yet another nightmare journey back to Orlando (where he could have taken a taxi to see the Dutch beat Morocco and become his next challenge) due to cancelled and diverted flights.

After the Norway game, Jim suddenly announced (although it was no real surprise) that he'd had enough of 'third world' America and would be flying home that night, accompanied by Hammy whose stint as guest UTV analyst had ended.

The rest of us flew south with a heavy heart and, as it was a scheduled flight this time, complimentary Mickey Mouse ears.

Bored out of our skulls, we found a new past-time: lying to Martin McCullough about who he'd just missed on his post-training returns to the hotel.

Jeekie: "Oh, Martin, you should have been here an hour ago; Bono turned up with Bob Dylan."

Martin: "Fuck, NO!"

Me: "Oh, Martin, you just missed Elle Macpherson; she was dancing up and down on the bar wearing a Republic of Ireland shirt – and those *legs*. They went on for *ever*."

Martin: "Fuck, no, NO!"

Terry: "Oh, Martin, if only you'd got here a few minutes ago: Chris de Burgh was in the bar, bold as brass, singing Lady in Red – except he'd changed the lyrics to 'My Nanny in Bed'. I'll tell you, that man's got balls..."

Martin: "Fuck, no, NO, NO!"

Malky: "Ah, ye shoulda been here, Martin: Pope John Paul II was givin' oot a blessin' and says he's excommunicating Bergkamp for bein a Taig wearin' an orange shirt..."

Martin: "Now I *know* you're lying."

Terry: "Malky, allow me to explain: in order for this subterfuge to work, it has to be *vaguely* plausible..."

On July 3, the day before the Netherlands game, an ITN crew asked me if I'd like to comment on remarks made by DUP deputy leader Peter Robinson back home about the Republic team: "I wouldn't like to see them go anywhere, but I see they are well travelled. They have got a few coloureds in the team now, too".

No, I don't think I will comment on that, if it's all right with you guys.

Jim may have *went*, but we still had a big, larger-than-life character to neck beer with in Florida: Dutchman Lex Muller, 54-year-old chief football writer for Algemeen Dagblad, Rotterdam's largest newspaper – and, of course, an old acquaintance of The Doyen.

"He's okay in small doses," warned Malky, who wasn't wrong; boy, could that man talk.

He was also intrigued by an up-and-coming mobile phone network's new catchphrase – "the future's bright, the future is Orange" – and vowed to shoehorn it into all his pieces as long as the Dutch stayed in.

The future wasn't so bright for the boul' Lex though: he was hauled off the Dutch team's Dallas-bound plane at Orlando Airport, banged up – suspended by his employers and ultimately sacked – after spooking passengers and crew by 'joking' he had a bomb and a gun inside his rucksack.

That incident, which delayed the fully-loaded Boeing 727's take-off for five hours (as bomb-disposal experts and sniffer dogs swept the plane), traumatised one passenger in particular – Dennis Bergkamp, who had to be given sedatives and coaxed into continuing the journey. He vowed, on returning from America, never to fly again.

Before becoming 'The Non-flying Dutchman', Bergkamp helped Dick Avocaat's *Oranje* beat the Green with an opportunist goal, which was followed by a speculative shot from Wim Jonk which Packie Bonner spilled into the net. A damp-squib of a finale as Independence Day fireworks began exploding over Lake Eola Park. Ten minutes after the final whistle, orange baseball caps bearing the scoreline were on sale for $10 outside the stadium.

"Always look on the bright side of life," sang the sunburnt, impoverished Irish fans in the 61,355 crowd.

But to quote one of Florida's favourite sons, legendary Doors frontman Jim Morrison, this is The End. The *Irexit*. A second successive tournament had ended with one win, two goals scored and a minus goal difference. In Italia 90, Jack's boys got better as time went on; it was the opposite on this occasion, with a more anticlimactic conclusion.

Philip Quinn: "John, how'd you start off your report?"

Me: "I wrote 'You've been Tangoed, Jack', or something like that."

Philip: "Mmm, rather topical. Not very subtle, though."

Me: "Well, sometimes if you're *too* subtle, people think you've missed the point. What did *you* write?"

Philip: "I started with 'They died with their boots on'... oi, what's so funny about *that*?"

Me: "Not a thing. It's a long story. Tell you what, I'll fill you in over a nice cold pint when we get to LA."

CHAPTER 43

BRAZILIANS ARE SPOT ON

It's over and out for Baggio as Italians pay the ultimate penalty

By John Laverty in Pasadena

He wouldn't miss it for the world.
But he did, and the world ended for Italy.
Over the crossbar it went, and over the moon went Brazil.
The genius who had the world at his feet let the World Cup slip out of his hands. The man who strived to have the last laugh in this competition merely had the last kick.
And it was Brazil, now four times world champions, who had the final say.

"Right, John, pay attention and take this down: The Langham, South Oak Knoll Drive, Pasadena."
"That sounds familiar; is this where the Fifa top brass are slumming it?"
"Aye, an' me too. Ah've got a suite there. It's the finest hotel Ah've ever been to, apart from the Sheraton in Perth, Australia.
Look, meet me for lunch on the 16th, ye got that? Call for me at reception."
"Okay. And what if I want to speak with you before that?"
"Leave a message wi' Sammy or whoever else answers the phone. Sure we'll both be ringin' the office every mornin'. Right, that's it. Arrivederci."
We'd agreed that Malky would follow the Dutch or whoever beat them, all the way to Pasadena; ditto myself with the Italians.
On the red-eye to Boston that July 5 morning, I didn't hold out much hope of Italy – the team I always support in tournaments when Northern Ireland aren't involved – progressing against surprise packets Nigeria. Somehow the 'cardiac kids', as one US commentator had referred to the Italians, had made it this far, but with The Divine Ponytail in poor form and goalless after eight internationals – hopes weren't high.
Roberto Baggio was already right up there with Cruyff, Beckenbauer, Van Basten, Matthaus, Zico, Scirea, Platini and Stielike in my list of favourite 'foreign' players.
But 27-year-old was having a mare in America. Never mind the best *player*, he wasn't even the best *Baggio;* team-mate Dino Baggio (no relation) was getting most of the plaudits.

Already embarrassed at being the unexpected fall guy (hauled off after only 22 minutes to make way for a substitute goalkeeper following Pagliuca's red card) against Norway, the £8m man was further humiliated by billionaire Juventus owner Gianni Agnelli, who labelled him a "coniglio bagnato" ("wet rabbit") after an ineffective showing against Mexico. Baggio was being upstaged in the States by Romario, Stoichkov and Hagi – all of whom he'd beaten to the Fifa World Player of the Year award and who, like him, were five feet nine or less in their stockings; this was quickly becoming the wee men's World Cup.

But I arrived at the heaving Foxboro (attendance 54,367; over 32,000 more than Northern Ireland v Colombia a month earlier) in time to witness the brilliant Buddhist finally take his place among the big boys – or, rather, the small ones.

A typical Baggio goal with just two minutes left on the clock, followed by a nerveless penalty in extra-time – the first time it had been required in USA 94… and suddenly the best player in the world, who had silenced his critics at long last, was celebrating just yards away from where I sat. Yep, THIS is the World Cup I'd imagined.

A one-hour hop took me from LaGuardia back to Boston four days later to see Baggio bag a late winner in the quarter-final against Spain, then another brace to sink surprise semi-final opponents Bulgaria in New Jersey.

Remarkably, all five of Baggio's efforts struck the interior side netting before nestling in the back of the onion bag; that's how precise this incredible player was.

In between those latter two Italian games, and alternating between Kennedy's and Jimmy's Corner on W44th (it's not on a corner, but heavyweight legend Floyd Patterson's old cornerman Jimmy Glenn owns it) I crossed the Hudson and saw Bulgarian 'bald eagle' Iordan Letchkov's brilliant diving header sink defending champions Germany and set up a last-four duel with Baggio and Co.

Malky, meanwhile, saw 'Brazil In Name Only' beat the Netherlands in a cracking quarter-final in Dallas (remember new dad Bebeto's 'rock the baby' goal celebration?), then polish off Sweden in Pasadena, where he was now well ensconced with Sepp and his cronies.

"They're talkin' aboot honourin' me wi' a centennial award for coverin' all them World Cups."

"That's brilliant, Malky. Are you going to get it here?"

255

"Nah, that's the problem. The FIFA centenary isnae til 2004; Ah'm gonna have to live at least another ten year… Oh, John, Ah forgot tae mention; Ah was introduced to yer man Johnnie Cochran in the lobby today."

"Who's Johnnie Cochran?"

"Ha-ha-ha-HA! 'Who's Johnnie Cochran'? MB knows more about music than his son Victor. Johnnie Cochran is the black civil rights lawyer who defended Mick Jackson last year."

"*Michael* Jackson, Malky. I'm a Prince fan; I couldn't care less about that other freak. Is Cochran here for the final?"

"Dunno. Ah've a funny feeling he's lookin' to get involved in the OJ trial."

"Well, he got Jacko off, and that pervert was guilty as sin. You don't pay off a kid 20 million dollars if you're white as the driven snow. And he isn't, no matter how much he bleaches his skin."

(In October 1995 Johnnie *(If it doesn't fit, you must acquit)* Cochran convinced the 'Trial of the Century' jury to deliver a 'not guilty verdict' on OJ – and ten years later, Fifa presented Malky with the Jules Rimet Centennial Award in recognition of him covering 13 World Cup tournaments.)

I arrived in the City of Angels – another sprawling, soulless concrete dump – on Friday, July 15, and booked myself into a downtown hotel which, like several others, had advertised 'special rates for World Cup journalists'.

Fortunately, I'd been warned that 'special rates' meant 'more than your ordinary Joe Bloggs would be paying'. So 'Mr Bloggs' booked himself in for three nights in La-La Land.

The standout moment was getting a word with the pony-tailed one at a press gathering near the Hollywood hills.

I asked Baggio if he felt inspired by similarities to 1982 legend Paolo Rossi; both were youngsters at Vicenza, both became Juve superstars and both were pants in the group games, yet had five goals by the time the final came round – including two each against east European opponents in the semis.

His response, through an interpreter, was immediate: "It's not the similarities that inspire me, it's the difference – Rossi has a World Cup winner's medal, and I don't. Hopefully that will change."

As we all know, it didn't.

The final was an absolute stinker; the worst in history, and that's saying something. Also the first goalless decider, and the first to require a penalty shoot-out; an insult to the 1970 classic between the same two countries, a dreadful anti-climax to what was, despite all the initial concerns about American apathy, the highest-attended tournament (52 matches, 3.6m fans) and one of the finest in terms of quality – and, ironically, goal-scoring.

It was the last tournament before the Premiership/Premier League became the go-to for foreign stars; before that, the only place you could regularly see the Gullits, Batistutas and Papins was on Channel 4's Football Italia. *Golaccio!*

Baggio, who'd sustained a hamstring injury in the semi-final and shouldn't have been on the ancient Rose Bowl's lush grass that scorching Sunday afternoon, will always be remembered principally for 'that miss' when, really, he deserves to be mentioned in the same breath as Maradona in Mexico 86. Fine margins, indeed.

I sat beside Martin Tyler, who'd been moonlighting for an Australian TV company, on the bus back to LA. Nice guy.

And that's all, folks; the final name drop from an epic seven-and-a-half-week adventure.

Apart from Malky (and Johnnie Cochran), no longer with us from that US adventure are Gordon Hanna, Noel Lemon, Jackie Charlton, Maurice Setters, Brian Madley, Michael Glynn, Gerry Toner, Joe McGorman, Roscoe Lee Browne and Andreas Escobar. God rest all your souls.

The Foxboro was demolished in 2002, with the 68,000-capacity Gillette Stadium (and Patriot Place shopping centre) replacing it; the Orange Bowl was demolished in 2008 and replaced by Marlins Park (capacity: 36,000); the Giants Stadium (which I quickly discovered you could see from the Twin Towers observation deck, 12 miles away) was levelled in 2010 and rebuilt as the fabulous $1.6bn, 82,550-capacity MetLife Stadium; the Citrus Bowl has been renovated (twice) and is now the 65,000-capacity Camping World Stadium; Kennedy's (capacity: wildly variable) closed in 2013 after its basic rent was doubled to $40k a month; closing time was even called (no doubt at 2am precisely) on the never-to-be-forgotten Why Not Lounge in 2015. As far as I know, the gay bar on Providence's Elbow Street is still going strong.

Thanks for the memories.

CHAPTER 44

Palermo, Sicily, January 1997.

At first I thought I was dreaming but no, there it is again.
Knock, knock.
"Mister John, Mister John… are you awake?"
I am *now*.
"Just a moment, please."
I padded groggily to the door.
"Who is *this*?"
"My name is Greta. Mister Brodie recruited me. Open up please, Mr John."
She strode confidently into the room; a slim, elegant-looking lady, maybe five years older than me. Dressed in a grey pencil skirt, white blouse and black high heels, she was carrying what looked like an overnight case.
"Look, Greta, I think there's been a breakdown in communications here. You're very nice, but this isn't what I'm looking for. It's really late and I'm tired. Look, if it's money…"
She started unzipping her case.
"Don't worry, Mister John, your friend Mister Brodie is taking care of everything. Now, switch on the light, lie on the bed and pull down your underpants…"

In September 1996, I was appointed sports editor. This was a surprise, not least to me.
The original ambition had been to 'take over from Malky', but that just meant being the main football man. Sports editor? Not a conscious aspiration.
And anyway, Sammy was doing a terrific job, both in terms of content and presentation.
It had been a difficult five years, too, with the paper going through the most dramatic shake-up in its history.
An American consultancy group – Brooks International – had been recruited, at a cost of £700k, to make the place 'more efficient'.
"We're givin' them 700 grand tae tell us we need tae shave the workforce by a quarter; Ah could have told them that for 70 quid," said Malky.
He was right, too. After all the talk, consultations, speeches, statements, euphemisms, blithe promises, civil service speak, suspicions, furtive collaboration, cooperation, non-cooperation and overt militancy, the

bottom line: 121 people (including many who had helped Brooks with the 'consultancy') were out of a job.

Among them was 55-year-old picture editor Norman Percy, a man I was particularly fond of. Norman's dry wit and droll sense of humour enlivened many a dull day.

"I'm about to be told what I'm *volunteering* for," Norman told me on the back corridor one day.

"How do you feel about that, Norman?"

"Ach, I'm okay about it. The money's decent and I've had a good run here; nearly 40 years. All good things come to an end, eh?"

Having slept on it, however, Norman changed his mind about the agreed redundancy package, and made frantic phone calls to that effect. He was told "the process" had gone too far ahead, and couldn't be reversed.

Norman had a shared "leaving do" with several others at the Ink Spot, bought me a drink and refused to accept one in return.

Four days later, Norman Percy was found dead in the garage of his Adelaide Park home, a hosepipe attached from the exhaust to the car's interior. A decent man who'd stepped off a world that was suddenly spinning too quickly for him.

To people of a certain age in the Tele, the word 'Brooks' still haunts; an evil that dare not speak its name. RIP Norman.

Apart from getting rid of people, one of the Yanks' bright ideas was abolishing deputies and assistants – so Sammy, having lost behemoths Malky, Walker and Jack in quick succession, also had to operate without a regular number two.

Instead, we took it in turns to 'act up' as boss; a thankless task. You commanded no respect from those 'under your watch' – and why should you? After all, the next day you were back as one of the lads.

Eventually, the system was deemed unworkable and deputies reinstated. All seemed 'normal' again – until Sammy suddenly announced that he'd been promoted to 'Assistant to the Editor' – fourth in command, behind Editor, Deputy Editor and Assistant Editor – and would therefore be leaving the sports desk.

We'd prepared for Malky's departure five years earlier, but this was was different.

I applied for the job – to 'show ambition' – but Jim, already a sports editor in another part of the building, was clear favourite.

Next to him, John 'The Captain' Taylor – Sammy's deputy; hugely popular and immensely capable. I'd happily work under either of those guys.

But the editor, Ed Curran, who replaced Roy Lilley in 1993, chose me.

I was delighted, of course, but genuinely shocked. I thought Ed might have held my earlier rejection (of his Sunday Life advances in 1988) against me, but no. Or maybe he was atoning for the phantom job offer (chief sports writer) from the previous year.

It wasn't long before I began thinking I'd made a terrible mistake. Naively, I believed I could be another Malky, jetting all over the place while The Captain and ultra-reliable assistant sports editor Graham 'The Mole' Hamilton (whose default expression was that of a man who'd just returned home to find someone else's car blocking his drive) ran the desk.

But things had moved on; the 'rivers of gold' had dried up.

This was primarily a desk-bound job, peppered with 'meetings about meetings' and invitations to events laced with insincerity and air-kisses; functions you'd never willingly attend but were required to. More money and 'perks', less job satisfaction.

Ed also seemed underwhelmed with my choice as new chief football writer – Steven Beacom.

He'd never heard of this guy but I'd researched 'Beaco' (who was then with the Irish News) meticulously – a workhorse, a story-getter, a team player and an ideas man.

There were too many hacks back then – and now – who'll do everything you tell them to do, and absolutely nothing you don't tell them to do. Beaco wasn't one of those.

"You might not have heard of him, Ed, but trust me; everyone will know who he is soon enough."

Sound advice to would-be sports editors, part 1: when you're invited to speak at a raucous all-male football dinner on a Saturday night, and at a prestigious ladies' hockey dinner the following day, don't cut corners by lazily gambling on one speech working equally well at both venues...

Dear Mr Curran,

I am writing on behalf of the President and Council of the Ulster Women's Hockey Union regarding an after-dinner speech by a member of your staff, Mr John Laverty.

Mr Laverty was invited to attend our Annual Presentation of Trophies and Lunch, held at Newforge Country Club on Sunday.

It was attended by distinguished guests such as the President of the IHA, President and Past President of the UBIHA, the Chairman of the Sports

Council for Northern Ireland, Life Members and members of most hockey clubs in Northern Ireland.

The event went extremely well until Mr Laverty made his speech. We found his remarks totally out of place, embarrassing, demeaning to women and unsuitable for such an occasion.

I was therefore instructed to write to you in the hope that you will perhaps ensure that Mr Laverty treats such occasions in the future with the respect they deserve.

Yours sincerely,
Ulster Women's Hockey Union

Sound advice, part 2: never miss an opportunity to wind up an oversensitive egomaniac...

Note to John Laverty of the Belfast Telegraph:

I saw your column on Tuesday, John.
The reason I don't write about Northern Irish football is that I don't see any.
Surely it makes sense to confine my observations to matters I know about?
I noticed you were writing about Manchester United. On Saturday I was at Old Trafford watching United and Chelsea. Yesterday, I saw Blackburn and Liverpool.
Who did YOU see over the weekend, John?

(Radio 5 Live commentator Alan Green)

On the other hand...

Dear Mr Curran,

I write to commend the work of John Laverty. I have admired John's work on many occasions. His work has a degree of thought and correct English form so sadly lacking in journalism generally.

Too many journalists wander back and forth between thoughts from paragraph to paragraph, filling half a page and saying very little.
John, on the other hand, has got the right idea; say it once, move on to the next point(s), shut up.

Not only does John put his thoughts together coherently, he usually has something worthwhile to say.

Yours faithfully,
Dessie Montgomery

By early 1997 I was really depressed; not feeling on top of the job, drinking too much, in a relationship heading for the rocks ("You're never here, John, even when you ARE here. Look, we need to talk; remember that guy at work I told you was just a friend..."), counting down the days until holidays, which was never me – and suspecting that something was definitely not right health-wise.

I was terrified it might be serious – and even more terrified to talk to my GP.

The depression/anxiety was at its height when myself and Malky boarded a plane for Sicily in January 1997.

Not even being voted 'Best Northern Ireland Journalist' a few days earlier by the Better Red Than Dead fanzine – with 65% of the votes, natch; 'Jackie Full-of-himself' (who he?) was second, with Coatesy third – lightened the mood. It wasn't easy feigning happiness when your addled brain was taunting the rest of you with words like 'worthless' and 'useless'.

Belfast Telegraph, Tuesday, January 21, 1997...

When the glamour wears thin

By John Laverty in Sicily

It's Tuesday, so it must be Palermo.
I've always wanted to say that. This is the life of the jet-setter, you know; exotic-sounding locations, beach parties, Ferraris for taxis.
Don't you wish you were here?
Well, don't. I made those first few lines up.
Today, we blow the lid on the foreign football trip.
If you think the lot of an international footballer – or the people who cover that lot – is something to be envied, you're sadly mistaken...

I'm still embarrassed at that self-pitying shite appearing on the back page. I may as well have started it with 'hello darkness, my old friend'. If

Sammy had still been in charge, he'd surely have asked: "What the fuck is *this*?"

I wrote it as an accompaniment to my preview of the Italy v Northern Ireland game, which had garnered more media attention than your average bog-standard friendly.

This was a new era for the home side; their first match under Cesare Maldini – father of veteran captain Paolo – and, as Italy would soon face England in a crucial World Cup qualifier, of significant interest to the national papers back home. England manager Glenn Hoddle would be an interested spectator at the compact Stadio La Favorita (where Italy would labour to a 2-0 win. Hod's got nothing to worry about, wrote the scribes. A month later Italy won 1-0 at Wembley.)

I rattled out that gawd-awful 'woe is me' diatribe shortly after arriving in the Sicilian capital on Monday, January 20.

Right, that's *that* out of the way. Libation beckoned; reversible suicide. Unlike me, my ex-boss was in fine fettle as we settled on a busy little hostelry on Via Vittorio Emanuele, near the seafront.

I think he enjoyed bumping into old pals like Paddy 'Patrick' Barclay from the Sunday Telegraph, who were staying at the same hotel near Quattro Canti. Frankly, though, even weirdo Hoddle would have been better company than me that night. But poor Malky did his best.

On Matt Busby: "Ah first met Matt when he played for the Army at Windsor during the war. Ah rang him in February 1945 after bein' tipped off that he was gettin' the United job. He said tae me: 'Yer a bit previous, laddie; I dinnae get demobbed until October, but they said they'd keep in touch. Dae ye think it's worth it for fifteen quid a week?'"

Me: "Mmm... fifteen quid."

On Tommy Dickson: "For everything he won wi' Linfield, his biggest regret was how badly he played for Northern Ireland against Scotland at Hampden in 1954. Ah couldnae believe it was the same player that day. He told me: 'I just froze, Malcolm. Instead of looking for the ball, I ran away from it. I just kept thinking I was out of my depth. It's no good others saying you're good enough if you don't think it yourself'. Who'd have thought the 'Duke of Windsor' would have a self-esteem problem?"

Me: "Mmm... self-esteem."

On Mary P: "After the Munich gold Ah interviewed her, then got her tae speak tae our managing director Tim Willis, who wanted to congratulate her in person. He says tae her: 'What would you like to mark your achievement?' and she says: 'A permanent running track in Belfast'. And

Willis goes: 'Consider it done'. Can ye believe that – and then Muggins here is tasked wi' raisin' the dough!

"Anyway, Ah didnae bother ma arse wi' that runnin' track because Mary P changed her surname to Poppins, married Dick Van Dyke and fucked off to California – John, you're not listening to a single fuckin' word Ah'm sayin', are ye?"

"Sorry, Malky. It's not you, it's me. I'm just not feeling the best."

"What the hell's wrong wi' ye? Out wi' it, right now."

I told him about the depression ("sometimes I want to stab myself, just to feel something other than this") and the ongoing health issue.

"Let's get out o' here," said Malky, "it's far too noisy."

He apologised to the bar manager for our abrupt departure: "Me and ma son are just goin' somewhere quieter tae talk; no offence."

Bar manager: "I'm not offended, Signori; this is Palermo... all these places are owned by the same people..."

Malky wasn't surprised by my office travails.

"Ah've already spoken to Colly about this," he said.

Really?

"Colly says yer tryin' too hard tae make yer staff like ye. He thinks ye've made a mistake by gettin' rid o' all the things they didnae like doin'. Look, John, that might make ye popular – for a while – but it won't earn ye respect, and that's the most important thing.

"Ye have tae understand that things have changed, that most o' the decisions ye make will be unpopular. If all ye care aboot is the boys likin' ye, yer on the path tae nowhere.

"Fray now on, ye say 'this is ma decision, this is the way it's gonna be, full point, end par'".

(My twisted mind harped back to the day Malky decreed that we had to "take it in turns to do the racing" when Colly and Bob were off. "Great idea, Malcolm", said John Campbell – GAA writer and master of hand grenade diplomacy – adding: "I'll do it the day after Jack does it...")

"It came naturally to you, Malky. There's not many folk can breeze through 40 years in that job."

"Ye think it was easy? Here's an exclusive for ye: Ah nearly left the Tele once. Nearly left the country. Bet ye didnae know *that*!

"A job came up wi' BBC Sport in Scotland; Ah was more than keen. Ah'd visions of movin' lock, stock and barrel tae Edinburgh, startin' anew – like the wheel comin' full circle, Ah suppose."

"What happened?"

"Margaret didnae like the idea one little bit. The boys were still at school; it was gonna cause all sorts o' upheaval. She said tae me: 'You keep talking and writing about Northern Ireland being the best country in the world, and now you're dreaming about upping sticks'. In the end, Ah let it go."

Another revelation: "Depression? Ye think it didnae hit me hard when ma final task wi' the Tele was collectin' me stuff in bin bags at the security desk?"

(He was referring to 1995. Malky, who'd been commissioned to write a book about the paper's history, had been granted use of a small office on the ground floor by Bob Crane, who'd been chief executive since 1979. But, according to Malky, "all bets were off" after Crane retired and, not long after the book – a superbly researched 300 pages – was published, the most accomplished journalist ever to walk through the Tele's doors walked out through its doors holding two black bin bags).

"That was just a wee while after Ah'd got that FIFA award from Blatter in the boardroom; maybe Ah should have ordered a reprint o' the book and added a bit aboot ma eviction..."

"But why'd that happen, Malky? You never said anything at the time."

"Ah think Ah was in shock, maybe denial. All Ah know is, Ah'd met a couple o' the new company bigwigs for lunch after Crane left, and thought it had been a convivial occasion; remember me tellin' ye aboot it the next day?

"Then suddenly Ah was persona-non-grata. Couldnae even get ma byline in the paper. Till the day Ah die, Ah'll never understand that."

(I'd heard that Malky had incensed the bigwigs with his 'vision for the future'. The sharp-suited, 'blue-sky thinking' blow-ins, who'd no previous newspaper background, didn't know Malky and were unaware of the respect he commanded, were unimpressed by a near-septuagenarian ex-employee advising them on company direction. They could have laughed it off as anachronistic ramblings but, instead, the bastards opted to make an example of him; to 'send a message'. I suspect, deep down, Malky knew that but, as usual, he masked his true feelings).

"But that wasnae the worst time. Folk think 1958 was a great year for me, but they forget what happened in Munich."

Malky knew several Busby Babes (and of course Busby himself, who was badly injured) but eight close friends – Alf Clarke (Manchester Evening Chronicle), Tom Jackson (Manchester Evening News), George Follows (Daily Herald), Archie Ledbrooke (Daily Mirror), Frank Swift (News of the World), Eric Thompson (Daily Mail), Donny Davies (*Manchester* Guardian) and the *doyen* of that time, Henry Rose (Daily Express) – perished in that plane crash.

"Ye keep me goin' aboot this, John, but Henry Rose really was 'larger than life'. He'd swan intae the press box wearin' his trademark trilby hat and smokin' a large Cuban cigar. He was ma hero, and even though Ah was 20 years younger and a nobody, he'd never pass me."

Malky said Rose was a rarity of his time; a Jew who flaunted his Jewishness instead of hiding it, a handsome bachelor with neatly trimmed moustache whose hedonistic lifestyle would have left even Bestie gasping in its wake.

"That man's ego knew no bounds; he was the only reporter introduced over the PA system at grounds, and outside they'd have a sign: 'Rose is here today'," said Malky.

"He earned a fortune too; drove a Jag with a personalised number plate {HR 470} in the days when only the Man U captain {Roger Byrne) could afford a car – and even then, it was only a Morris Minor.

"Henry was the people's champion; the Alex Higgins of journalism, ye might say, except folk still liked Henry after meetin' him. His was the biggest funeral Ah've ever been tae; they lined the streets for six miles between the Express office and the Southern Cemetery."

He added: "George Follows' death hit me hardest, though. We were really close; he'd even promised to write a piece for the Pink on his return to Manchester that very week.

"Ah was in a trance for maybe two month afterwards; Ah'd have been on that plane, except the 1958 World Cup draw in Sweden was two days later so Ah couldnae manage both.

"Every time Ah saw Harry {Gregg) or Jackie {Blanchflower} after that, I thought of Henry, George and the other boys. We'd all have been in Sweden together that summer."

Then: "And then there was Sam English?"

"Who?"

"Sam English. He was from here."

"What, Palermo?"

"Nah, ye diddy! He was from Aghadowey. One of the greatest ever Rangers centre-forwards. Ma father worshipped him. Ah never saw him play, but met him a few times. A really nice man."

Me (getting impatient): "Yes, but what about him?"

"It was Sam who crashed intae Celtic keeper John Thomson at Ibrox in 1931, an' Thomson later died. Sam never lived it down."

"I would think not, after killing someone."

"Nah, yer no gettin' me. He was cleared of any wrongdoin' and even Thomson's family said it were a complete accident. But the abuse was non-stop.

"He had tae leave Glasgow for Liverpool. Even then, Celtic supporters got the train south tae brand him 'a murderer' from the Anfield stands. Rival players too."

"So, how'd it all turn out?" I asked, anticipating a happy ending to this grimmest of tales.

Malky: "He never once spoke about that day at Ibrox. He quit football when was 28, and ended up in the Clyde shipyard as a sheet metal worker. He suffered from depression for the rest o' his days, and died in 1967 aged 58."

Me: "Oh, brilliant. That's the sort of uplifting tale I really need right now."

Malky: "Look, John, Ah probably didnae articulate that very well. What I mean is, there comes a time when ye have tae stop wallowin' in misery and just deal wi' the cards ye've been dealt."

"Says the retired multi-millionaire. Christ, Malky, I'm only 34."

"Aye, but that's the thing aboot depression. When yer in its grip, ye think ye'll never get away from it.

"On the other hand, and just remember this, John, when yer happy, ye never think yer gonnae be sad. What Ah mean is, it all balances out..."

Ironically, that conversation, although laced with dark moments, helped cheer me up. So the great Malcolm Brodie wasn't mentally indestructible after all; maybe there was hope for the rest of us.

Nostalgic anecdotes were reprised; I got the impression Malky searched his remarkable brain that Monday evening for appropriate, light-hearted ones.

On Jackie Blanchflower: "Ah loved it when a punter walked up to him on Royal Avenue and said: 'Tell me, Jackie; was it you or your brother Danny who was killed at Munich?'".

On Norman Whiteside (forced to quit football through injury at 26): "Not long after he retired – around the same time as me in '91 – he was guest o' honour at a do in County Antrim. They'd got some *for-till merchant* {Malky's description of elderly administrators} tae introduce him, and yer man was not only nervous but inarticulate." (When Malky attempted an Ulster accent, he sounded more like one of those aliens in the Smash potato ads).

"All ye heard was: 'Tonight, we're here to honour the youngest man ever to play at the World Cup – even younger than your man *Peel* from Brazil. Norman played over 200 matches for United, scoring nearly 50 goals, including an FA Cup final winner'.

"Then yer man went off script and attempted to ad lib: 'I don't know what went wrong at United; I think he must have got fat from drinking all that beer, ha-ha. Anyway, he ended up at Everton for a couple of years. And now he's fucked'..."

On Sion Mills (when Ireland famously bowled the Windies out for 25 in 1969): "There was a do in the clubhouse for both teams afterwards, and everyone was congratulatin' the Irish players. Then one oul' boy stood up and announced: 'I think the real heroes today were the ground staff; they worked like blacks to get the place ready...'"

My turn: "Hey, John, tell me that story again about yer man Grattan."

Legend has it that, as a cub reporter with the Tele, Gary Grattan was sent to interview an elderly Newry couple who'd been robbed overnight. The traumatised pair told Gary that they only thing the robbers left was a tenner for the gas, which had been left behind the clock on the mantelpiece.

Naturally, Newtownabbey man Gary thought this was 'a great line' for his story.

Shortly after leaving the pensioners' house, he realised his car was almost out of petrol – and that he'd left his wallet in the office and had no access to money...

"He didn't, did he? Ha-ha-ha-Ha!"

Malky loved hearing that story, which I rarely got to finish. For him, imagining the *denouement* was more amusing that actually hearing it. I knew what he was up to; if I was in the mood to tell the Gary Grattan story, then I was in good form. It was one of Malky's litmus tests.

Even so: "Ye go see a doctor, John – pronto. Ongoin' anxiety over somethin' like that isnae gonna help yer depression, mark ma words. Anxiety and booze are a bad mix, and ye can bottle somethin' up for so long that it's too big tae let oot. Don't keep burying yer head and pretending there's no sand in yer ears afterwards. What was it George Bernard Shaw said about booze bein' the anesthesia by which we endure the operation of life?"

Then Malky – who wouldn't normally walk the length of himself – accompanied me to the magnificent Teatro Massimo; I wanted to see where the climactic scene in Godfather III was filmed. After that, hotel nightcap, beddy-byes and an unexpected knock on the door...

Greta – full title Doctor Greta Vittoria Cardelli – gave my nether regions a thorough examination later that night.

"You don't have testicular cancer," said the on-call *medico* while washing her hands in the en suite sink afterwards.

"You may, however, have epididyitis."

"*Epi*... what?"

"It's an inflammation that can cause pain and swelling in the testicles. I'm leaving you some antibiotics and some anti-inflammatory pills. In the meantime, wear boxer shorts and see your GP back home if the problem persists. Good night, Mister John."

CHAPTER 45

How journalism works:

1. In a live BBC Radio 5 Live debate about our paper's GAA coverage in July 1998, I make a comment to the effect that, if Gaelic games replaced football on the Tele's back page, we might gain 6,000 new readers while losing 10,000 existing ones.
2. This comment is misquoted on the front page of the Irish News on Saturday, August 1 as: "If I improved the Belfast Telegraph's GAA coverage, the paper would lose 100,000 readers".
3. Concerned Tele editor Ed Curran gets a recording of the 5 Live programme, which proves that the comment in question wasn't made.
4. Sunday Independent journalist writes an excoriating piece about me (and, bizarrely, Jim Gracey), based on the misquote.
5. The Ulster GAA Writers Association votes to have myself and Jim banned from their forthcoming annual dinner at Bundoran's Great Northern Hotel.
6. Bass Ireland PR manager Brian Houston warns the GAA writers that if two personal friends of his aren't welcome at the dinner, he would withdraw all his company's sponsorship.
7. The GAA writers rescind their decision.
8. Great Northern owner Brian McEniff personally greets myself and Jim like returning battle heroes as we stride into the foyer prior to the dinner.
9. The Sunday Independent journalist is named Northern Ireland Sports Journalist of the Year, beating me into second place.

As a head of department, you have to be extra careful about what you write or say; the footprint (or, rather, your chances of putting said foot in it) is considerably larger.

December 5, 2000...

I hope Lennon realises what he's let himself in for

By John Laverty

...Lennon is at the peak of his career, and can look forward to regular title-chasing and European forays with the Bhoys from Glasgow.

Already a very wealthy young man, his coffers will be boosted further by this lucrative move to 'Paradise'.

But God doesn't deal you all the aces – and I have a funny feeling this move will mark the beginning of the end of Neil Lennon's international career.

Lenny isn't stupid; he's well aware of the kind of 'reception' Celtic players get at Windsor Park, even if they're playing for the home team. Just ask Anton Rogan.

It would be nice to think that things had changed since those dark days in the 80s when Rogan was subjected to appalling terrace abuse because he was one of the Bhoys, and not one of the boys.

But none of us are that naive, and Lennon knows that his relationship with a hard core of Northern Ireland supporters will never be the same again.

Our next game, against Norway at Windsor in February, will be a litmus test. I have a funny feeling Lenny will find out what it means to go from Paradise to Hell in a matter of days...

Lenny being hounded out by brainless bigots is, arguably, the biggest story I was involved in during a nine-year stint as sports editor.

I say 'involved', but everyone at Windsor Park that night in February 2001 – and there were over 7,000 of us – witnessed the naked sectarian abuse the new Celtic midfielder had to endure.

Well, maybe not the Northern Ireland manager Sammy McIlroy, who clearly needed his ears syringed: "It was mixed. One minute there was cheering, and then there was booing. I didn't think it was anything bad, to be honest with you, and I'm sure Neil didn't".

Lenny carried on, the jeering subsided – but, 18 months later, loyalist death threats issued prior to a friendly with Cyprus brought a premature end to his 40-cap international career.

After the earlier Norway debacle, however, fingers were pointed at me, and in particular a comment piece I'd written a couple of months earlier. Was that piece provocative or prescient? Realistic or reckless? Many were convinced it had played a part in Lenny's disgraceful demonisation.

One of those was Celtic manager Martin O'Neill, who boned me about it at a Europa Hotel football dinner in May 2001.

Martin suggested I'd set Lenny up – even quoting my article. When I suggested the sentiments hadn't been expressed *quite like that*, Martin produced a photocopy from his jacket pocket.

"No, John, you wrote *this*..."

I felt like one of those rabble-rousing 'Ulster' politicians who, in the words of the Kaiser Chiefs, 'predict a riot' and then get blamed for stoking it up in the first place.

With hindsight, I wouldn't have published that Lenny piece. Stating the obvious is one thing; giving arseholes an excuse to be arseholes is something else.

The Lenny stuff notwithstanding, Sammy Mac's Northern Ireland – and the McMenemy-Jordan-Jennings 'dream team' that preceded it – weren't much kop.

McMenemy, who took over from Hammy in early 1998, bore little resemblance to the inspirational 'Big Lawrie' who'd led Southampton to an unlikely 1976 FA Cup final win over United, and whose charisma had persuaded Kevin Keegan to choose the unfashionable Saints after leaving SV Hamburg in 1980.

Ditto Joe 'Jaws' Jordan, the marauding, mesmerising, orthodontically-challenged United hero of my youth. At least Big Pat was, well, Pat.

The 'highlight' of McMenemy's excruciating but mercifully short reign (14 games, four wins, only one of which was in a competitive fixture, seven defeats, win ratio 35.7%) was the announcement of his first squad – which included Dele Adebola, a Nigerian striker with no Northern Ireland connections whatsoever but who qualified for selection through possession of a British passport.

Alas, the Birmingham City player felt he could do better than our wee country, and held out for an invitation from England which never came. There was also a bizarre 'off the record' briefing in Helsinki prior to a Euro 2000 qualifier in September 1999, when the ex-England assistant manager briefly morphed back into the Lawrie we knew and loved – dismissing some of his underperforming players as "toe-rags" and referring to one in particular as "someone I wouldn't piss on if he was on fire."

I remember Malky whispering in my ear: "Either yer man's lost his marbles – or he's finally found them".

Not surprisingly, the subsequent 4-1 loss to Finland was McMenemy's last game in charge, his resignation a blessed relief for those GAWA diehards horrified that the IFA had actually offered him a new contract. Lawrie was a strict disciplinarian, though, as exemplified by the time he drummed Tags out of the squad following an, um, *incident* involving a shocked stewardess on the flight back from a 4-1 friendly defeat by Spain in June 1998. Let's just say she'll not look at a ham sandwich the same way ever again.

My last 'away trip' was Estonia in March 2004, with another Lawrie. It was Sanchez's second game in charge, following a 4-1 home defeat by Norway – which sounds demoralising, but Healy's second half strike in the February 18 friendly got the champagne corks popping – having finally ended a world record run of two years and five days (thirteen and a half games and 1,298 minutes) without a goal.

Then Healy scored again at a sparsely populated Lillekuka Stadium in Tallinn to give Northern Ireland their first win since the same player's penalty saw off Malta in October 2001 – 16 games earlier.

Those games marked the start of a brief but golden Sanchez/Healy era, but that friendly in Estonia was an end game for me.

Sanchez, whose father was Ecuadorian but whose mother hailed from Belfast, won three caps in the late 80s and, prior to landing the Northern Ireland job, was best known for scoring the scrappy but seismic 1988 FA Cup-winning goal for Wimbledon against Liverpool.

He got the nod from Windsor Avenue after history repeated itself and Jimmy Nick – just like a decade earlier – priced himself out of the running. Guess what: I didn't write a word about *that*.

Not long after his appointment was ratified in January 2004, Lawrie accepted my invitation to the Tele Sports Awards at the Ramada Hotel, Shaw's Bridge.

We must have imbibed until 4am; honestly, we bonded so well that night, I'm surprised we didn't end up in bed together.

Or so I thought. En route to the Baltic republic's delightful capital, and needing 'a line' for the paper, I boned Lawrie about who would be captaining the side. His answer: "I'll announce that at a press conference tomorrow."

You know what – fuck you, Lawrie. And fuck this for a game of soldiers, period.

How in God's name did Malky wade through over half a century of this crap? It was only 15 years for me, but I knew I'd had enough.

Beaco, who'd been sharing the Northern Ireland matches with me, could have them all from now on.

When I got back to my desk on the Friday, all my Have a Rattle letters were sitting on my keyboard, unopened – ergo, not brought to the copytakers for transcription; an essential midweek task, because Joyce and Co were up to their eyes on Fridays.

I was beyond angry, ranting and raving to no one in particular about how it was against the laws of physics for handwritten letters to print themselves, and all it would have taken to make me happy was for some

273

lazy bastard to get off his fat arse for just 30 seconds; instead, I come back to this shit.

Around that time, I publicly humiliated a well-meaning but impressionable young journalist who'd recently applied for a job in our place.

At a stretch, you could argue it was partly his fault; he buttonholed me at a function, demanding to know why he hadn't been taken on – and hinting that it might have more to do with his Catholicism than his ability.

"Tell me the truth, John – right now. Why'd you overlook me?"

"You really want to know the truth... right here, right now? In front of all these people?"

"Yes, I do. Out with it."

"It's because I've read your stuff."

"And what does *that* mean?"

"It means it's absolute shite. And, presumably, that was *after* an experienced sub had worked on it, so I shudder to think what crap you'd offered up before that. You applied for a job which involved improving other people's copy when, Christ, you can barely write your own name."

He turned on his heel, moved quickly towards the toilets, and wasn't seen again that evening.

Not long after that, I quit The Best Job In The World.

CHAPTER 46

One thing I loved about Malky; he always cut to the chase. No bull with that wee man. He never lost his accent either; the pair of us spoke Glaswegian when we needed a quiet word. No one had a clue what we were saying...
(Sir Alex Ferguson)

June 2004, Sesimbra.

"Let me tell ye this, Jim, absolutely straight: MB does NOT eat chicken curry."

"Well, let *me* tell you *this*, Malky: MB *will* eat chicken curry, or MB will go without."

"Och, come on, Jim, that isnae fair."

"Look Malky, Mrs Ferreira is coming up specially to cook us chicken curry – and that's what we're going to have."

Me: "Jim, if ye don't mind me saying, that's a bit draconian."

Jim: "No, it's not. I know *his* game; 'let's cancel Mrs Ferreira and book yet another table down at the square for steako-well-done-o'. Not happening this time."

Malky: "Oi, stop talkin' aboot me like Ah wasnae here. Ah'm nae a bairn, ye know..."

June 1998, Paris...

It was a balmy evening. The Auld Alliance in lower Marais was a bear pit. We'd been alternating between the hitherto cosy Scottish bar and Le Pick-Clops on Rue Vieille du Temple (which would ultimately charge us 'regulars' *prix du resident* instead of *prix touristique; merci, mes amis*) since arriving in the host's capital a few days earlier.

But this was a bad call; June 9 – the day before Scotland took on champions Brazil in the opening game of *Mundial 98* at the brand-new Stade Francais.

This was more Souchiehall Street at Hogmanay than Rue Francois Miron in early summer.

Still, we'd commandeered a wee table outside, and there was always Le Pick-Clops if the 500th drunken rendition of Flower of Scotland to the skirl of bagpipes proved to be too much.

Not long after 11pm, the Caledonian singers were silenced by a French police siren – urgency and emotion expressed in two unique notes – as a small blue and white Renault, bearing two officers of the law, parted the Tartan Sea.

"Some header's been talking when he should've been listening, and getting a Glasgow kiss for his trouble" (My synopsis).

Jim: "Let's go back to Le Pick-Clops. Nothing to see here, *Monsieur,* and no chance of another pint, now that the cops are here."

The following day I rang Malky (who was staying five miles away near the Parc des Princes) to finalise our pre-match travel plans.

"Have ye been listenin' to the World Service?" he asked.

"Funnily enough, no."

"There was some fun an' games in the Auld Alliance last night; Stan Collymore beat the crap out o' his girlfriend – ah cannae remember her name, Eureka or somethin' like that – after she'd walked intae the place wi' Ally McCoist. The Sun's gonna run five pages on it tomorrow..."

France 98 was easier to cover than USA 94; mobile phones with compatible, reliable laptops were *de rigueur,* the *Train a Grande Vitesse* was transport of choice; no wi-fi, but internet cafes existed (*bonne chance* trying to find one, though), and no infuriating time difference. Oh, and Malky was four years older.

Collymore's unforgivable public assault on Ulrika Johnsson wasn't the only thing 'Dumb and Dumber' were oblivious to in Paris, a place where even the trees look pleased with themselves.

After a surprisingly hard-fought World Cup opener, which Brazil edged 2-1 in front of 80,000, we opted to skedaddle early, beat the crowds and catch a train back into town.

The station at St Denis – a drab, industrial northern suburb – was over half a mile away, but we set a Sir Roger-like early pace.

Then: "Stop, STOP! What the fuck are we doing?"

Me (panting): "What do you mean, Jim?"

"I mean *this*: we're in our thirties and poor Malky is 72 this year. Christ, are we trying to kill him for the sake of an empty seat on a stinking train?"

Malky – additionally burdened by his trademark heavy black leather document case – was wheezing uncontrollably, rivulets of sweat lashing off him. I felt guilty and utterly ashamed, not least because he didn't complain. Maybe he hadn't enough breath left in his body.

Our obsession with rail travel harped back to the day we arrived when, having initially planned to get from the strike-affected, delay-addled CDG Airport by rail, we lazily switched to sharing a cab with Malky – knowing full well that (1) there'd be a significant detour to accommodate us and (2) the fare, which Malky would pick up, would be astronomical. (I think it amounted to £93).

We'd taken advantage of our esteemed colleague's patent dislike of public transport, graphically illustrated during Euro 96 when the then 69-year-old attempted to exit a Wembley-bound tube train, believing he'd sufficient time to purchase a Daily Telegraph.

Jim: "Malky, this is clearly the first time you've travelled by Tube in your long and distinguished career."

That was June 15; the day Gazza scored that wonderful volley against Scotland. I was actually sitting beside Sheryl Failes, the woman who would become his wife two weeks later, when that goal went in. (Another priceless Euro 96 moment: Malky asking Birmingham policeman for directions while said officer was busy beating a football hooligan senseless with his baton).

So we weren't blind to *everything*: you couldn't fail to notice that, during the spectacular, magical-garden-themed ceremony in Paris (when colourful mechanical insects flew around giant buds that burst open, releasing huge footballs), Malky, bored out of his mind, proceeded to read an outdated copy of the DT.

He'd performed a similar trick in Rotterdam on Sunday, August 31 the previous year – the day Diana died – when we were corporate guests at an Eredivisie game between Feyenoord and De Graafschap.

Euro 2004 in Portugal was the most revelatory, though; the first in which we shared a rented house.

A beautiful place it was too; Casa de Nossa Senhora, a spacious, sunkissed villa (complete with outdoor pool) in the foothills of the Serra da Arrabida overlooking the quaint fishing village of Sesimbra, 25 miles from Lisbon.

To be honest, only Jim and Steven Beacom – Malky jokingly called him 'Stephanie Beacham' – were there in a 'working' capacity; the Tele's first and third sports editors did bits and pieces, but for us it was predominantly a football-themed vacation.

A short list of MB epiphanies in Portugal:

1. When he said "Cuppa tea, John?", what he meant was "*make* me a cuppa tea, John". This request would be made at least six times a day.

2. He doesn't like sunbathing. Doesn't buy expensive suncream either – but rubs copious amounts of ours onto his body before muttering (less than three minutes later) "Och, Ah've had enough o' this heat" and skulking back inside.

3. The man's a thief. One day he wandered into my en suite for a nosy.

"What's *that*, John?"

"It's a shower mat. It has wee suction cups for a secure grip."

"Tidy job, that thing..."

Next day, 'that thing' disappeared. It wasn't hard to find, but I let it stay where it had been relocated – in Malky's bathroom.

4. His name-dropping skills remained legendary. Prior to Sesimbra, the unbeatable, oft-repeated, default MB trump card had always been "as Irving Berlin said tae me..."

But, after a particularly heavy night at the Largo da Marinha, and having endured relentless *Eleven-erife* taunting from his younger colleagues ("Liam Neeson used to come round to my house in Ballymena"; "Really? I had a drink with Noel Gallagher the other day..."), a tired and emotional Malky delivered the ultimate, unbeatable *piece de resistance* when it *really* mattered: "Who do YOU know who has walked on the Moon?"

(Apart from that distinction, another of Apollo 17 commander Gene Cernan's claims to fame was having his number in Malky's contacts book).

5. He isn't a football fan. No, you're not reading that wrong. Although most of his life was spent *covering* football, Malky had little or no interest in matches he wasn't directly involved in through work – hence the boredom displayed in Rotterdam and Paris, and the obvious apathy towards watching televised affairs at the four World Cups we both attended.

A one-time Rangers supporter, he gave that up after leaving Glasgow. "Ah'm nae a fan wi' a laptop, like Stephanie Beacham over there," he'd say; "Ah believe ma sense of detachment makes ma writin' better. Tae be a good writer, you need tae be courageous an' expose yerself... metaphorically."

Cricket was the sporting love of Malky's life; that old black leather bag always contained at least two autobiographies, and Bradman was right up there with Sinatra, Churchill and Berlin on his shortlist of all-time heroes.

For me, Portugal was the most memorable trip of all. For the first time, we were all there as bona fide *mates*. Malky had been boss to both Jim and me, but that was now a distant memory; I was still Beaco's boss, but had been (secretly) working on an exit strategy.

(I turned down a tempting job with The Sun in 1997 – ironically it would have made their NI 'stringer' Malky redundant, although that didn't enter my thoughts at the time. My reasons were similar to Malky's when he rejected BBC Scotland.)

Indefatigable Fermanagh native Beaco – whose work ethic, according to Colly, mirrored that of a young Brodie – became one of Malky's adopted sons.

Mark McIntosh – like Beaco a prodigy of the post-Brodie era, and mentored by myself and Jim – was another.

Considering their relative youth, 'grandsons' was a more apt appellation; after all, Malky had finally become a grandfather, to Claire, apple of his eye, in the late 90s.

The 'chicken curry row', although light-hearted, was further evidence of a sea change at the seaside in Sesimbra.

Malky had turned 77 then – not exactly in a second childhood, but not as sharp as he was, physically or mentally. Even Dumb and Dumber could see that.

But after the work was done and the laptops put away, the craic, be it in villa or village, was just like old times.

Beaco listened rapt one night as the other three reminisced about the 'O'Driscoll sisters', whom we'd met in Paris.

Malky was mesmerised by Anne-Sophie and Dorothee who, despite their surnames, were unmistakeably French (their great grandfather hailed from Cork).

For reasons unexplained, and despite limited English, the twenty-something pair enjoyed sitting with us oldies in Les Chimeres on Rue Saint-Antoine – and were more than useful as translators when required, which was often.

Malky enjoyed their company because they laughed hysterically at everything he said, although I doubt if they understood a word of it.

Remarkably and purely coincidentally, we bumped into the O'Driscolls again, two years later, while walking though Paris en route to the 2000 Champions League final between Real Madrid and Valencia.

A darker episode recalled from the 1998 Paris sortie was joining Malky for breakfast in his quaint little family-owned hotel – "the people here are first class; they really look after me" – and discovering that those "first class" people had been mercilessly fleecing him.

279

Jim spotted this after seeing *l'addition* that morning; £70 for toasted sarnies and coffee. Even by central Parisian standards, that was eyewatering – and this was no Ritz.

"Christ, Malky; no wonder these people hug you every morning."

Let's just say we 'suggested' that *Gaspard et Camille* take a closer look at the bills in future, lest similar 'mistakes' occur.

That aside, Malky was in great form in France. Those pricks who had so callously turfed him out of the building three years earlier had moved on to destroy morale somewhere else; the paper's biggest living legend instantly had his renown, self-esteem, security pass – and, perhaps most importantly, MB byline – reinstated.

Yes, we'll always have Paris – and Bordeaux, and several other cities the sleek TGV propelled us to. France 98 was the only tournament all three of us covered from start to finish; by the time Japan-Korea 2002 came around Beaco was the sole Tele football man although, through the generosity of Budweiser, I got to spend quality time with him, Malky and Jim in both Seoul and Tokyo.

Ditto Germany 2006 – Malky's 14th and final tournament. I'd left sport by then, having been promoted to Assistant Editor; a move that clearly shocked some of the younger hacks on the third floor who saw me as 'that bloke who writes stuff about Linfield and Glentoran.'

"Ah remember it bein' a big surprise when ye first moved fray news tae sport; now they're surprised at ye goin' the opposite direction," said Malky.

Beaco – who was appointed sports editor shortly after I left – told me: "I got to know Malky best in Germany when we travelled all over the place by car. You and Jim had left; it was just the pair of us; I'd known him for years, but this was the first time we'd had personal conversations.

"Although he was getting on, the competitive spirit was still there. One day in Germany, we had to climb four flights of steps to the press box. It was a sweltering day and MB was hitting 80 – but his pace quickened when he saw {72-year-old} Hugh McIlvanney and {62-year-old} Jim Lawton ahead of us.

"Before reaching the third level we'd overtaken them; I remember thinking Malky would rather die than let those two get there first."

In 2008, shortly after Spain became European champions in Vienna, Beaco was informed that production of the Pink would cease for good later that month.

It was/wasn't a shock; everybody loved the legendary sports paper but not enough of them were buying it.

Despite its dynamic, world-record production speed, by the time the ISN hit the streets its basic match reports had been rendered old-hat by knocked-on pieces and analysis on TV, radio and internet. If that hadn't killed it off, the imminent arrival of 'smartphones' in the mid-Noughties undoubtedly would have.

Also, the company that took over from our previous owners, Thomson, in 2001 – Independent News and Media – had become major players in contract printing. The small-circulation 'Pink' was taking up valuable time and space on the huge Goss Metroliners.

On July 26, 2008, the last Pink rolled off the Royal Avenue presses; the end of an era, for sure. It first hit the streets as a four-page publication, printed on distinctive pink paper, in November 1894.

Malky had been its boss for 40 years, Sammy (who oversaw it switching from broadsheet to tabloid in 1993) for five, myself for nine and Beaco for just three.

"I knew Malky was gutted about the Pink folding, but he was pragmatic about it too," said Beaco.

"He told me: 'It's had a good run, Stevie; all good things must come tae an end'. It had been a major part of our lives, but his especially."

Remember in Portugal when Malky tea-leafed my shower mat?

There was something else I noticed in his bathroom that day; the number of different pills he was taking. Similar evidence was on display in Germany two years later.

I've no idea what the drugs were, but it was clear Malky was no longer in rude health.

He had his first heart attack in 2007, was rushed to hospital and had a short wire-mesh tube, or stent, inserted to promote better blood flow. Naturally he played the whole thing down.

"Thousands o' folk have this done every week," he told me the day after he was discharged.

"It's a routine procedure; sure, didnae Alec Ferguson get it done a couple o' year ago, and he's only in his mid-sixties."

Malcolm's son Kenneth: "we realised in 2007 that 'Big Mal' was in fact a mortal being, and getting towards the end of the line. I think we cherished every moment after that. We were blessed to get another six years.

"And, certainly, he grew even closer to Claire. He realised these precious family moments couldn't go on for ever. You know what he ate, what he drank; the man was a walking miracle."

281

In April 2011, Malky got hold of a major story that, for once in his life, he opted not to share with anyone.

He left the surgery of Cameron Ramsay (also the Linfield club doctor and long-time friend), having been informed that he had an incurable, degenerative heart condition.

Dr Cameron didn't sugar-coat the pill; two years at most, Malky was told. But he kept that bombshell to himself, and carried on as usual.

Actually, that's not true.

He still attended the odd Irish League game, still wrote bits and pieces for the Sun and DT, but the unparalleled, unbroken coverage of Northern Ireland internationals came to an end in 2012, not long after Michael O'Neill became manager.

According to master statistician Marshall Gillespie, Malky attended 416 Northern Ireland games, home and away, over 66 years, the first a 7-2 defeat by England at Windsor on September 28, 1946 – the day after his 20th birthday.

He witnessed 114 wins, 195 defeats, 107 draws. He's the only person to have covered matches involving all 12 Northern Ireland managers (and, prior to Peter Doherty, the IFA selection committee).

When Malky started this odyssey, George VI was King, Sir Basil Brooke was NI Prime Minister, Perry Como, Frank Sinatra, Dinah Shore and Bing Crosby were the best-selling musicians, Frank Capra's new movie, It's A Wonderful Life, was in pre-production and the Tele's main news included the 'Iron Curtain' descending on Europe, the hanging of nine top Nazis after the Nuremberg trials, the launch of the huge HMS Eagle aircraft carrier from Harland and Wolff shipyard and Nutt's Corner becoming the province's principal airport.

When his stint ended, Barack Obama was US President, David Cameron PM, Skyfall had just hit the cinemas, London was about to host the Olympics, the best-selling pop stars were Adele and One Direction and the big local yarns were the Queen shaking hands with Northern Ireland Deputy First Minister Martin McGuinness, the Titanic centenary 'celebrations' and the tragic death of Ulster rugby star Nevin Spence who perished, along with his father and brother, in a slurry tank accident.

By the time he walked out of 'The Shrine' for the last time, he'd seen an astonishing 72% of all Northern Ireland matches ever played.

"He once told me that, despite everywhere he'd been, Windsor remained his favourite stadium," said Beaco.

"I think he'd have hated the outdoor press box {at the rebuilt 'National Football Stadium at Windsor Park'} while at the same time glowing about

282

the new place's Malcolm Brodie Press Centre {which opened in January 2017, bearing a huge picture of the great man and a list of his unprecedented achievements}."

(The press room at the refurbished Mary Peters Track was also named in his memory, with a commemorative plaque and inscribed picture. The original track, set in a natural amphitheatre in leafy south Belfast, was completed four years after the success of an MB-driven campaign, backed a personal fund-raising drive by Dame Mary, his close friend and confidante.)

Beaco: "It isn't the same without MB sitting near you and roaring 'time?' after every noteworthy incident."

Me? I suspect Malky would have had press centres named after him even if was still with us. What a proud moment that would have been at Windsor especially; it was certainly a poignant one for Margaret and the 'three boys'.

It might even have been up there with receiving the MBE at Buckingham Palace on March 27, 1979.

"You couldn't annoy him in the run-up to that day," said Steven Brodie. (I'll spare blushes by not revealing which son skipped accompanying his parents to Buck House in favour of an Elton John concert at the Whitla Hall...)

You often hear of people who bear a terminal illness with great dignity and courage, but few do while keeping it a secret from their loved ones. In was only in the last two weeks of Malky's extraordinary life that he admitted to Margaret, the boys and Claire just how ill he really was.

Towards the end of 2012, David Martin, local football administrator and future IFA president, invited Malky's to speak at the Co Antrim FA's 125th anniversary celebrations at Belfast City Hall.

It would be right up the old man's street; big crowd, lashings of nostalgia – and Uefa president Michel Platini sitting alongside him.

But Malky said no.

"I was really taken aback," David told me.

"When we started planning the dinner, Malcolm was the obvious choice. His breadth of knowledge, global respect, oratory skills and sense of humour would have been perfect for that day.

"But he just said: 'Nah, David. Those big speaking engagements are behind me now'.

"Looking back... I suppose, deep down, he believed he wouldn't be around in April 2013. Sadly, he was right about that."

CHAPTER 47

Sometimes you will never know the value of a moment until it becomes a memory.
(Theodor Seuss Geisel)

Friday, January 25, 2013...

"Bout ye?"

"Oh I'm grand, Malky, but a much more important question: how are *you*?"

"Agh, fair tae middlin'. Frankly, a wee bit pally-wally on it. The oul' ticker's been givin' me a bit o' jip so they're havin' a good hoke around."

"But they'll be letting you out soon, right?"

"Aye, Ah'll be oot o' here soon enough."

"But not in time for Burns Night."

"Whaaa?"

"That's one of the reasons I'm calling... it's the 25th of January."

"Och, so it is! Do ye remember those great nights at the Ink Spot, when Ah stood everyone a dram for Burns Night?"

"Never missed one, Malky... until of course those unmentionables closed it down."

"Aye, but they'd banned me by then anyway. Remember that? Ma picture on the wall, me the president o' the club, and some 18-carat gold diddy had decreed Ah wasnae welcome in the place."

"Well, it's good to know that, nearly 18 years later, you've finally got over..."

"John, John, listen; the consultant's here. Ah have tae go. Ah'll give ye a ring when Ah get oot; we'll go tae the Potted Hen. Ah like that place. See ye anon."

Wednesday, January 30, 2013.

JL's Malky Obit, part 1

By John Laverty

Malcolm Brodie wouldn't have wanted me to write this. For years, he hinted that he'd already composed his own obituary; all that was missing was the publication date.

A bit morbid, Malky?

"Not really," he once told me. "I mean, who knows MB better than MB himself?"

Who indeed. And, come to think of it, did we know a better obituary writer?

His were always so readable; he had that knack of striking the right balance between reverence and nostalgia.

I enjoyed reading them — if you could 'enjoy' such things.

Another question. Malky, why do you use phrases such as "larger than life" and words like "immortal" to describe someone who has just passed away? A little on the ironic side, don't you think?

He set down his Johnnie Walker Black and water, shot me yet another of those despairing 'You just don't get it' looks and said: "Listen, Schemer, I'm talking about the spirit *of the person. Some day you'll get it..."*

Well, I never did get it. The self-penned obituary, that is.

Did it ever exist? Was it just Malky winding us all up?

*We'll never know. The thing is, it doesn't matter. The obit story is just one of many that invite 'legend' to join the cacophony of kind words being used to describe Dr Malcolm McPhail Brodie MBE since he passed away yesterday evening... **(more follows later...)***

Unofficial MB grandson Mark McIntosh, who'd been helping Malky with his 'Steve Smyth' Sun copy, was the last non-family member to speak to him. It was around 5pm on Tuesday, January 29.

"I was telling him about the squad that would be heading off to Malta for a friendly," Mark told me.

"He didn't sound particularly well, but no different than he'd been sounding for weeks. We chatted about the squad, and about who'd be covering Irish League games that weekend.

"I knew he was gravely ill, of course, but I honestly didn't think that would be the last time we'd speak. Like everyone else, you grew up thinking this man was immortal."

Shortly after that phone call, Margaret, Iain and Kenneth arrived at Belfast's City Hospital. Steven, who'd been detained at work, had arranged to join them later.

"As we approached his ward, we saw an old man being wheeled away, an oxygen mask clamped to his face," said Kenneth.

"I remember thinking 'God help that poor guy, he's not in good shape'. At that point I hadn't realised it was my own father on that gurney."

The medics worked on Malky for hours as the family waited, hoped, for positive news. None came.

Malky suffered not one, but a series of sustained heart attacks that Tuesday evening. At around 10pm, the final, fatal one came calling.

"We sort of knew at Christmas that things were bad," said Kenneth.

"He loved playing Santa but he really struggled this time; in the end Claire had to help him. He was so courageous, keeping the full extent of his illness to himself until virtually the last minute.

"He just didn't want to be a burden to anyone."

Obituaries appeared all over the world, including Canada where Malky's name had been atop sports and news pieces that catered for Ulster ex-pats.

To be frank, as Malky would say, many of the obits were lazily written; full of unchallenged, generic anecdotes, recycled, apocryphal stories, urban myths and irritating inaccuracies.

Even the Tele itself, in its first report about Malky's passing, erroneously referred to him being "evacuated from Glasgow to *Portadown, Co Armagh*, during the Second World War".

I remember wondering at that time who outside his close family – myself included – could genuinely say they knew this man.

My wife, Claire: "I've heard you tell people that you couldn't speak for a couple of minutes after hearing the news about Malky. It was more like a couple of hours. You couldn't sleep either, which is highly unusual."

What no one saw: me in the shower the next morning, crying my eyes out.

It's only happened twice before: on September 26, 1971, when Mum told her eight-year-old that his best friend, Adrian Swann, had succumbed to leukaemia, and when Mum herself passed away, aged 70, on December 29, 1993. None of them remembered for the length of their lives, but for the difference they made to mine.

Malky's service was at Cregagh Presbyterian Church (packed to the rafters; the adjoining hall took the overspill) on Monday, February 4, 2013.

Iain Brodie said the family had opted against a Saturday funeral because they could 'hear' Malky saying it would affect that weekend's football coverage – which of course he'd helped organise.

My first thought on arriving at the 85-year-old, distinctive red brick church: Good God; Malky will be gutted he's not here in person, only in spirit.

Those who were there that cold, wet afternoon included Harry Gregg, Pat Jennings, Terry Neill, Billy Hamilton, Gerry Armstrong, Iain Dowie, Mary P, Coyler, Big Ronnie, BJ 'Barney' Eastwood, Jeekie, Jim Boyce, Janet Gray, ex-Tele editors Roy Lilley, Ed Curran and Martin Lindsay, a host of media folk and a myriad of ex-colleagues from print and broadcasting.

(Later that day, the 'Copyboys' website published a list of mourners from local journalism. It mentioned virtually everyone who'd ever held a pen – but not me. I could imagine Malky laughing his head off at that; "Ha-ha-ha-HA! Folk Ah've never broken breath to in ma life are gettin' a namecheck, and ma own son Victor didnae...")

Jeekie, Mary P and Jim (now the company's Group Sports Editor) led the tributes, along with Rev Paul Dalzell, who read out special messages from Iain, Kenneth, Steven and Claire.

Jim was relieved to be speaking ahead of Mary and Jeekie; as he pointed out to congregational laughter, how do you follow an Olympic pentathlon gold medalist and a singer?

Malky's coffin, bearing white lilies, carnations and roses, had entered the church to the strains of Highland Cathedral, and was carried out to Amazing Grace; the cortège then made its way to City of Belfast Crematorium at Roselawn Cemetery.

I'd love to report that I paid full attention to everything in that church but my mind drifted at times; stories from the pulpit interspersed with personal reminiscences.

Two in particular stood out.

November 7, 2002...

Malky had treated me to dinner at the iconic Morning Star on Pottingers Entry ("first class steak"); it was my invite, but that hardly mattered because he never let you pay.

We hadn't long finished eating when he said "Ah've somethin' for ye". With this, a waiter arrived with a large rectangular object, bound in brown paper.

"What's this, Malky?"

"Open it and see."

Like a kid on Christmas morning, I tore the paper open – but was then momentarily confused by what emerged.

It was a framed back page of the Tele and – quelle surprise – the main story had Malky's byline on it.

Thing is, it wasn't much of a story; something about Wales making changes to their squad prior to a match against England. Not what the doyen was renowned for.

I didn't want to say this; my expression said it for me.

"Ah take it yer unimpressed wi' ma story?" he said.

"Ah'm nae surprised; it was a quiet, unmemorable day for me... but maybe not for yer mother."

The penny finally dropped: Monday, November 12, 1962 – the day I came into this world.

"Ah know it's a wee bit early, but happy 40th birthday," he said.

"Ah thought about gettin' your World Cup final report fray Paris framed – it's one o' the best things ye've ever written – but then Ah remembered; they forgot tae put yer byline on that."

(Monday, July 13, 1998. The mistake was spotted immediately – but this was technically 'The Twelfth', and only one edition goes out that day. I'm no byline junkie, but the one thing you don't want it missing from is the World Cup final. I was devastated).

"This is perfect, Malky. Honestly, I'm really touched by this. I'll treasure it."

After that, we were joined by old pals Pierre (Smirnoff) and Johnnie (Walker).

I haven't told anyone this before, but the following morning I realised to my horror that I'd left the framed page in the taxi.

The driver swore he never saw it in his cab. Really? It was a broadsheet page: 29.5 inches by 23.5 inches. Hard to miss, don't you think? That was a bitter pill.

Ten years later, another milestone birthday. Malky, looking pale and gaunt, took me for lunch at the Potted Hen in Cathedral Quarter and presented a hard-back copy of The Dark Side of Camelot by Seymour Hersh; the definitive JFK biography – and this copy was signed by the author.

"Ah remember ye sayin' ye wanted tae read that," he said, his voice weak and rasping.

"Good God, Malky; that was 15 YEARS ago!"

"Aye, but Ah'll bet ye didnae bother yer arse buyin' it..."

That was the last time I saw Malky alive.

July 17, 1994...

We'd just reached our seats in the heaving Rose Bowl as Kenny G was wrapping up his unique version of the Star Spangled Banner.
It was time for the real star of the closing ceremony to take centre stage – literally. Whitney Houston, wearing brown shorts and black ankle boots, ran onto the middle of the pitch, accompanied by a white-suited Pele, and started into I Wanna Dance With Somebody.
Notwithstanding the terrible acoustics, the world's biggest pop star (who was nursing a throat infection) was nowhere near her brilliant best (for what became the most watched live 'concert' in history; an estimated two billion tuned in).
But hey, it's still Whitney, and she was standing only a few yards away.
Acoustics and mega-diva somehow found an acceptable aural accommodation by the time The Greatest Love of All started (in a stadium which the record books say accommodated 94,194 people that sun-drenched Californian afternoon, but has since been re-estimated at having housed 10,000 more).
When the 30-year-old rose above the inadequate sound system for...

I decided long ago
Never to walk in anyone's shadow
If I fail, if I succeed
At least I'll live as I believe

...I remembered something Jeekie had said a couple of weeks earlier: "Who'd have thought it, eh? Two wee men, from the backstreets of Ballymena, at the greatest show on earth."
And then the tears came. As Irving Berlin *didn't* say to me, but articulated in song, my defences were down.
The enormity of the occasion hit like a tsunami.
Having been in the US for nearly two months by then, and seemingly inured to the import of the World Cup, this had suddenly become a magical, enchanted kingdom, a wondrous, Narnia-like fusion of real and surreal.
Was this what I had in mind 17 years earlier when I sat reading the back page of the Tele and fantasising about travelling the world writing about big football matches like Malcolm Brodie?
And there he was, sitting in a seat the same size and no more important than mine – that literally had my name on it: *John Laverty, Belfast*

289

Telegraph, FIFA WCF, 07-17-94.

For the first (and perhaps only) time in my life, I felt *equal* to him. At the age of 31, my personal Nirvana had been reached (of course Malky was younger – a mere stripling of 27 – at his first *Mundial* final in Bern, Switzerland, on July 4, 1954). I may have got as far up the journalism ladder as him – technically – and there would be two other Tele sports editors after me.

As far as synonymousness with the job title is concerned, however – and to quote that memorable line from Russell Mulcahy's Caledonian-themed fantasy The Highlander – there *can be only one.*

There'd be other World Cups to cover, further wonderful sporting moments to cherish; all 'forever videoed in memory', to borrow from you-know-who.

Nothing to top this, though; the apex, zenith, pinnacle and apogee. Over 5,000 miles from home but, just then, there was nowhere I'd rather be, nothing I'd rather be doing, no one I'd rather be with.

I loved Malky. Friend, colleague, mentor, inspiration, proxy parent. Disarming, peerless, kind, generous, mischievous, charismatic, ingenious, proud, sporadically vainglorious, extraordinarily intelligent, diverting, droll, astute, charming, jocular, combative, incomparable, irrepressible... irreplaceable.

The man I adored, revered, admired, envied, trusted, mistrusted, fought with, made up with, trusted again and would spend so many more unforgettable years with, was flattered to be called a son of (albeit in jest), yet would still bitch to Jim and Colly about – but would tear the face off anyone who dared speak ill of 'Malcolm'. Unless he's 'Malky', your opinion means nothing.

As long as I have memory, I'll remember the wee man from Glasgow's Dumbarton Road who was living proof that you don't need to reach a great height to become a colossus.

To borrow a lyric from a US number one single of that era, co-written by Jeff Silbar – a man who grew up not far from the Rose Bowl – *Thank you, thank God for you.*

Malky stood up (maybe there *was* wind beneath his wings on that hot, airless day) after realising what an emotional state I was in.

"Sit back doon here beside me, like a fella," he said.

"Ah wasnae gonna mention this until later, but Ah've arranged that we spend our last couple o' days in San Francisco."

"Really?"

"Aye. Why, ye dinnae wanna stay here, do ye? Quite frankly, Ah think this place is a dump."

"Me too, Malky. No, I think leaving LA is a brilliant idea."

"Yer woman from FIFA's gonna get the flights changed an' sort out everythin' else. We fly tae Frisco in the mornin' and are booked intae the hotel near Union Square where Sinatra stayed for the Golden Gate Theatre concerts in '46. He was aboot yer age back then. We'll have a wee bite tae eat at the Grotto in Fisherman's Wharf."

"That sounds like a seafood place."

"Aye, it is, but they do first class steaks too. Ah know the guy who owns it."

"Why are you doing this, Malky?"

"Ye *know* why, John. Right, that's it. Ah can hardly read that team-sheet. Did Baggio make it?"

Wednesday, January 30, 2013.

JL's Malky obit, part 2

It was just before midnight when the call came through; a call from someone who would never phone you that late.

No explanatory words were necessary then. There simply aren't enough now.

The world is suddenly a lesser place for not having Malky in it.

How many individuals, beyond your parents, can you say have genuinely shaped — indeed, changed the course of — your life?

What can you say about this remarkable man that hasn't already been said so many times over the past 86 years?

Perhaps Malcolm Brodie has already told me. Like he said: "Some day you'll get it." And now I finally have.

Larger than life. Immortal. **(Ends)**

Right, that's it.

ACKNOWLEDGEMENTS

For help, advice and the provision of precious memories: Sammy Hamill, Bob Fenton, Colin McMullan, Jim Stokes, Graham Hamilton, John Campbell, Jim Gracey, Roy Winter, Eddie Stirling, William Cherry, Mark McIntosh, Steven Beacom, Iain Brodie, Steven Brodie, Claire McNeilly, Roy France, Raymond Esteban and Marshall Gillespie.

... and in loving memory of Malcolm Brodie, Jimmy Walker, Jack Magowan, Ronnie Harper and John Taylor. RIP.

ABOUT THE AUTHOR

John Laverty is an award-winning journalist from Ballymena, Co Antrim.

After a stint as a news reporter in his hometown, he was appointed the Belfast Telegraph's north west regional correspondent, then football correspondent, sports editor, assistant editor, morning edition editor, night editor and executive editor.

His first association with the 'Tele', however, came as a teenage paper boy and, after finishing his round, he would turn to the back pages and devour the latest reports from legendary globe-trotting sports editor Malcolm Brodie.

Less than a decade later, 'Malky' would appoint the young man who would eventually succeed him as boss of the hugely successful Telegraph sports desk... and the adventure of a lifetime would begin.

John lives in Belfast with his wife Claire and daughter Soley.

ABOUT *dimedio*

From Latin, dimedio is "in the middle"

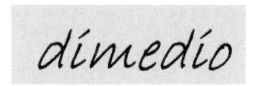

dimedio, formed in 2016, provide high quality sports and travel writing. Please contact us if you have a requirement in this area via:

e: dimedio2016@gmail.com
p: 0114-2480086
m: 07771-358944
f: dimedio
t: dimedio
l: dimedio Limited

dimedio's chosen charity for 2020 is The Gorilla Organisation

dimedio supports Guide Dogs for the Blind by donating all received used stamps

dimedio supports the fight against plastic waste in our oceans

Printed in Great Britain
by Amazon

68955605R00169